THE USSR TODAY: FACTS AND INTERPRETATIONS

Third Revised Edition

Leo Hecht
George Mason University

"Scholasticus" Publishing 1987

Library of Congress Cataloging-in-Publication Data

Hecht, Leo.
The USSR today.

Bibliography: p.
Includes index.
1. Soviet Union. I. Title.
DK17.H4 1987 947 87-13041
ISBN 0-9606754-3-4

"Scholasticus" Publishing
P.O. BOX 2727 • SPRINGFIELD, VIRGINIA 22152

Table of Contents

Table of Charts

Preface to the Third Edition

In the prefaces to the first and second editions the main theme consisted of the monotony of the Soviet system and its leadership. The years 1982/83 in which the second edition appeared were primarily ushered in by a change of leadership from Brezhnev to Andropov to Chernenko. It appeared that prospects for change in the future were quite dismal.

This Third Edition is, therefore, quite different. With the ascention of Mikhail Gorbachev to the leadership of the Party matters have changed a great deal — at least overtly, on the surface. These changes not only encompas economic and cultural innovations, but also political ones which, if instituted permanently, would have extremely far reaching repercussions. During the life of this edition then, that is, during the next four or five years, the possibilities for both internal and foreign policy metamorphoses are definitely there. These years will prove or disprove a number of important propositions: Will Gorbachev be able to consolidate his power completely, in detriment to the objectives of the "Old Guard" in the Party? Will the Soviet economy finally be able to stand on its own two feet and, in fact, become competitive with the West? Will the recent initial efforts towards human rights and free choice continue and gather momentum? Will the Soviet disarmament proposals be expanded and accepted by the West, thereby offering the Soviets the opportunity to concentrate more fully on improving internal affairs? Finally, are Gorbachev's proposed reforms only a momentary abberation awaiting the imposition of severe restrictions in the future, or will the Soviet people be able to hold on to their gains? This edition cannot offer solutions but will, however, attempt to support a variety of opinions on either side of the political spectrum. The answers will have to await the Fourth Edition in 1991/92.

Leo Hecht, George Mason University

I. Geography

The Soviet Union covers an area of 22.4 million square kilometers (8,650,000 square miles), and encompasses one-third of Asia and half of Europe. Its dimensions from north to south are approximately five thousand kilometers and from east to west approximately ten thousand kilometers and span 11 time zones. It is approximately two and one-half times the size of the United States. About one-fourth of Soviet territory is in Europe and about three-fourths in Northern Asia.

The USSR has the world's longest frontiers and the largest number of foreign neighbors: To the west and northwest, Finland, Norway, Poland, Czechoslovakia, Hungary and Romania; to the south, Turkey, Iran, Afghanistan, China, Mongolia and Korea. On the north and the east it is bounded by seas. It is washed in the northwest by the Baltic Sea; in the east by the Pacific Ocean and its seas (The Sea of Okhotsk, the Sea of Japan and the Bering Sea); in the north by the Arctic Ocean and its seas (the White Sea, the Laptev, Kara, East Siberian, Chukchi and Barents Seas); and in the south by the Caspian Sea, the Sea of Azov and the Black Sea.

Relief: The major elevations are in the south and the east. The elevation falls off towards the north and the west. The highest points are in the Pamirs; the lowest on the east coast of the Caspian Sea. The following are the mountains over five thousand meters tall:

Peak Communism	7,495
Peak Pobeda	7,439
Lenin Peak	7,134
Khan Tengri	6,995
Elbrus	5,642
Kykh Tau	5,198
Kazbek	5,047

Drainage: The USSR possesses more than one-half million kilometers of navigable waterways, and 150,000 rivers more than ten kilometers long. There are more than one-quarter million lakes, mostly in the northwest and southeast. The longest rivers include the following: (in kilometers)

Ob	5,410
Lena	4,440
Amur	4,416
Yenisei	4,092
Volga	3,531
Syr-Darya	2,991
Amu-Darya	2,600
Kolyma	2,513
Ural	2,428
Dniepr	2,201

Chart 1 European USSR

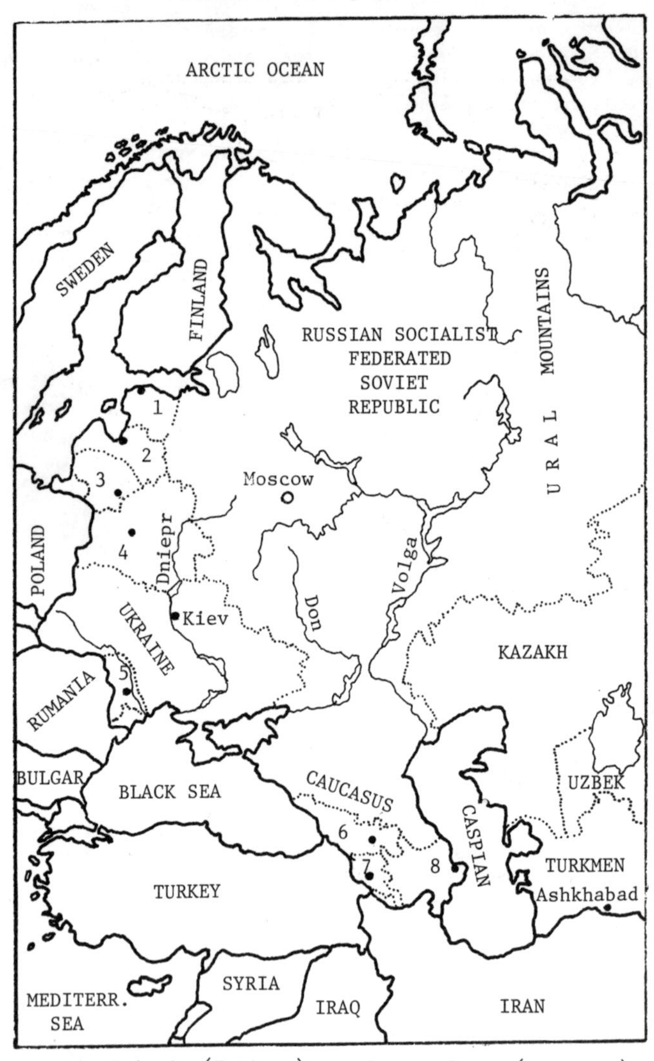

1. Estonia (Tallinn)
2. Latvia (Riga)
3. Lithuania (Vilnius)
4. Belorussia (Minsk)
5. Moldavia (Kishinev)
6. Georgia (Tbilisi)
7. Armenia (Erevan)
8. Azerbaidzhan (Baku)

Chart 2 Asian USSR

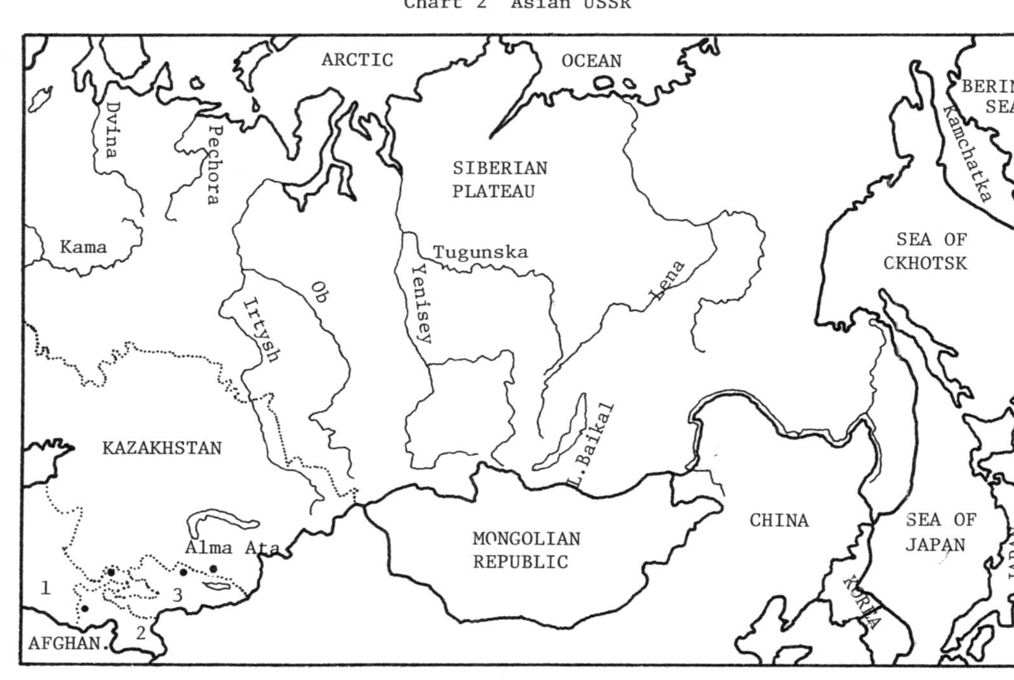

1. Uzbekistan (Tashkent) 2. Tadzhikistan (Dushanbe) 3. Kirgizia (Frunze)

The largest lakes include the following: (in square kilometers)

Caspian Sea	371,000
Sea of Aral	66,500
Baikal	31,500
Ladoga	18,400
Balkhash	18,200
Onega	9,610
Issyk-Kul	6,280

Temperature: There is a vast difference in the temperatures of the various regions. It varies from a high of 50 degrees centigrade in Central Asia to minus 75 degrees centigrade in Yakutia (northern Siberia). The European part of the USSR has the most temperate climate ranging from relatively cold weather in the north to relatively warm weather in the south. This area also has the greatest amount of precipitation.

Flora and Fauna: The Soviet Union is the world's biggest producer of timber; it owns nearly one-third of the world's forests. One-third of the USSR is covered by forests, mainly the northern areas. Most trees are coniferous, however there are also significant numbers of birch, chestnut, spruce, cedar and ash trees. In the north the forests merge into tundra - in the south into the steppe. It also possesses approximately 17,000 different plant species. The fauna are similarly diverse. There are 1,500 species of fish alone. There are 104 nature preserves located in different geographic zones for the study and preservation of both flora and fauna.

Mineral Resources: Most of the nation's natural resources are yet untapped since they seem to be concentrated in the relatively inaccessible areas of the north and the east. Nevertheless, the nation's resources are vast with new exploration and development being conducted on an accellerated basis. The USSR has the world's largest deposits of coal, natural gas, iron, manganese, and other materials. There are especially large deposits of copper, lead, zinc, aluminum, nickel, phosphorites, potassium salts and mica. The USSR also has a good share of the world's gold, silver and of precious and semi-precious stones. In addition, there seem to be indications of vast oil reserves.

Population: The Soviet Union has a population of approximately 280 million according to latest figures. There is an approximately one-percent growth per year, but not in those areas where the authorities would like to see it. While the Russians have reached a zero population growth, the non-Russian areas have been increasing their growth. For this reason, for the first time in history, the Russian share was recorded as less than half of the Soviet population in 1987.

As an after-effect of World War II, there are still considerably more women than men in the country (53.6% vs. 46.4%). The gap is narrowing, however, since there are 6% more male infants than female infants being born.

The average population density for the entire nation is 11.6 inhabitants per square kilometer Although settlements in the Asian part of the USSR have been

Chart 3

Winter and Summer Climate

Location	January Mean Temp. Fahrenheit	Minimum	July Mean Temp. Fahrenheit	Maximum	Range Fahrenheit
Russian Plain:					
Moscow	12	-44	66	99	54
Leningrad	15	-35	64	97	49
Sub-Tropical Zone:					
Tashkent	30	-15	81	109	51
Batumi	43	18	74	95	31
Siberia:					
Yakutsk	-46	-84	66	102	112
Tomsk	-3	-60	66	95	69
Verkhoyansk	-59	-90	60	93	119

Chart 4

Nature Preserves

Names (and Locations) of Largest Preserves	Size (in hectars)
Pechora-Il'ich (Northern Urals)	721,300
Barguzin (East Shore of Lake Baikal and the Barguzin Mountain Range)	248,200
Belovezhakaia Pushcha (Belorussia)	74,200
Astrakhan (Volga Delta)	60,500
Ilmen (Eastern Slopes of the Southern Ural Mountains)	32,000
Voronezh (near the city of Voronezh, European RSFSR)	30,800
Total Number of Preserves in the USSR:	104
Total Preserve Territory:	8 million hectars
Number of Plant Species:	17,000
Number of Fish Species:	1,500

Chart 5

Most Common Fauna

	Region	Fauna
a.	In the North:	Polar bear; various species of seals; walrus; polar fox; wolf; ermine; blue hare; reindeer.
b.	Forest Zone:	Brown bear; black bear; lynx; fox; wolverine; sable; squirrel; chipmunk; kolinsky; wild boar; marten; Siberian stag; roe deer.
c.	Southern Steppes and Deserts:	Tiger; cheetah; hyena; deer; steppe arkhar; Dzheiran antelope; great bustard; hare; saiga.
d.	Ussuri taiga and Far East:	Leopard and tiger.
e.	Caucasus:	Red deer; roe deer;chamois; mountain goat; ibex; moufflon.
f.	Mountains of Central Asia:	Mountain goat; arkhar; ermine; red wolf; snow leopard; spiral-horned mountain goat.

Most important fur-bearing animals for commercial reasons:
Sable; polar fox; squirrel; muskrat; mink.

strongly encouraged and have increased many-fold over the last twenty years, the great preponderance of the population is still in the European part of the Soviet Union

The nation has taken significant steps toward urbanization. There are now 22 cities with over a million population (Baku, Erevan, Gorkii, Kharkov, Kiev, Kuibyshev, Leningrad, Minsk, Moscow, Novosibirsk, Odessa, Omsk, Sverdlovsk, Tashkent, Tbilisi and others). There are 279 cities with over 100,000 population, including 45 cities with more than a half million inhabitants. There is increased urbanization with 184 million city dwellers against 96 million rural population. According to the most recent figures the social composition of the population is as follows (percent):

Workers (includes blue collar factory workers and lower level management)	61.5
Collective farmers and cooperative craftsmen	12.5
White collar workers and management	26.0

READINGS

Atlas avtomobil'nykh dorog SSSR. Moscow: Glav. uprav. geodesii i kartografii, 1987.

Armstrong, T. E. Russian Settlements in the North. Cambridge: Cambridge University Press, 1965.

Bacon, Elizabeth E. Central Asia under Russian Rule: A Study in Culture Change. Cornell University Press, 1966.

Bechtel, Marilyn and Rosenberg, Daniel (eds.) Nations & Peoples: The Soviet Experience. New York: MWR Publications, 1984.

Botting, D. One Chilly Siberian Morning. London: Hodder and Stoughton, 1965.

Fodor, Eugene and Fischer, Robert C. (eds.) Fodor's Soviet Union 1980/81. New York: David McKay, 1980.

Goldhagen, Erich (ed.) Ethnic Minorities in the Soviet Union. New York: Praeger, 1968.

Gregory. James S. Russian Land, Soviet People New York: Pegasus, 1968.

Kolarz, W. Peoples of the Soviet Far East. London: George Philip, 1954.

Kolesnik, S. V. and Pavlenko, V. F. The Soviet Union: A Geographic Survey. Moscow: Progress, 1976.

Lydolph, Paul E. Geography of the U.S.S.R. New York: Wiley and Sons, 1975.

Maly atlas SSSR. Moscow: Glav. uprav. geodesii i kartografii, 1975.

Matthews, W. K. Languages of the U.S.S.R. Cambridge: Cambridge University Press, 1951.

Nove, A. and Newth, J. A. The Soviet Middle East. London: Allen and Unwin, 1967.

Salishchev, K. A. Kartovedenie. Moscow: Izd. Moskovskogo universiteta, 1976.

Smith, Jessica (ed.) A Family of Peoples: The USSR after 50 Years. New York: NWR Publications, 1973.

USSR: The Land and the People. Moscow: Novosti Press, 1975.

Wheller, G. A Modern History of Soviet Central Asia. London: Weidenfeld and Nicholson, 1965.

Wixman, Ronald. The Peoples of the USSR: An Ethnographic Handbook. University of Oregon, 1983.

II. The Republics

The USSR is a federal state composed of fifteen sovereign republics (SSRs). Each Union Republic is a state with its own constitution (based on the federal constitution); its own judicial system; flag; national anthem; citizenship; and legislative mechanism. Each Union Republic borders on a foreign nation or international body of water, may have direct relations with foreign powers, may conclude agreements with them and may even exchange consular and diplomatic representatives with them. Its territory may not be altered without its consent. It may even secede. In reality its policies are very much tied to the Kremlin. Although the republics do have some degree of separate authority and responsibility, they cannot act independently in any situation which may even remotely affect the Soviet Union as a whole. It is up to the federal government to determine when this is so; thereby it retains total control over the republics.

Although all republics are said to be equal, this is certainly not the case since power must be measured along economic terms. If this is so, then it should be quite obvious that the power lies in the Slavic group, followed by the Trans-Caucasian group and the Baltic group. The Asian group has very little to say in matters affecting the nation as a whole.

a. The Slavic Group: The three Union Republics listed, share a common Slavic heritage and speak languages within the Slavic linguistic group. These are, however, totally separate languages and not dialects To emphasize their character as independent states, all three of these republics were granted separate memberships in the United Nations.

The Russian Soviet Federated Socialist Republic (RSFSR) is pre-eminent among all the Union Republics. It contains the seat of the national government and the Party, and has an absolute majority in all national governmental and Party bodies except the Supreme Soviet. It has the largest population (139,600,000) and an immense amount of territory (17,075,418 square kilometers) covering 76% of the total land mass of the USSR. After World War II the RSFSR annexed the northern part of East Prussia although, geographically, the new acquisition should have been absorbed by the immediately neighboring Union Republic, Lithuania. At least, this adjustment should have been logically made after Lithuania became a Soviet Republic. However, although this strategic piece of land is not contiguous to the RSFSR, it is still retained by it Possibly the RSFSR prefers to have a direct border with Poland. Shortly thereafter, it similarly annexed the entire 16th republic, the Karelian SSR, formerly Finnish territory. Approximately 83% of its population is Russian. The other 17% are divided among many other nationalities, with no one significant minority. This Union Republic also contains sixteen Autonomous Republics, the importance of which will be discussed later. The capital is Moscow (8.6 million); the second largest city is Leningrad (4.9 million). It also contains the following cities with more than one-half-million population: Gorkii, Novosibirsk, Kuibyshev, Sverdlovsk, Kazan', Cheliabinsk, Perm, Omsk, Volgograd (formerly Stalingrad), Rostov, Ufa, Saratov, Voronezh, Krasnoiarsk, Iaroslavl' and Novokuznetsk. The republic enjoys by far the highest standard of living. Shortages of consumer items do exist, but are felt to a much lesser degree than in the rest of the country. This republic also has the best educational facilities, medical care, publishing enterprises, cultural activities and entertainment. The RSFSR became a Union Republic when the federal state of the Soviet Union was created.

The Ukrainian Soviet Socialist Republic is the second most important Union Republic and second most populous (50.3 million). It occupies an area of 603,700 square kilometers. Approximately 75% of the population is Ukrainian. There is a sizeable Russian minority (approaching 20%) and one may do quite well in the main centers of population if one speaks only Russian. The capital is Kiev (2.4 million). Other cities with over a half-million population are: Kharkov, Odessa, Donetsk, Dnepropetrovsk, Zaporozhe, Krivoi Rog and Lvov. This republic also has a relatively high standard of living, second only to the RSFSR. It produces more than 20 percent of the industrial output of the USSR, and 25 percent of its grain. After World War II, when Poland annexed a large part of Germany, an equally large part of Poland was annexed by the Ukraine and was dubbed the Western Ukraine. Although some of the ethnic roots of the annexed area and the Ukrainian Republic are the same, these are certainly not the same people now. Not only are there definite linguistic differences, but also more important cultural ones. The annexed area is devoutly Roman Catholic or Uniate, while the Ukraine has traditionally been devoutly Orthodox and violently anti-Catholic and anti-Polish. In addition the Ukraine also annexed land in Eastern Czechoslovakia and Eastern Hungary for purely military reasons, i.e., to give the Soviet Armed Forces a direct path of entry to those countries. Historical events during the past three decades have borne out the effectiveness of this planning. The Ukraine too, is one of the original Soviet Republics.

The Belorussian Soviet Socialist Republic is by far the smallest of the three. It encompasses an area of 207,600 square kilometers. Its population is predominantly indigenous, however, it, too, is establishing a sizable Russian minority (10 1/2%). Its total population on numbers slightly more than 9 million. Its capital, which was totally rebuilt after having been destroyed by the Germans, is Minsk (1,300,000). It has numerous medium size cities, but few large ones. It, also, enjoys a relatively high standard of living. Generally, it is considered a rather docile pawn of the RSFSR. Minsk was rebuilt to become one of the most important centers of heavy industry. In addition, the Republic is rich in resources such as high-quality oil, coal, peat and salt. Its extensive forests are not only a resource, but also harbor varieties of animals and birds which have become extinct elsewhere. Belorussia, too, is one of the original Republics.

b. The Trans-Caucasian Group: Each of these three Republics has a cultural heritage dating back much further than that of the Russians and has developed a measure of superior feeling because of this. Traditionally, the Soviet state has given them more freedom of action than any of the other non-Slavic states. This group also enjoys a relatively high standard of living primarily because of its extremely fertile land, its agricultural prowess, and its significant food industry.

The Armenian Soviet Socialist Republic, the smallest of the fifteen, has an area of 29,800 square kilometers. Its total population is 3,000,000, which is heavily indigenous (88.6%). The capital is Erevan with a population of 1,000,000. Most Armenians are easily identified by their names which end in "ian." Historically ancient Armenia encompassed a large section of northern Turkey, including Mount Ararat. The present day Armenians have not forgotten the massacre of Armenians

Chart 6

Names and Locations of Principal Ethnic Groups

Slavic Groups — *Great Russians* (Western RSFSR, a fairly wide belt in the western and southern part of RSFSR, thinning across central Siberia with "islands" in northern and eastern Siberia, in Kamchatka, Magadan, along the upper Ob, Yenisey and Lena Rivers, and in the southern Ukraine, including Crimea); *Ukrainians* (Ukrainian SSR, in bordering regions of the RSFSR, and in northern Caucasus); *Byelorussians* (Byelorussian SSR).

Moldavian -- *Moldavians* (Moldavian SSR), Rumanian origin.

Turkic Groups — *Tatars* (main concentration in Volga Region, others widely scattered); *Bashkirs* ("islands" in the west of the Urals); *Kazakhs, Uzbeks, Kirghiz, Turkmen, Kara-Kalpaks, Uygurs, Dungans* (Central Asia); *Yakuts,* (N. and E. Siberia); *Dolgans* (N. Siberia); *Khakass, Tuvinians* (S. Siberia); *Azers, Kumyks, Karapapakhs* (Caucasus).

Finno-Ugrian Groups — *Mordovinians, Udmurt, Mari* (between Volga and the Urals); *Komi* (N. Urals); *Karels, Finns* (extreme northwest); *Estonians* (Estonian SSR).

Baltic Groups — *Latvians, Latgals, Lithuanians* (along the Baltic, North of Byelorussia).

Caucasian Groups — *Georgians, Armenians, Dagestanians, Chechen-Ingush, Cherkess, Kabardinians, Abkhaz* (the Caucasus area).

Iranian Groups — *Osetins, Kurds, Talysh, Tats, Yezids* (the Caucasus); *Tadzhiks* (Central Asia).

Mongol Groups — *Buryats* (several large islands north of the Mongolian Peoples' Republic); *Kalmyks* (some remnants along the Caspian Sea).

Tungus — Manchurian Groups — *Tungus* (N. Siberia); *Evenki* (Krasnoyarsk Krai).

Palaeo — Asiatic Groups — *Chukchi, Koryaks, Kamchadals* (N. E. Siberia); *Ainos* (Sakhalin).

by the Turks in the 1920's. The entire northern section of Iran has a heavy Armenian population which fled there from Turkey and which has close family ties with Armenia in the USSR. The anti-Christian fundamentalism of the present Iranian government has frightened Armenians on both sides of the border. Although the use of Russian is quite prevalent, the native Armenians communicate in the Armenian language and writing system. Besides a flourishing food industry, to include excellent brandies and wines, Armenia has also, in a very short time, built a respectible chemical, non-ferrous metal, textile and machinery industry. Armenia became a Union Republic in November, 1920.

The Azerbaidzhan Soviet Socialist Republic occupies an area of 86,000 square kilometers. It has a total population of six million with sizable Russian and Armenian minorities of approximately 10% each. Its capital is Baku (1,700,000 people), and is located on the Caspian Sea. It is the only Trans-Caucasian Republic which is predominantly Moslem. Approximately 70 percent of the population are indigenous. Baku owes its existence to the oil industry. It is surrounded with thousands of oil derricks, even on its Caspian Sea shore, where small oil towns have been constructed as far as one hundred kilometers into the sea itself for offshore drilling operations. Other than oil, the Republic has some natural gas deposits and stone quarries for construction purposes, but little else. Most of the region is quite arrid and bare. Azerbaidzhan became a Union Republic in April, 1920.

The Georgian Soviet Socialist Republic has an area of 69,700 square kilometers. It has a total population of 5 million, and sizable minorities of Armenians and Russians (10% and 9% respectively). Its capital is Tbilisi with 1,100,00 population. It is fondly remembered by many as the birthplace of Stalin. It has beautiful scenery, excellent climate and areas (e.g. Abkhazia) with lengendary longevity. Most Georgians may be identified by their family names which end in "shvili" or "adze." Approximately 85 percent of the Republic is mountainous and one-third is covered by forest. Georgia, too, has been able to industrialize in a relatively short time. It is no longer restricted to producing tea, wine and tobacco, but has been able to develop its non-metallic mineral mines and the processing of ores, through a remarkable development of its power resources. During the past decade, Georgia constructed a heavy industry which produces sheet metal, locomotives and earth moving equipment. It became a Union Republic in 1921.

c. The Baltic Group: These three republics were constituted by the USSR in July 1940. None of them have any linguistic, ethnic or cultural relationship with any other entity in the Soviet Union. They were annexed ostensibly for territorial security reasons, and because a portion of their territory had previously been (forcibly) occupied by Tsarist Russia. In reality, this act of annexation was a purely imperialistic move which took place during the Hitler-Stalin pact period and which was later passively sanctioned by the United States at the Helsinki Accords

The Estonian Soviet Socialist Republic covers an area of 45,100 square kilometers. Its total population is 1,500,000. It is the intent of the Soviet regime that the strong ethnic feelings of the Estonians be eroded. There is therefore a very clever design in operation, which offers Estonians considerable educational and work benefits in other parts of the USSR. At the same time, there has been a strong influx of Russians into Estonia, so that by now fully one-fourth of the population of the Republic is Russian. This is especially true in the capital, Tallinn, which has a population of 430,000 and is a fashionable spa for the Russian upper class. The economy of Estonia is primarily based on industry of the following categories: Machine construction including oil refining equipment; electronics; agricultural machinery; mining and excavating machinery; and scientific instruments. It also possesses a highly productive agriculture.

The Latvian Soviet Socialist Republic encompasses an area of 63,700 square kilometers. Its total population is two and one-half million. Much of what was said about Estonia is also true for Latvia. Only slightly more than half of the population is now Latvian. Approximately one-third of the population is Russian. There are also considerable numbers of Belorussians and Ukrainians present. The capital is Riga with a population of 835,000. The economy is based on both industry and agriculture. It produces refrigerators, washing machines, bicycles, ships, streetcars, generators and agricultural machinery. It also specializes in diversified crops, animal husbandry and fisheries.

The Lithuanian Soviet Socialist Republic occupies an area of 65,200 square kilometers. Its total population is 3,500,000, with its capital, Vilnius, populated by 481,000 inhabitants. The two significant minorities are Russians and Poles, with 10% of the population respectively. Lithuania has a wide range of mineral deposits including gypsum, sulfates, chalk, peat, phosphorites and iron. It is heavily industrialized and produces both heavy and light machinery. Like the other two Baltic Republics, it also has a well producing agriculture, primarily in animal husbandry.

d. The Asian Group: These Union Republics are by far the most backward and economically deprived. Yet, the Russians regard this area much in the same light as the Americans regarded their West in the late nineteenth century. This is an area with great potential. There are vast projects of land reclamation and exploration being conducted at the present. Many young Russians with pioneer spirit prefer the heat of this area to the bitter cold of Eastern Siberia.

The Kazakh Soviet Socialist Republic is the second largest Union Republic, with an area of 2,717,335 square kilometers. Its total population is not quite 16 million The capital is Alma Ata with a population of 930,000. This is the Republic with the greatest economic and political potential in Asia. Not only is it a major supplier of raw materials, but it is also the site of major agricultural land reclamation projects. It is expected that the grain and cotton production of the republic will soon be second only to that of the RSFSR. There is little doubt this republic is fast becoming an internal colony of the RSFSR and a solid pro-Russian voting block in both the government and the Party. Only 32% of the population is indigenous, while 43% is Russian and 7% Ukrainian. There is considerable enmity between the Russians and the Kazakhs which came to a head in early 1987. The indigenous chairman of the Communist Party of Kazakhstan, D. Kunaev, was relieved from that position and removed from the Politburo. More significantly, his duties and Party head were given to an ethnic Russian. These actions brought about severe riots in Alma Ata in which many thousands of Kazakh university students participated. Slogans protested the "Russification" of their homeland and the imposition of Russian colonial rule. They insisted upon the reinstatement of Kunaev but were, of course, unsuccessful. Since Kazakhstan is a great mineral reservoir and has untold economic potential for the nation, Gorbachev did not want its future to remain in the hands of Kunaev, whom he considered to be a corrupt and inefficient crony of Brezhnev. Kazakhstan became a Union Republic in December, 1936.

The Kirgizian Soviet Socialist Republic comprises an area of 198,500 square kilometers. Its total population of 3,500,000 encompasses 43.5% Kirghizians, 30% Russians, 11.0% Uzbeks and 4.2% Ukrainians. The capital is Frunze with a population of 533,000. This Republic, too, is fast becoming a sphere of influence of the Russian Federation. Kirghizia has immense coal reserves and other major deposits including oil, gas and non-ferrous metals. It also produces a large amount of mutton and wool, cotton, and various other agricultural products, mostly as a result of a major irrigation project. It also became a Union Republic in 1936.

The Tadzhik Soviet Republic occupies an area of 143,100 square kilometers. Its population of 3.8 million includes 56.2% Tadzhiks, 23% Uzbeks and 12% Russians. The capital is Dushanbe with 500,000 inhabitants. There are definite attempts towards industrialization and there are major deposits of natural resources including oil, coal and metallic ores in Tadzhikistan. It possesses the largest hydro-electric power station in Central Asia. Although great strides have been made in developing this Republic, it is still one of the poorest and most backward. It was founded in 1929.

The Turkmen Soviet Socialist Republic has an area of 488,100 square kilometers. Its population of 2,800,000 includes 65% Turkmen, 16% Russian and 8% Uzbeks. Here, too, Russian influence is steadily growing. The capital is Ashkhabad with 312,000 inhabitants. Its major products include iodine, bromine, a great deal of natural gas, oil and cotton. Most of the upper stratum of technicians is Russian, while the indiginous population has rather low standards of living and education. Turkmenistan was formed in October, 1924.

The Uzbek Soviet Socialist Republic comprises an area of 447,400 square kilometers. Its total population of 15.5 million includes 64.5% Uzbeks, 13% Russians, and a 13% total of Tatars, Kazakhs and Tadzhiks. Its capital is Tashkent, with 1.8 million population. Uzbekistan is among the most interesting Republics due to its cultural heritage which is exposed in cities such as Samarkand and Bukhara. It is the second largest silk producer in the world. It has great oil, coal and gas reserves. The latter is piped to the European parts of the USSR. It is also the main producer of heavy machinery and equipment in Central Asia. The Republic also has a thriving cotton-growing and cattle-raising agriculture. It, too, was founded in October, 1924.

e. The fifteenth republic is one which cannot be included in any of the other groups. It is the Moldavian Soviet Socialist Republic which became part of the USSR in 1940. It, too, is an excellent example of Soviet expansionism. It was taken away from Rumania although the population has no ethnic or cultural common roots with any part of the Soviet Union. By now, fully a third of the population is Russian or Ukrainian. It has a highly productive food and alcohol industry and is therefore of considerable economic importance. Its total population is 3,900,000 of which 504,000 reside in the capital, Kishinev. It has the highest population density of any Republic. The SSR was established in August, 1940.

READINGS

Armstrong, J. A. Ukrainian Nationalism. New York: Columbia University Press, 1963.

Barghoorn, Frederick C. Soviet Russian Nationalism New York: Oxford University Press, 1956.

Bilinsky, Yaroslav. The Second Soviet Republic: The Ukraine After World War II. New Brunswick: Rutgers University Press, 1964.

Borys, Jurij. The Russian Communist Party and the Sovietization of the Ukraine. A Study in the Communist Doctrine of the Self-Determination of Nations. Stockholm: Norstedt and Soner, 1960.

Browne, Michael, (ed.). Ferment in the Ukraine. London: Macmillan, 1970.

Davies, R. W., (ed). The Soviet Union. London: George Allen and Unwin, 1978.

Dzyuba, I. Internationalism or Russification. London: Weidenfeld and Nicolson, 1968.

Karklins, Rasma. Ethnic Relations in the USSR: The Perspective from Below. Winchester: Allen & Unwin, 1986.

Lang, D. M. A Modern History of Georgia. New York: Grove Press, 1962.

Matossian, M. The Impact of Soviet Policies in Armenia. Leiden: Brill, 1962.

Rutkis, Janis, (ed.). Latvia: Country and People. Stockholm: Latvian National Foundation, 1967.

Schuyler, Eugene. Turkistan. New York: Praeger, 1966.

Sprudzs, Adolf and Rusis (eds.) Res Baltica. Leiden: Sijthoff, 1968.

Sullivant, Robert S. Soviet Politics and the Ukraine. New York: Columbia University Press, 1962.

Vaidyanath, R. The Formation of the Soviet Central Asian Republics. New Delhi: People's Publishing House, 1967.

Vardys, V. Stanley. Lithuania under the Soviets. New York: Praeger, 1965

III. Political Subdivisions

Each Union Republic (SSR) is a national, sovereign state. It sends 32 deputies to the Soviet of Nationalities of the Supreme Soviet of the USSR. Within these Republics, there may be other subdivisions which do retain a certain degree of autonomy, but are nevertheless integral parts of the Union Republic in which they are located. In order of significance, they are as follows:

a. The Autonomous Republic (ASSR): This republic also has it own constitution which is patterned after the national constitution but adds certain specific provisions pertaining to the ASSR; its own citizenship; national emblem; flag; capital city; parliament; executive branch; and judicial system. Its territory may not be altered without its consent. It has no direct relations with foreign countries, nor may it engage in any activities which have a direct or indirect effect on the SSR or the USSR. There are twenty ASSR's in the Soviet Union, sixteen of them located in the RSFSR. This is certainly not by chance. Although one of the prerequisites of an ASSR is the existence of a relatively large ethnic group in a relatively large area, there are several other SSR's which contain groups that would fulfill this requirement. It is, however, to the great political advantage of the RSFSR to possess the vast majority of ASSR's on their own territory for a very simple reason: each ASSR may send an additional eleven delegates to the Soviet of Nationalities of the USSR Supreme Soviet. This gives the Russian Republic a disproportionately stronger voice than would be warranted by its population figures.

b. The Autonomous Region (Oblast; AO): This is a national territory which, due to its national composition and other special features, is granted a degree of political and administrative autonomy. An AO is an integral part of an SSR. Its governing body is the Oblast' Council, which is empowered to consider only local questions. There is a total of eight AO's in the Soviet Union, five of which are in the RSFSR. Again, this is understandable, since each AO sends five deputies to the national parliament.

c. The National Area (Okrug; NO): An NO is normally populated by several, numerically weak nationalities. Most commonly, the area is relatively large and extremely sparsely populated. There are ten NO's in the Soviet Union, all of them located in the RSFSR. Except for the normal duties of their local authorities, NO's have no political or administrative autonomy. Each does, however, send one delegate to the national parliament.

d. The Territory (Kray): This subdivision incorporates some of the functions of the AO and the ASSR but is not represented in the national parliament. It is usually quite large in territory and rather sparsely populated. Its boundaries have been laid out rather arbitrarily, primarly for administrative facility. A Kray may contain NO's, AO's or both. There are six Krays in the Soviet Union:

Chart 7

Political Subdivisions

ASSR's:

In RSFSR	In Azerbaidzhan	In Georgia	In Uzbekistan
Bashkir	Nakhichevan	Abkhazian	Kara-Kalpak
Buriat		Adzharian	
Chechen-Ingush			
Chuvash			
Dagestan			
Kabardion-Balkar			
Kalmyk			
Karelian			
Komi			
Mari			
Mordovian			
North Ossetian			
Tatar			
Tuva			
Udmurt			
Yakut			

Autonomous Oblast':

In RSFSR	In Azerbaidzhan	In Georgia
Adygei	Nagornyi Karabakh	South Ossetian
Gornyi Altai		
Jewish	In Tadzhikistan	
Karachai-Cherkess		
Khakass	Gornyi Badakhshan	

National Areas (Okrug); All located in the RSFSR.

Agin-Buriat	Nenets	Khanty-Mansi
Komi-Permiak	Taimyr	Chukchi
Koriak	Ust-Ordin Buriat	Evenki
		Yamalo-Nenets

Altai
Krasnodar
Krasnoiarsk
Maritime
Stavropol
Khabarovsk

e. The District (Rayon): At the lowest level of administration, all areas are divided into Rayons. There are City Rayons and Rural Rayons. All economic report is normally broken down to the Oblast' level, and virtually never down to the Rayon level.

f. A number of cities of special importance, although they fall within the territory of a Rayon, do not have to report through the normal chain of command, but are responsible directly to the Union Republic. All the cities listed as having more than a million population fall into this category.

READINGS

Anderson, Thornton. Russian Political Thought. Ithaca: Cornell University Press, 1967.

Cattell, David T. Leningrad: A Cast Study of Soviet Urban Government. New York: Praeger, 1968.

Conquest, Robert (ed.) Soviet Nationalities Policy in Practice. New York: Praeger, 1967.

_______. The Soviet Deportation of Nationalities. New York: St. Martin's Press, 1960.

______. The Politics of Ideas in the USSR. New York: Praeger, 1967.

Farrell, R. Barry (ed.) Political Leadership in Eastern Europe and the Soviet Union. Chicago: Aldine Publishing Company, 1970.

Goldhagen, E. (ed.) Ethnic Minorities in the Soviet Union. New York: Praeger, 1968.

Gutnov, Alexei et. al. The Ideal Communist City. New York: George Braziller, 1968.

Hammer, Darrell P. The USSR: The Politics of Oligarchy. Boulder: Westview, 1986.

Millar, James R. The Soviet Rural Community. Urbana: University of Illinois Press, 1971.

Mote, Max E. Soviet Local and Republic Elections. Stanford: Hoover Institution, 1965.

Pipes, Richard. The Formation of the Soviet Union. Cambridge: Harvard University Press, 1964.

Rakowska-Harmstone, Teresa. Russia and Nationalism in Central Asia. Baltimore: Johns Hopkins University Press, 1970.

IV. The System of Elections and The Governmental Structure

The term "soviet" means council. There are soviets on all levels of governmental subdivisions. Every citizen of the Soviet Union who is eighteen years old may be elected deputy to a local soviet; at the age of twenty-one he may be elected to the Supreme Soviet of a Republic (SSR), an ASSR and, in accordance with a new law, even to the Supreme Soviet of the USSR. All Soviet citizens who have reached the age of eighteen, except for those who have been declared legally insane, have the right to vote.

The nominating process, according to Soviet thinking, is relatively simple. On the local level, candidates are nominated by plant workers, the Party, military units, public organizations or collective farm members. The candidates are then discussed by all those present. Collectively, the decision is reached by the nominators as to which candidate is best. This is the one candidate who is then placed on the ballot. There is a minimum of electioneering at absolutely no expense to the candidate. There is no conflict between two or more persons, accompanied by destructive mud-slinging and false promises. The single individual selected has been nominated not by outside interests, but by his own peer group. The ballot then reflects only one name for each open position. The voters then have the right to vote either yes or no. Since the candidate has the support of all nominators and of the Party, it very rarely happens that a no-vote predominates. In the last series of elections at which more than two million deputies were to be chosen, fewer than a hundred received a predominance of no-votes. All elections are by secret ballot.

Although the above process appears to be quite logical, orderly and inexpensive, it does have a number of shortcomings. During the initial nominating procedures, it is quite obvious that only those persons are nominated who would be acceptable for political reasons. In addition, a powerful majority will always impose its will upon a weaker minority. By the same token, a strong minority, e.g., a Party organization, may impose its selection upon a weak majority. In early 1987 Gorbachev announced that he was going to propose a gradual change of the system of elections and that he intended to investigate the possibility of extending this tentative system to general governmental elections. The major element in the innovation is to be a change from the single candidate system to a multiple candidate system. In other words, the ballots will no longer contain one name with boxes to check which say "yes" or "no", but rather the names of at least two candidates for each position to be filled. The first trial elections using this system, on a limited basis, were scheduled for June, 1987. A new law governing elections is to be promulgated in early 1988.

A "deputy" is the elected representative of his constituency on any level. He is accountable to his constituency and has to report to it regularly. He is obliged to participate in the work of his soviet and any of its committees to the best of his ability. No matter on what level he may be, his work as a deputy is not considered to be his profession. He still remains on the rolls of his original job which he held when he was first elected. He is paid by his original place of work, not by the soviet. He works at his duties as a delegate only when the soviet is in session.

Otherwise, he works at whatever job he holds permanently. Therefore, contrary to the system in capitalist countries, being elected to a legislature does not mean a raise in income, but rather an increase in work. Soviet citizens therefore become delegates only because of their dedication and their desire to serve, according to Soviet official pronouncements. This is all not quite true, however. Although Soviet delegates still receive their old pay, it is strongly augmented with bonuses for volunteer activities. In addition, delegates enjoy numerous prestigious privileges, e.g. travel, special stores, promotions, which result in considerable financial benefit

A deputy has certain rights: He may not be hindered by anyone in the fulfillment of his duties, under penalty of the law. If he sits in any of the Supreme Soviets, it is his right to introduce legislation. He has the right to submit inquiries to the government echelon on his level. He enjoys immunity and may not be arrested and prosecuted without the consent of the soviet to which he has been elected. He has free use of all rail, water, motor and air transport. He is reimbursed for all personnel expenses.

The pertinent chart outlines the various levels of government from the local to the national level. We will concern ourselves primarily with the composition of the Supreme Soviet of the USSR. It consist of two chambers: the Soviet of the Union (750 deputies) and the Soviet of Nationalities (750 deputies). The Soviet of the Union concerns itself with the common interests of all Soviet citizens, regardless of their nationality. The Soviet of Nationalities does likewise, but also represents the specific interests of the many nationalities and national groups in matters concerning their economies and cultures.

The Soviet of the Union is elected on the basis of one deputy for a specified number of population. The Soviet of Nationalities is elected in the following manner: 32 deputies from each of the SSR's; 11 deputies from each ASSR; 5 deputies from each autonomous region; and one deputy from each National Area.

The two chambers have equal rights. They are elected at the same time and have concurrent terms of four years. They have the same right to initiate legislation and to vote The following are the functions of the Supreme Soviet:

Endorses the State Budget.
Approves national economic plans.
Concludes, ratifies and abrogates international treaties.
Decides on declaration of war
Initiates new republics into the USSR
Controls the observance of the Constitution of the USSR.
Controls the conformity of the Constitution of the SSR's to the
Constitution of the USSR.
Approves border changes between Republics.
Approves formation of new ASSR's and AO's.
Defines use of national raw materials.
Health, labor and education legislation.
Defines legislation on judicial procedures.
Lays basis for civil and criminal legislation.
Declares amnesties.
Legislates rights of foreigners.

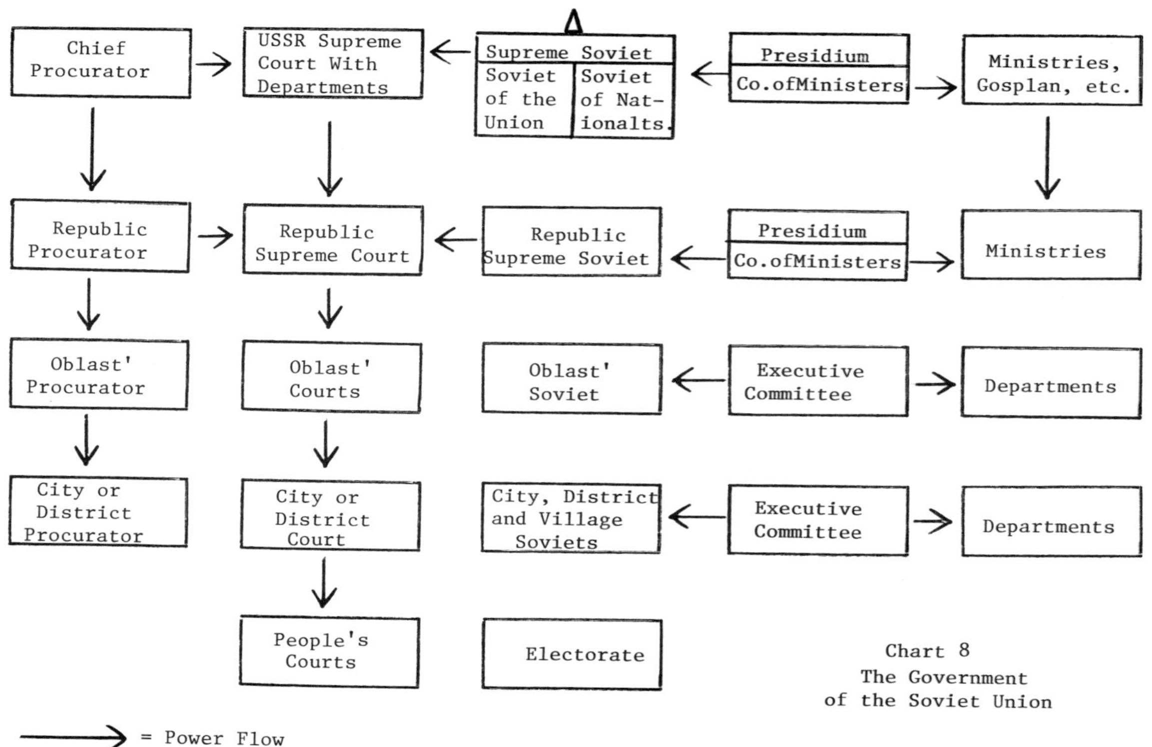

Chart 8
The Government
of the Soviet Union

Legislates procedures of attaining citizenship.
Exercises highest control over all government bodies.

At a joint meeting of the two chambers, the Presidium of the Supreme Soviet of the USSR is elected. This is a permanently operating body which straddles the line between legislative and executive and is theoretically the highest state authority in the land. The make-up of the Presidium is as follows:

The Chairman of the Presidium (often referred to as the President of the USSR)
The First Vice-Chairman of the Presidium
The Secretary of the Presidium
15 Vice Chairmen of the Presidium, each representing an SSR.
21 additional members.

The Presidium acts primarily in those lengthy and frequent intervals when the Supreme Soviet is not in session. It has the power to appoint or remove members of the government; appoint or dismiss members of the Supreme Court; and to introduce legislation. In all cases, the decisions of the Presidium are presented for approval to the next session of the Supreme Soviet, after the fact. It would be difficult to recall an instance when such decisions were not approved, since all decisions of importance, no matter by whom they are made, must first be cleared by the Party. The functions of the Chairman of the Presidium are primarily ceremonial.

Each of the two chambers also has standing committees whose responsibility it is to draft bills, to control the activities of administrative bodies, and to control the implementation of legislation. Some of these committees are as follows:

Committee for legislative proposals.
Committee for planning and budget.
Committee for credentials.
Committee for foreign affairs.
Committee for youth affairs.
Committee for nature conservation.
Committee for industry.
Committee for public services.
Committee for municipal economy.
Committee for transport and communications.
Committee for trade.
Committee for construction and building materials
Committee for science and cultural affairs
Committee for agriculture.
Committee for education.
Committee for consumer goods.
Committee for public health and social security.

In reality, the most powerful governmental entity is the Council of Ministers. Its members are appointed by the Supreme Soviet at a joint session. In fact, the composition of this body is predetermined by the Party. This is the body which issues day to day operational instructions to all divisions of the national government. Its many members include:

Chart 9

The Supreme Soviet of the USSR

Women	475	(31.3%)
Armed Forces	56	
Party Members	1,096	(72.2%)
Young Communist League	174	(11.5%)
Under 30 years old	279	(18.4%)
Workers	498	
Collective farmers	271	
Engineers and Technicians	77	
Science, Culture Literature, Art	142	
Employees of the State labor union, and Party	473	
Total deputies:	1,500	

Chart 10
The Council of Ministers of the USSR:
Composition

a. Ministries: (Those which are marked with an asterisk exist only on the All-Union level. The other have counterparts on the SSR level).

Ministry (of) (for)	Agriculture
"	Agricultural Procurement
"	Assembly and Special Construction Work
"	Aviation Industry *
"	Automobile and Truck Industry *
"	Building Materials Industry
"	Cellulose Paper Industry *
"	Chemical Industry *
"	Chemical and Petroleum Machinery Industry *
"	Civil Aviation *
"	Coal Industry
"	Construction
"	Construction in the Oils and Gas Industry *
"	Construction of Heavy Industrial Enterprises
"	Construction, Road and Communal Machinery Industries *
"	Culture
"	Defense *
"	Defense Industry *
"	Education
"	Energy and Electrification
"	Energy Machinery Industry *
"	Finance
"	Fisheries
"	Food Industry
"	Foreign Affairs
"	Foreign Trade *
"	Gas Industry *
"	General Machinery Industry *
"	Geology
"	Health
"	Heavy and Transportation Machinery Industries *
	Higher and Specialized Secondary Education
	Industrial Construction
"	Instrumentation, Automation Method and Control Systems Industries *
"	Justice
	Light Industry *
"	Machine Tool and Tool Industries *
"	Machinery Industry *
	Machinery for Livestock-Raising and Feed Industry *
"	Machinery for Light Industry, Food Industry and for Consumer Appliances *

Chart 10 (Cont.)

Ministry (of) (for)	Means of Communication Industry *
"	Meat and Dairy Industry
	Medical Industry *
	Medium Machinery Industry *
"	Merchant Marine *
"	Non-Ferrous Metals Industry
	Oil Industry *
"	Oil-Refining and Petro-Chemical Industry
	Procurements
"	Radio-Technical Industry *
"	Railroads *
"	Reclamation and Water Management
"	Rural Construction
"	Shipbuilding Industry *
"	Timber and Wood Products Industry
"	Tractor and Agricultural Machinery Industry *
"	Trade
"	Transportation Construction *

b. State committees or Commissions:

Committee for	Construction
"	Films
"	Forestry
"	Foreign Economic Ties
"	KGB (Committee for State Security)
"	Labor and Social Questions
"	Planning GOSPLAN
"	Prices
"	Publishing, Printing and Book Trade
"	Science and Technology
"	Sports and Physical Culture
"	Standards
"	Supplies Procurement
"	Television and Radio

c. Other Member Bodies:

All-Union Agricultural Supply Agency
Central Statistical Administration
People's Control
Procuracy
State Bank
Supreme Court

The Chairman of the Council of Ministers;
Four First Deputy Chairmen;
Several Deputy Chairmen (the number fluctuates);
The Chairmen of the standing committees;
The Ministers;
The Chairmen of the Councils of Ministers of each of the fifteen SSR's.

Because of the large number of members of the Council of Ministers, there is a "kitchen cabinet" called the Presidium of the Council of Ministers composed of the Chairman and First Deputy Chairman; the Minister of Defense; head of the KGB; head of GOSPLAN; Minister of Foreign Affairs; Procurator General; and any one else called in for a special discussion. The actual composition of this Presidium is never discussed in the press.

The national government is also responsible for the appointment of the Supreme Court and of the Procurator. These offices will be discussed in the chapter on the Judiciary. In addition, possibly the busiest hierarchy in the government is the State Planning Commission. It, too, will be discussed later in the chapter on Economic Planning.

The Supreme Soviets of the SSR's consist of only one chamber. The number of delegates to each of these Supreme Soviets depends on individual population figures and republic laws. For example, the RSFSR has a Supreme Soviet with 904 deputies, while the Turkmen SSR has only 229 deputies. Its powers are restricted to problems contained within the borders of the pertinent SSR. It, also, has a Presidium, standing committees and a Council of Ministers.

The ASSR's have a governmental system nearly identical to that of the SSR's. Its numerical composition is, however, considerably smaller than that of the SSR's.

The local soviets are those that exist on regional, rural district, city district, town and village level. Their governing body is the Executive Committee. It incorporates all the functions of a Council of Ministers, on a highly localized level. Depending on the population, local soviets may have a membership of anywhere from 20 to 150. Nation-wide, there are approximately 2 million delegates to local soviets.

READINGS

Berman, Harold J. and Quigley, John B., Jr. Basic Laws on the Structure of the Soviet State. Cambridge: Harvard University Press, 1969.

Brzezinski, Zbigniew (ed.) Dilemmas of Change in Soviet Politics. New York: Columbia University Press, 1969.

_____ Ideology and Power in Soviet Politics. New York: Praeger, 1962.

Gureev, P. P. and Sedugin, P. I., eds. Legislation in the USSR. Moscow: Progress, 1977.

Hough, Jerry F. and Fainsod, Merle. How the Soviet Union is Governed. Cambridge: Harvard University Press, 1979.

Hough, Jerry F. Soviet Leadership in Transition. Washington, D.C.: The Brookings Institution, 1980.

Lane, David. Politics and Society in the U.S.S.R. New York: New York University Press, 1978.

Matthews, Mervyn (ed.) Soviet Government. New York: Taplinger Publishing, 1974.

Rahr, Alexander G A Biographic Directory of 100 Leading Sovioet Officials. Munich: Radio Liberty Research, 3rd. Ed., 1986.

Reshetar, John S. Jr The Soviet Polity. New York: Harper and Row, 1978.

Rush, Myron. Political Succession in the USSR. New York: Columbia University Press, 1965.

Schapiro, Leonard. The Government and Politics of the Soviet Union. New York: Random House, 1967.

Steward, Philip D. Political Power in the Soviet Union. Indianapolis: Bobbs-Merrill, 1968.

Vanneman, Peter. The Supreme Soviet: Politics and Legislative Process. Consortium for Comparative Legislative Studies, Duke University, 1977.

Wesson, Robert G. The Soviet Russian State. New York: John Wiley & Sons, 1972.

V. The Judiciary and Law Enforcement

The Soviet legislative process requires that the following stages be carefully followed in the process of making laws:

a. Legislative Initiative:

The right to initiate legislation is vested in those persons and groups who are authorized to express the views and desires of large segments of the population of the USSR. Such persons and groups include the following:

members of the Supreme Soviet;
the Presidium of the Supreme Soviet;
members of the Council of Ministers;
mass organizations (e.g., trade unions, Komsomol, women's organization, Red Cross society, etc);
the Supreme Court;
the Procurator General;
the Party (CPSU).

b. Consideration by a Legislative Body:

Once legislation has been initiated, it is considered by a body or bodies which are best qualified to judge the quality and pertinence of the legislation and which are able to compose the final version of a draft law. In most cases this duty is assigned to the standing committees of the Supreme Soviet whose area is most pertinent to the subject of the proposed law. The committee would also work closely together with the Legislative Proposals Committee whose function it is to supervise the promulgation of the final draft

c. Adoption and Promulgation:

Once the law is in the required format, it is voted on by both chambers of the Supreme Soviet of the USSR. A two-thirds majority is required for approval. It is then signed by the Chairman and the Secretary of the Presidium of the Supreme Soviet. It must then be published. Most important laws are published in the Party newspaper Pravda or the government newspaper Izvestia. All laws must also be published in the Gazette of the Supreme Soviet. In some cases, where classified information is involved, they are published only in classified publications.

According to the precepts of the USSR, "Soviet justice defends the social and state order, the socialist economic system and socialist property, the political, labor, housing, property and other rights of citizens, and teaches citizens to observe the law strictly and undeviatingly and to be honest in regard to their national and civic duties." Evidently this statement indicates definite differences between the Soviet system and ours. The Soviet system of justice is there primarily to uphold the political and economic system. It is more concerned with a citizen's duties than his rights.

The Soviet judiciary has to follow the following regulations:
No arrests may be made without a court decision or a Procurator's warrant.
No person may be declared guilty or subjected to penalty unless convicted by a court of law.

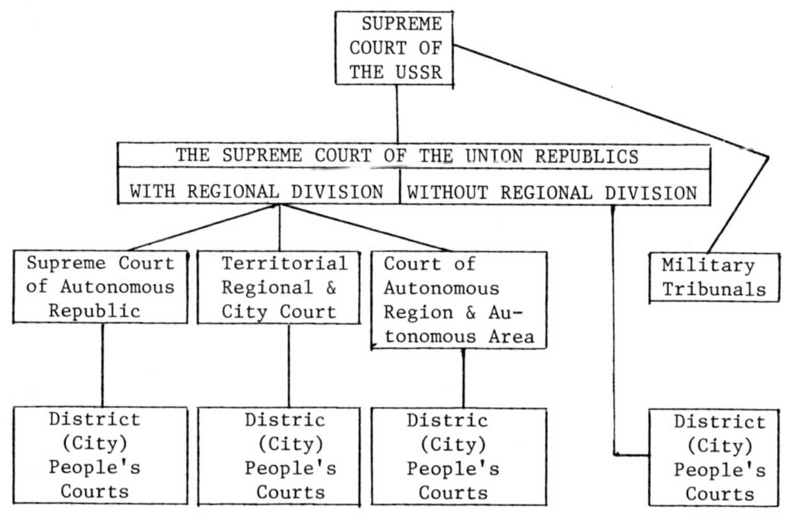

Chart 11

THE SOVIET COURT SYSTEM - ALL LEVELS

All citizens are equal before the law and the court.
Legal proceedings must be in a language which the accused understands.
The accused must be given the opportunity to study the case thoroughly before the trial.
The trial is open and the accused has the right to defense.

Quite obviously, there are numerous exceptions made to the above regulations. Certainly not all KGB officials wait for court action or a warrant before they arrest a suspect. Many persons suffer a penalty before they are convicted, for example, many lose their livelihood for dissident activities without ever having appeared before a court of law. It is also untrue that all citizens are treated equally by the court. A Russian, all other things being equal, receives much better treatment by the court than a Jew or a Tartar. It is also untrue that all trials are open. The most important political trials are definitely closed to the public under the pretense that an open trial may adversely affect the public order.

The following are the levels of Soviet courts:

a. The Supreme Court of the USSR: This is the highest judicial body in the country. It consists of:

(1) The Plenum of the Supreme Court of the USSR, which is composed of the Chairmen of the Supreme Courts of the Union Republics. The task of this body is to codify judicial practices and draw up directives for the lower courts to follow. It makes recommendations which the Supreme Court of the USSR submits to the Supreme Soviet, for the improvement of legislative practices. It also reviews appeals of Supreme Court decisions. The Plenum convenes every three months.

(2) The Judicial Board of Criminal Cases.
(3) The Judicial Board for Civil Cases.
(4) The Military Judicial Board.

All three judicial boards examine only cases of extreme importance which are brought before them as a court of first instance. They handle cases that are too involved or politically dangerous for lower courts to handle.

b. The Supreme Court of the Union Republics: Just as in the case of the Supreme Court of the USSR, the law does not specify exactly what cases fall under the jurisdiction of this court. It has the right to take over any case within the jurisdiction of a lower court, when it is felt that the importance of the case warrants special attention. It, too, has a Plenum which supervises the activities of all the subordinate courts in the SSR.

c. City, Regional, AO, NO, and ASSR Courts: These courts handle more important cases which would better not be handled by the People's Courts. They are also the approving authority for cases concluded by the People's Courts.

d. The People's Courts: These courts are the workhorse of the Soviet judicial system. They handle nearly 96% of all cases of civil or criminal nature. There are People's Courts in every city district and town.

The composition of Soviet courts of first instance does not vary. There is always one judge and two lay assessors. All judges are elected for a term of five years. Assessors serve for one or two years. The Supreme Courts are elected by the appropriate Supreme Soviets. District, regional and city courts are elected by the appropriate local soviets. People's Courts are elected by the local citizenry in a secret election. The only qualification for judges is that they must be 25 years of age or more. Neither they nor the assessors require any formal judicial training or prior experience although most judges do now have law degrees. They must administer justice in accordance with their conscience, intellect and life experience, and not in accordance with some dry letter of the law noted in some lawbook. Precedents are not admissible evidence. It is therefore quite common that two different individuals may receive totally different sentences for the same transgression. More than 85% of all cases are civil suits arising from labor, housing or family disputes.

Verdicts in civil suits may be appealed within seven days after they have been pronounced; in criminal suits, after ten days. There may be only one appeal to the next higher court. During the appeal, the execution of sentence is suspended. The court of the second instance reviews the case completely and then makes a decision whether to let the judgement remain in force or to send the case back to the lower court. This appellate court has a panel of judges without assessors. Most higher courts function primarily as courts of appeal with expanded membership.

The accused has the right to be represented by counsel at preliminary investigations and at court. In minor civil suits, this is rarely the case. However, according to law, in criminal cases where a prosecuting attorney is required, the accused must be represented by counsel. If he cannot afford one, the court provides him one free of charge. In the entire USSR there is a total of 15 thousand barristers, more than 40% of whom are women, a rather recent development in a profession which was traditionally male in the Soviet Union. Most graduates with law degrees from universities or law institutes go into governmental administration. Others become judges or procurators. A rather large number of lawyers go into legal counseling. Every geographic jurisdiction has a number of lawyers who work out of a collective which may be loosely compared with a local bar association. They work in a suite of offices which is accessible to citizens who need legal advice. Specific fees are charged for this service which is paid by the citizen at a joint cash register. The total sum is then divided among all the lawyers who work at that specific station.

Members of the barristry (trial lawyers) constitute the best paid segment of the legal profession. Although trial lawyers' fees are specified by the state, these fees are comparatively high. Normal fees range from five rubles for an extremely short and simple court appearance to sixty rubles for a complicated one. Most barristers have "special" clients who pay them with monies and goods far above the going rate. Some of these clients are major black-marketeers who are in constant need of legal advice; others may be plant managers, for example. Although such behavior on the part of a lawyer constitutes grounds for disbarment procedures, many are nevertheless tempted. Most judges and lower-level procurators endeavor to become barristers to improve their standard of living and to work with a semblance of free pursuit of their profession which they do not have in their present jobs.

The courts have the right to impose the following punishment, in ascending order of gravity:

Social condemnation.
Fines.
Deprivation of rights to hold certain posts or to engage in certain activities.
Exile.
Banishment.
Corrective labor without imprisonment.
Imprisonment: (Normal maximum: 10 years. For especially heinous crimes: 15 years).
Deprivation of any title of honor or military rank. (Only in conjunction with another sentence).
Confiscation of property. (Only in conjuntion with another sentence).
Death. (Only for murder and "encroachment upon the foundation of the socialist system").

The most powerful entity in the entire Soviet legal system is the office of the Procurator. The Procurator General of the USSR is appointed by the Supreme Soviet of the USSR for a period of seven years. The Constitution charges him with "supreme supervision over the observance of the law by all institutions, persons in office, and all citizens." The Procurator General also personally appoints the Procurators of the SSR's, the ASSR's, territories, regions and major cities for a period of five years. The more specific charges of the office of the Procurator on all levels are:

Exercising supervision over the observance of the law by all ministries and departments, the institutions and enterprises under them, by the executive bodies of the local soviets, by persons in office, and by citizens;
Bringing to trial those who have committed an offense;
Seeing to it that legality is observed during the investigation of crimes so that no citizen is improperly convicted or restricted in his rights;
Exercising supervision over the validity and justice of sentences and judgments passed by judicial bodies;
Exercising supervision over legality in the execution of sentences.

More simply stated, the Procurator has the right to have anyone arrested and tried. By the same token, he may have anyone released. Since there is no law forbidding double jeopardy, he may see to it that citizens are tried more than once for the same transgression. He may see to it that a sentence imposed by a court is reduced. By the same token, when he feels that the sentence of a court is too lenient, he can appeal to have it made more severe. When a case comes before a court on any level, he may decide that it is too important or difficult for that level to handle, and he may personally move it to a higher court. He has a direct line to the top through the procurator system and is not dependent upon anyone laterally for support. He actually has a great deal more power than any court.

It would seem logical that the Ministry of Justice have some say in matters involving the judicial process. This is not the case in the Soviet Union. The primary functions of this ministry are to supervise the election of People's Judges and assessors, and to care for the physical courtroom installations. Neither the courts nor the procurators receive any orders or guidance of significant substance from this ministry.

The Militia in the USSR fulfills the function of the local and state police forces. It is charged with public security and order, protects the personal safety of the citizens, protects state, public and private property, and sees that traffic rules are obeyed. Although the militia does receive some local guidance from the executive committees of the local soviets, they are really subordinated to the Ministries of Internal Affairs of the SSR's. This assures the same operational method in the entire republic, facilitates assignment policies and establishes a headquarters for possible mobilization.

The Public Order Squads are volunteer organizations throughout the country. Each volunteer spends several hours, once a month, patrolling public places, especially during rallies, holidays and other major events when crowds gather. They are charged with preventing public disorder and are empowered to detain offenders and bring them to the militia. These squads also appear to be a likely reservoir for strategic mobilization in case of war.

Most Recent Changes

The Kremlin leadership has turned its drive for reform to the Soviet Union's legal system, exposing and condemning cases of police brutality, false arrest and imprisonment in a bid to buttress public faith in the country's standard-bearers of law and order. In early 1987 Soviet journalists launched a veritable expose of glaring legal abuses, documenting everything from the 1986 execution of an innocent man in a mass-murder case in the Byelorussian city of Vitebsk to the implication of militia veterans in the armed robbery of a Moscow department store two months ago.

In a television appearance, Vladimir Terebilov, the chairman of the Soviet court system, conceded that 5 percent of all court cases here are marred by judicial impropriety, putting the number of judicial abuses every year in the thousands, at least. The legal reform drive ranges wide, advocating greater independence of judges, increased public accountability of Soviet militiamen and other issues not raised in decades. The more controversial measures, such as major personnel shakeups in the courts and changes in the Soviet criminal code, are still in the discussion stage, however. As dozens of Soviet political prisoners return home, pardoned by recent decrees of the Supreme Soviet, the overhaul of the legal system is a logical step in Moscow's highly publicized exercise in expanding what it calls socialist democracy.

The Kremlin leadership, including the Politburo and Central Committee, has already embraced some aspects of the drive for legal reform. When Soviet leader Mikhail Gorbachev redoubled his calls for "reconstruction" of Soviet society and broadening of Soviet democracy in a major speech to the Central Committee last month, he embraced the cause of judicial reforms, too. The Soviet Union needs "measures to raise the role and prestige of the Soviet court," Gorbachev told party leaders. He announced the imminent release of a draft law to give Soviet citizens the right to sue party officials for illegal actions.

Resistance to efforts at reforming this country's laws and legal bodies has already emerged.

The top officials in the procurator's office and the supreme court are against any changes. They are against any reform. They think it suffices to change a few people and to have minor changes in the code, rather than to have any major reforms. When Foreign Ministry press spokesman Gennadi Gerasimov announced in April, 1987 weeks ago that a review of the Soviet criminal code was taking place, he said, "There is a tendency nowadays in the review toward a softening, although there are some comrades who think the stricter it is, the better."

According to the Soviet advocates of legal reforms, the tendency for abuse stems from some weaknesses in the very bases of the Soviet legal system, including the presumption that once arrested, an individual is guilty until proven innocent. Under such circumstances, the judge is not very likely to even consider the evidence presented by the defense very seriously. Often, the abuses start at the level of the local militia, according to recent articles in the Soviet press. The weekly magazine Ogonyok documented widespread police brutality in Petrozavodsk, north of Leningrad, including beatings to bring on false confessions.

The biggest cause of abuse from the level of police through the courts is the overwhelming tendency, particularly in the provinces, to bow to the demands of party officials, thus undercutting the principle of an independent legal and judicial system. Locat authorities can't find the real criminal, so they pick up anyone and charge him. The most stunning example involves a murderer of more than 30 people in Vitebsk. Under pressure to solve the case, local police picked up several suspects and beat them until they confessed to the crimes. One of those who confessed was sentenced and executed last year before authorities admitted that they had made a mistake. The real murderer has yet to be tried, but nine court officials involved in the earlier case have been reprimanded.

Given the resistance within the system, major reforms will be achieved gradually, at best. One expected change is that defense attorneys, now barred from interrogations and the investigation and permitted to represent the witness only when the trial begins, will be given permission to enter the process at an earlier stage. Another is that the jury of judges in major cases will be expanded in an attempt to encourage impartiality. Some Soviets have noted that the reform drive has already resulted in some small changes in the behavior of local militias.

READINGS

Berman, Harold J. Justice in the USSR, 2nd ed. Cambridge: Harvard University Press, 1963.

Butler, William E. The Soviet Union and the Law of the Sea. Baltimore: John Hopkins, 1971.

Chkhivadze, V. M., (ed.) The Soviet State and Law. Moscow: Progress, 1969.

Conquest, Robert (ed.) Justice and the Legal System in the USSR. London: The Bodley Heard, 1968.

______. The Soviet Police System. New York: Praeger, 1968.

Denisov, A. and Kirichenko, M. Soviet State Law. Moscow: Foreign Languages Publishing House, 1960.

Feifer, George. Justice in Moscow. New York: Delta, 1965.

Feofanov, Y. Soviet Citizens and the Law. Moscow: Novosti Press, 1976.

Genkin, D. M. and Kunik, Ia. A. Sovetsko-grazhdanskoe pravo. Moscow: Izd. "Vysshaia shkola," 1967.

Gsovski, V. and Grzybowski, K. Government, Law and Courts in the Soviet Union and Eastern Europe. New York: Praeger, 1960.

Gureev, P. P. and Sedugin, P. I., (eds.). Legislation in the USSR. Moscow: Progress, 1977.

Hazard, John and Shapiro, Isaak. The Soviet Legal System. Dobbs Ferry: Oceana, 1962.

Lapenna, Ivo Soviet Penal Policy. Chester Springs: Dufour, 1968.

LeFave, W. R. Law in the Soviet Society. Urbana: University of Illinois Press, 1965.

VI. The Communist Party

One of the most popular misconceptions is that, although the Soviets hypocritically claim that the Government runs the country, it is in reality the Communist Party which has the final say so. This is certainly not true; the Soviets have never tried to hide this fact. Moreover, it is the cornerstone of the system that the Party is the one great controlling mechanism for all political, economic and social activities. This is clearly spelled out in the Constitution and the Party Statutes. The way that this is accomplished is by having a parallel structure in which there is a Party organization for every level on which a government organization functions. Most often than not, the senior personnel of government offices will, at the same time, be functionaries of the Party. It is these Party organizations which must be consulted by the same level government offices before major decisions may be reached. This is true for the lowest level, e.g., in the determination as to who will take over management of a collective farm; it is just as true on the highest level, e g., who will be appointed to the Council of Ministers or to the Supreme Court. Local and national elections are also strongly influenced. A candidate for an office nominated by the local Party chief is virtually assured of being elected.

The Party ostensibly has a definite degree of flexibility. It is, in fact, named the "Party of Creative Marxism." This means, that although Marxist principles are inviolate, the Party should make provisions for adaptive changes to fit the times and new situations. In reality, however, Party organizations, be they local or national, are still led primarily by old functionaries who resist any attempts at change. They brand these attempts as deviationism, which is sufficient to purge any member from the Party ranks.

The membership in the Party is not as great as one may expect There are a total of 15,700,000 members, which is barely 6% of the population. The membership breakdown is as follows:

Industrial workers	41.5%
Collective and State farmers	20.0%
Engineers and scientists	20.0%
Cultural workers, military and Government	18.5%
Women	24.0%

One is normally invited to become a candidate for party membership when one has a good record in the youth movement and one has been politically active. Members of the intelligentsia are also invited to join. After a trial period of one year, this candidacy is either changed into full membership status, or the individual is notified that he is no longer considered likely material. Membership in the Party assures one of a relatively good and influential life. Expulsion from the Party assures one of a life of strife and deprivation. It is estimated that more than 70,000 members lose their Party membership each year.

The organization of the Party is relatively simple. The primary organizations, and there are 391,000 of them, exist on the lowest level where governmental

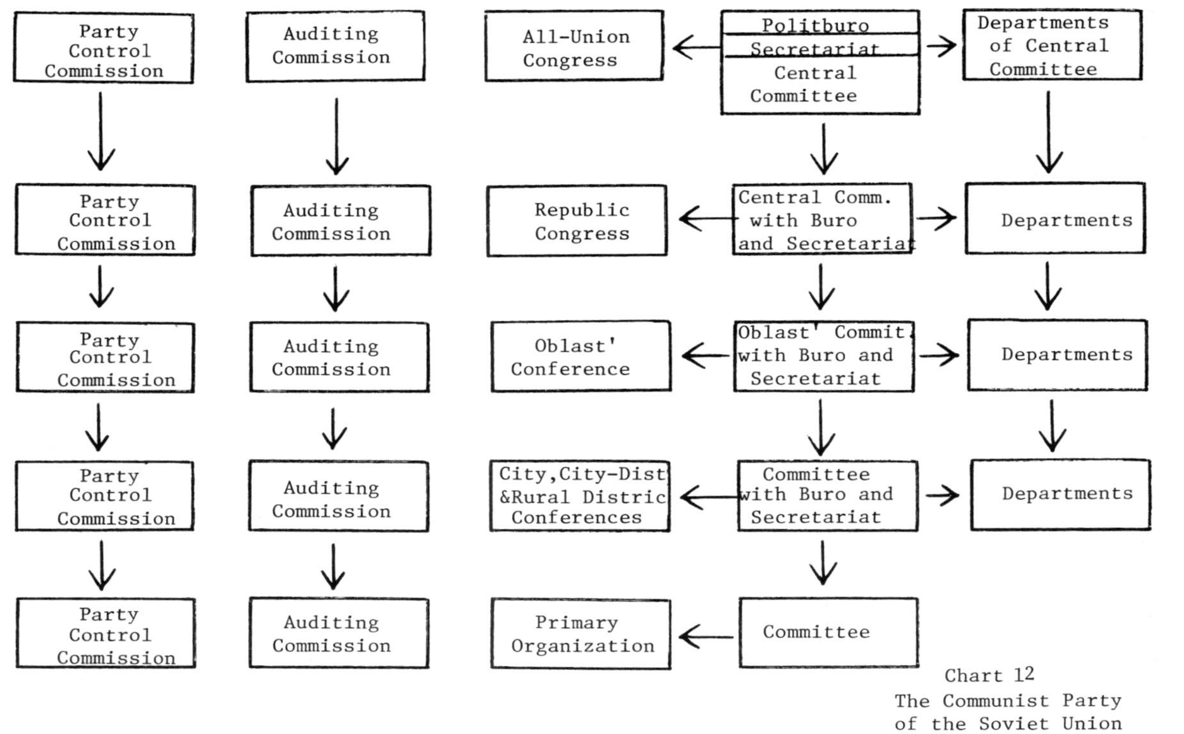

Chart 12
The Communist Party
of the Soviet Union

agencies may be found. This is the territorial production level which is used as a basis for the establishment of virtually all organizations. It simply means that the Party membership of a means of production (e.g., of a factory, department stores, schools, administrative offices) in a territory, i.e., geographic area (e.g. town, State Farm, city borough) gets together to form an organization and elect its leadership. This is the same territorial production principle which governs all voting, nominations and elections of deputies. The smallest organizations with fewer than 15 members elect a Secretary and a Deputy Secretary to carry on the day-to-day activities; where there are more than 15 members, a "buro" is elected; and those organizations with more than 300 members elect a Party Committee. These buros and committees guide the day-to-day work of the Party unit, call party meetings, and deal with the next higher Party echelon. Buros are elected every year; committees every two or three years.

The next level, above the primary organizations, is composed of city, district, regional and territorial Party Committees which are elected by Party Conferences attended by the leadership of the subordinate primary organizations. The next higher level is the Party Congress of the SSR, which convenes every five years and elects its governing bodies, i.e., the Central Committee and the Central Auditing Commission. The highest body is the Party Congress of the USSR, which also convenes at least once every five years (or sooner, if urgent business is to be conducted). Membership of this congress is restricted to leading functionaries of secondary and higher organizations. Approximately 5,000 members attended the most recent congress (the XVII Party Congress of 1986). The purpose of the congress is to hear the reports of the General Secretary, the outgoing Central Committee, and the Auditing Commission. They then elect the new bodies for the next five years. The Congress determines the numerical membership of these bodies. These elections are by open show of hands.

Between the rare meetings of the Congress, the business of the Party is conducted by the Central Committee which meets at least every six months. To handle business in the interim, the Central Committee elects the Politburo and the members of the Secretariat including the General Secretary of the Party. Membership in either of the above bodies may be eliminated either by death or by purge.

There is considerable disagreement among Soviet experts in the West as to which body incorporates the greatest amount of power in running the country. Some maintain that it is the Politburo, which establishes policy for both internal and international procedures and relations; others claim that the power is concentrated within the Secretariat, since this office controls the actual membership and has the responsibility of installing or eliminating local Party leaders. A third version contends that the actual power is in the hands of the Central Committee, despite its relatively large membership, since it is this body which really appoints the Politburo and the Secretariat. There is no doubt that this Central Committee, when the definite majority is of an opinion different from the Politburo or the Secretariat, will have its way. It was, in fact, the Central Committee which toppled Khrushchev. A unanimity of opinion within the Central Committee is extremely rare, however Most of the time there is a great deal of factionalism within it, - the hawks against the doves; the theoreticians against the pragmatists; the intellectuals against the uneducated; the Ukrainians against the Russians; the young against the old, etc. This is the case despite the much hallowed principle of democratic centralism. This principle states that persons must be elected and decisions arrived at purely democratically. However, after this step has been taken, it becomes binding. The body must stand as a central, solid monolith. There is no room for argument and no provision for a loyal opposition. All opposition is, by definition, disloyal.

In other words, the leadership of the Party is undergoing an identity crisis at the present time which is being mirrored in several ways. For instance, there are reports of deviationism from within the Party ranks in the Urals, in the Ukraine, in Georgia and Armenia, in Kazakhstan, and other geographic areas. There also seems to be some degree of instability between the Party and certain areas within the government. All things considered, it is nevertheless still true that the Party retains absolute power over all fields of endeavor in the country.

In accordance with the Soviet concept of control, every entity must, in some form, be subject to the inspection of another body. Even the Party is not exempt from this system. There are two inspecting bodies which fall into this category:

a. The Party Auditing Commission: This body is represented on all levels Since Party membership dues are relatively high and a great deal of money flows into the Party coffers, there must be tight control over the hundreds of millions of rubles which are taken each year. There must also be a careful audit of all expenditures to eliminate any illegalities. Much of this money is used to support communist underground organizations abroad.

b. The Party Control Commission: Again, this body is represented at all levels. Its purpose is to make certain that Party organizations conform to the Statutes. It also sees to it that required activities are performed and that no attempt is made by one Party unit to thwart another or to compete unfairly. Attention is also paid to the caliber of recruits and to make sure that a Party unit does not grow beyond its normal pace. The Control Commission has the right to inspect all Party records and makes regular reports to the next higher echelon of the Party. (NOTE: This organization should not be confused with the People's Control Commission or Committees which are not Party organizations but are, of course, Party controlled. This organization, which is represented in the Council of Ministers, is composed of an extremely large number of members throughout the USSR and on all levels of Government and mass organizations. This is an attempt to involve as many people as possible in the process, and also to establish another control mechanism. People's Control are authorized to inspect all governmental and organizational activities and to determine whether they are in consonance with the benefits to society and the will of the people. They are charged with reporting all violations to the next higher echelon and to the appropriate Party level.)

Chart 13
Departments of the
Central Committee of the CPSU

Department	Area of Responsibility and Supervision
Administrative Organs	Most important department. Supervises all intelligence, defense and judiciary bodies.
Agriculture	All agriculture-connected ministries and agencies and water conservation.
Chemical Industry	Chemical, paper and oil refining industry.
Construction	All ministries connected with construction; academies and unions of architects.
Culture	Unions of cultural workers; movies; Ministry of Culture.
Defense Industry	All ministries and committees which are connected with defense industry.
Foreign Cadres	Responsible for personnel decisions for ministries which have units abroad.
General	Internal security of the Central Committee; housekeeping chores for the Central Committee.
Heavy Industry	Energy industry; geology and mining.

Departments of the
Central Committee of the CPSU
(cont)

Information	Novosti; TASS; Pravda; other information services.
International	Activities of foreign service; relations with communist organizations in capitalist countries.
Light Industry and Food Industry	Ministries connected with food production.
Machinery Industry	Eleven ministries which encompass the machinery industry.
Organizational Party Work	People's Control; local Party organs; membership and statistics; trade unions; Komsomol.
Planning and Financial	Finance; procurement; labor; GOSPLAN; State Bank; statistics.
Political Administration of the Ministry of Defense	The Party within the military.
Propaganda	Publications and books; newspapers and journals; media; agitation and propaganda by Party units.
Science and Education	Ministries of education and of health; the Academies of Science.
Socialist Countries	Communist parties in socialist countries.
Trade and Consumer Services	Consumer items and utilities.
Transportation and Communications	All forms of transportation on land, sea or air; communications.

THE LEADERSHIP OF THE COMMUNIST PARTY OF THE SOVIET UNION (CPSU)

(NOTE: The numbers refer to the chart of photographs)

The Politburo of the Central Committee, CPSU

a. Full Members:

1. Mikhail Sergeevich GORBACHEV. Born March 2, 1931 in Privolnoe, Stavropol Territory. Nationality — Russian. Positions include: General Secretary of the Central Committee of the CPSU; Member of the Presidium of the Supreme Soviet of the USSR; Chairman, USSR Defense Council.

2. Geidar Alievich ALIEV. Born May 10, 1923 in Nakhichevan. Nationality — Azeri (Azerbaidzhan). Positions include: Major General; First Deputy Chairman, USSR Council of Ministers.

3 Vitalii Ivanovich VOROTNIKOV. Born January 20, 1926 in Voronezh. Nationality — Russian. Positions include: Chairman of the Council of Ministers of the RSFSR.

4. Andrei Andreevich GROMYKO. Born July 18, 1909 in Starye Gromyki, Belorussia. Nationality — Russian. Positions include: Chairman of the Presidium of the Supreme Soviet of the USSR.

5. Lev Nikolaevich ZAIKOV. Born April 3, 1923 in the RSFSR. Nationality — Russian. Positions include: Member of the Presidium of the Supreme Soviet of the USSR; member of the Secretariat of the Central Committee of the CPSU.

6. Egor Kuzmich LIGACHEV. Born November 29, 1920 in the RSFSR. Nationality — Russian Positions include: Party ideologue and second ranking member of the Politburo; member of the Secretariat of the Central Committee of the CPSU.

7. Nikolai Ivanovich RYZHKOV. Born September 28, 1929 in the RSFSR. Nationality — Russian. Positions include: Chairman, Council of Ministers of the USSR.

8. Mikhail Sergeevich SOLOMENTSEV. Born November 7, 1913 in Erilovka, Lipetsk Region. Nationality — Russian. Positions include: Chairman of the Party Control Committee of the Central Committee of the CPSU.

9. Viktor Mikhailovich CHEBRIKOV. Born April 27, 1923 in the RSFSR. Nationality — Russian Positions include: Army General; Chairman, USSR Committee for State Security (KGB).

10. Edvard Amvrosievich SHEVARDNADZE. Born January 25, 1928 in Mamati, Lanchkhuti District. Nationality — Georgian. Positions include: Minister for Foreign Affairs of the USSR.

11. Vladimir Vasilevich SHCHERBITSKII. Born February 17, 1918 in the Dnepropetrovsk Region. Nationality — Ukrainian. Positions include: First Secretary of the Communist Party of the Ukraine.

Candidate Members:

12. Petr Nilovich DEMICHEV. Born January 3, 1918 in Kirov. Nationality -- Russian. Positions include: First Deputy Chairman of the Presidium of the Supreme Soviet of the USSR.

13. Vladimir Ivanovich DOLGIKH. Born December 5, 1924 in Ilanskii in Krasnoiarsk. Nationality — Russian. Positions include: Member of the Secretariat of the Central Committee, CPSU.

14. Boris Nikolaevich ELTSIN. Born February 1, 1931 in the RSFSR. Nationality — Russian. Positions include: First Secretary of the Moscow Party Organization.

15. Nikolai Nikitovich SLIUNKOV. Born April 26, 1929 in Gorodets in the Gomel Region. Nationality — Belorussian. Positions include: First Secretary of the Belorussian Party Organization. SEE ADDENDUM, p. 51.

16. Sergei Leonidovich SOKOLOV. Born July 1, 1911 in the Crimea. Nationality — Russian. Positions include: Marshal of the Soviet Union; Minister of Defense of the USSR. Eliminated June 1987. Replaced by General D. Iazov.

17. Iurii Filippovich SOLOVEV. Born August 20, 1925 in the RSFSR. Nationality — Russian. Positions include: First Secretary, Leningrad Party Organization.

18. Nikolai Vladimirovich TALYZIN. Born January 28, 1929 in Moscow. Nationality — Russian. Positions include: First Deputy Chairman of the Council of Ministers of the USSR; Chairman, State Planning Committee of the USSR (GOSPLAN).

The Secretariat of the Central Committee, CPSU
(In addition to those who are also members of the Politburo)

19. Aleksandra Pavlovna BIRIUKOVA. Born February 25, 1929 in Moscow. Nationality — Russian.

20. Anatolii Fedorovich DOBRYNIN. Born November 16, 1919 in Moscow. Nationality — Russian. Former Ambassador to the U.S.A.

21. Mikhail Vasilevich ZIMIANIN. Born November 12, 1914 in Vitebsk. Nationality -- Belorussian.

22 Vadim Andreevich MEDVEDEV. Born March 29, 1929 in the RSFSR. Nationality -- Russian.

23. Viktor Petrovich NIKONOV. Born February 28, 1929 in the RSFSR. Nationality -- Russian. SEE ADDENDUM, P. 51.

24. Georgii Petrovich RAZUMOVSKII. Born January 19, 1936 in the RSFS. Nationality -- Russian.

25. Aleksandr Nikolaevich IAKOVLEV. Born December 2, 1923 in the RSFSR. Nationality -- Russian. SEE ADDENDUM, p. 51.

26. Ivan Vasilevich KAPITONOV. Born February 23, 1915 in the Riazan Region. Nationality -- Russian. Is also the Chairman of the Central Auditing Commission of the CPSU.

NOTE: There have been radical changes in the membership of these bodies, particularly the Politburo, since the ascention of Gorbachev. More changes may be expected in the near future. There are still a number of members (e.g. Shcherbitskii), who are "hangers on" from the Brezhnev era and whom Gorbachev would like to get rid of. Also, a number of members are approaching eighty and will be replaced soon.

The Central Committee:

At the Party Congress of 1986 the membership was expanded to 319 full members and 151 non-voting members respectively. Of the 319 full members 44% are full-time Party functionaries; another 29% are leading functionaries in USSR and SSR government; nearly 9% are military officers; 4% are ambassadors; and 4% are intelligentsia. A number of token workers constitute less than 5% of the membership. The remaining 4% are trade union officials and factory managers. Less than 3% of the full members and 5% of the candidate members are women.

M.S. GORBACHEV

It should by now be quite clear to every observer that the future of the Soviet Union, both as it affects foreign and domestic affairs, is intricately tied to one man -- Mikhail Sergeevich Gorbachev. The purpose of these comments is to promote a better understanding of the man, his strengths and weaknesses, his protagonists and antagonists, and his visions for the future. It would be helpful at this point to start with a bit of biographical information.

Gorbachev was born on March 2, 1931 in the small town of Privolnoe in the Krasnogvardeiskii District of the Stavropol Territory in the RSFSR. His family background is normally listed as "peasant." His first job was as a laborer at a machine tractor station in his home district. In 1950 he was selected to become a student at the Law Faculty of Moscow State University. Because of his activism as a Komsomol organizer he became a Party member in 1952. He received his degree in 1955 and returned to his home district where he filled several, progressively more important, functions in the Komsomol and the Party. In 1967 he also completed a correspondence certificate at the Stavropol Agricultural Institute. In 1970 he became a deputy to the Supreme Soviet of the USSR and, for the next several years, was active as member and chair in a number of its most important sub-committees including the one on foreign relations. In 1971 he gained membership in the Central Committee of the Communist Party of the Soviet Union. In 1978 he became the member responsible for agriculture in the Secretariat of the Central Committee. In 1979 he was made a candidate member of the Politburo which was changed to a full membership in 1980. From 1983 to 1985 his responsibilities on the Party Secretariat included economics, cadre affairs, ideology, culture, and world communism affairs. Under Chernenko, in 1984, one of his major duties in the Politburo was chairing the committee to reform the system of higher education and vocational training. In 1985 he succeeded Chernenko as General Secretary of the Party. His primary mentors were Party ideologue M. A. Suslov and the former chairman of the KGB and later General Secretary of the Party Iurii Andropov.

His travels abroad included trips to Belgium, Bulgaria, Canada, Czechoslovakia, France, West Germany, Great Britain, Iceland, Italy, Mongolia, Poland, Portugal, Switzerland and Vietnam.

Without a doubt, Gorbachev is the brightest and best educated leader the Soviets have had since Lenin. He has traditionally allied himself with intelligent people, rather than "yes men." This list would include Ryzhkov, Dobrynin, Aliev and Shevardnadze. His wife, Raisa, is also an intellectual and occasionally lectures on philosophy at Moscow State University from which she holds two degrees.

Quite clearly, Gorbachev sees himself in the function of a reformer. The mistake should not be made, however, that he intends to stray from the communist objective -- he simply wants to streamline it and make it more effective. In order to do this, he has to identify inefficiency, corruption, ignorance, needless repression of personal initiative, sloth, and complacency. His projected reforms reflect this thinking.

For example, he wants to reform the economy by introducing incentives for production increase. In order to accomplish this, he must give the individual production facilities a greater hand in decision making. He is interested in not only quantity of production, but also in quality control. He must therefore induce the individual worker to produce better products by making it worth his while

He wants to reconstruct the social order by permitting the population greater freedoms. These would include fewer travel restrictions both domestically and abroad, less censorship, a call for "glasnost," that is, the obligation to speak up if the Party or government do anything not considered equitable. Included in this category are projected election reforms and an increase in popular referenda. The most propagandized act in this general category was the release of dissidents including Sakharov and Begun, and the increase in the number of exit visas.

The cultural area has taken on added significance. The heavy-handed supporter of censorship, the "Tsar of the arts" Demichev, has been "kicked upstairs" to make way for a new openness in theatre and film. Gorbachev has also created a committee on the arts and has appointed his wife one of its members thereby increasing its importance.

Gorbachev's international propaganda, his public relations exercises, have also been varied and wide-spread. In support of his cultural initiatives, he has invited a number of defectors to return to the Soviet Union either permanently or temporarily, with no travel restrictions. Included in this invitation are Liubimov, Aksenov, Baryshnikov, Rostropovich and many others. He has also made it known that he wants an increase in cultural exchanges with the West. On the political scene, he is attempting to play the benign, peace-loving leader who wants disarmament and is willing to compromise even with an intransigent United States. This has gained him many supporters in Western Europe.

In order to accomplish these difficult objectives, Gorbachev must gain the support of wide segments of the population. The one which is dearest to his heart is the intelligentsia. Gorbachev considers himself one of them and sees in them the hope for the Soviet future. This is why so many of his reforms are targeted towards this group. This includes his reforms in the arts, his insistence on cultural exchanges, increased travel abroad, and his reinstatement of Sakharov in his work for the Academy and Sciences. His economic reforms are geared to win over the industrial management. His insistence on efficiency would promote the better educated staffers in government and public organizations. Also, generally speaking, younger people see a great deal of hope for themselves in Gorbachev's philosophy for the future.

Nevertheless, although there has been a great number of announcements and discussions of a great variety of reforms, very little concrete has been accomplished by this writing. There is no question that Gorbachev, by virtue of his position in the Secretariat, is firmly in control, and that he is in little danger of being replaced. Why is it then, that he is finding it so difficult to get his reforms initiated? The answer is quite simple. His opposition is concentrated in those groups which have the most to lose.

The Party "old guard" which has been in firm control for so many years, is loathe to give up any of its prerogatives. They view a liberalization with suspicion and would even oppose a call to open discussion or controversial questions which may end up in adverse criticism. Many consider Gorbachev a young upstart who is willing to dissipate central authority which always has been and should always remain within the purvue of senior Party functionaries.

The Five-Year-Planners are opposed to a revamping of the economy since it would deprive them of control over the economy. An increase in private enterprise would diminish their authority over the means of production and distribution and would make central planning horrendously complicated. In addition, the many who are involved in the underground economy and are becoming millionaires because of it, would have to forfeit their lucrative involvements.

Those in agriculture, who are responsible for horrendous mismanagement over the past few decades, would hate to be shown up for the inefficient managers they are They, also, would suffer economically from a revamping of the agricultural segment of the Five-Year-Plan which would eliminate cheating on the required quotas.

Generally, then, the opposition to Gorbachev has been by special vested interests who do not wish to give up their control over the society. They are therefore attempting to undermine Gorbachev in order to stay in power. Some of these internal struggles Gorbachev has won, for example, the elimination from the Politburo of Kunaev from Kazakhstan. Some, he has lost, for example, his failure to eliminate from the Politburo The Ukrainian Party chief Shcherbitskii, an original Brezhnev appointee.

It has been said that Gorbachev will win out in the end because he is younger than his opposition and will outlive them. It has, however, also been said that even young men get older and more conservative as time passes, and that they develop a taste for power which causes them to resist any efforts to diminish it. It has also been said that Gorbachev is the hope for peace and has a more "liberal" attitude than his predecessors. It must again be pointed out that he is not an American-style liberal, but that he is a very bright pragmatist who understands the concept of power and how to use it. He is also a Soviet nationalist who will do everything to bolster the best interests of his nation to the detriment of all others, if need be. All his projected reforms, many of which will probably never be realized, may be eliminated with a stroke of the pen if the need arises. It should also be pointed out that he possesses one quality very rare in a Soviet leader — impatience — which may work against him.

READINGS

Adams, Jan S. Citizen Inspectors in the Soviet Union. New York: Praeger, 1977.

Avtorkhanov, A. The Communist Party Apparatus. Chicago: Henry Regnery Co., 1966.

Burks, R. V. The Dynamics of Communism in Eastern Europe. London: Oxford University Press, 1961.

Carew-Hunt, R. N. A Guide to Communist Jargon. London: Geoffrey Bles, 1957.

Dallin, Alexander and Larson, Thomas B. (eds.) Soviet Politics Since Khrushchev. Englewood Cliffs: Prentice-Hall, 1968.

Dallin, Alexander and Rice, Condoleezza (eds.) The Gorbachev Era. Standord: Stanford Press, 1986.

Dornberg, John. Brezhnev: The Masks of Power. New York: Basic Books, 1974.

Gehlen, Michael P. The Communist Party of the Soviet Union. Bloomington: Indiana University Press, 1969.

Hill, Ronald J. and Frank, Peter. The Soviet Communist Party. 3rd Ed. Winchester: Allen & Unwin, 1986.

Hunt, Robert N. Carew. The Theory and Practice of Communism. New York: Macmillan, 1957.

Juviler, Peter and Morton, Henry. Soviet Policy Making. London: Pall Mall Press, 1967.

Partiinoe stroitel'stvo. Moscow: Mysl', 1968.

Reshetar, John S. A Concise History of the Communist Party of the Soviet Union. New York: Praeger, 1964.

Schapiro, Leonard. The Communist Party of the Soviet Union. 2nd ed. New York: Random House, 1971.

Slovo o partii. Moscow: Izd. polit. lit., 1967.

THE POLITBURO
(Full Members)

1. GORBACHEV 2. ALIEV 3. VOROTNIKOV 4. GROMYKO

5. ZAIKOV 6. LIGACHEV 7. RYZHKOV 8. SOLOMENTSEV

9. CHEBRIKOV 10. SHEVARDNADZE 11. SHCHERBITSKII

Chart 14 The Party Leadership

THE POLITBURO
(Candidate Members)

12. DEMICHEV

13. DOLGIKH

14. ELTSIN

15. SLIUNKOV

16. SOKOLOV

17. SOLOVEV

18. TALYZIN

****

ADDENDUM
Politburo Appointments
June 26, 1987

a. A.N. Iakovlev and V.P. Nikonov, both members of the Secretariat (see p. 46), were given full Politburo membership.

b. N.N. Sliunkov, Candidate Member, Politburo, was promoted to full Politburo membership (see p. 45).

c. General Dmitrii Iazov has succeeded Marshall Sokolov as Minister of Defense and as a Candidate Member, Politburo (see p. 45).

****

Chart 14 (Cont.)

THE SECRETARIAT

19. BIRIUKOVA 20. DOBRYNIN 21. ZIMIANIN

22. MEDVEDEV 23. NIKONOV 24. RAZUMOVSKII

25. IAKOVLEV 26. KAPITONOV

Chart 14 (Cont.)

Smith, Laibman and Bechtel (eds.) Building a New Society: the 25th Congress of the Communist Party of the Soviet Union. New York: MWR Publications, 1977.

Spravochnik partiinogo rabotnika. 9th ed. Moscow: 1976.

Strong, John. The Soviet Union Under Brezhnev and Kosygin: The Transition Years. New York: Van Nostand, Reinhold, 1971.

Ustav kommunisticheskoi partii Sovetskogo soiuza. Moscow: Izd. polit. lit., 1971.

Voslensky, Michael. Nomenklatura. New York, Doubleday, 1984.

Wolfe, Thomas W. Soviet Strategy at the Crossroads. Cambridge: Harvard University Press, 1964.

VII. Public Organizations and Institutions

Every human endeavor, avocation, activity and field of interest, is carefully organized into a series of clubs, associations and interest groups. It is a fact that no totalitarian state can tolerate the creation of organizations or groups on a private level, without control by the authorities. And this is the key word, control. Any grouping of persons not under control may engage in activities detrimental to the system despite the fact that this was not the original purpose of the grouping. Quite clearly, a dissident organization which would propagate the necessity to overthrow the authorities would be strongly persecuted. However, even if a private Soviet group attempted to form a "Society for the Celebration of Lenin and Marx," they would be just as severely persecuted since this society would not be under state control. The system tells the individual that there is some kind of organization for anything that he may want to engage in, but that he may not look outside the system for satisfaction of his desires.

Obviously an exhaustive listing of all organizations and societies would run into the hundreds of pages and would not be especially valuable to the reader. The following list therefore contains only several of the most important organizations, plus a number of representative societies:

The Trade Unions: These compose the largest single organization. Nearly all working people, with the exception of a number of collective farmers, belong to it, although membership is not compulsory. These trade unions have a variety of functions:

a. They may propose labor legislation to the Supreme Soviets.

b. They are consulted by the means of production as to production processes.

c. They negotiate with management on questions of supplemental bonuses and fringe benefits.

d. They own hundreds of thousands of athletic fields, theaters, libraries and club houses for the workers' use.

e. They publish their own newspapers, periodicals and books.

f. They are primarily responsible for the assignment of vacation space to workers, and they own many thousands of sanatoria and hotels in vacation areas all over the country. (Those workers who do not belong to the union "voluntarily" cannot be assigned such vacation space.) These vacations are either free or carry a minimal charge.

g. They establish policy concerning the administration of the social security and pension system.

h. They establish relationships with foreign labor unions.

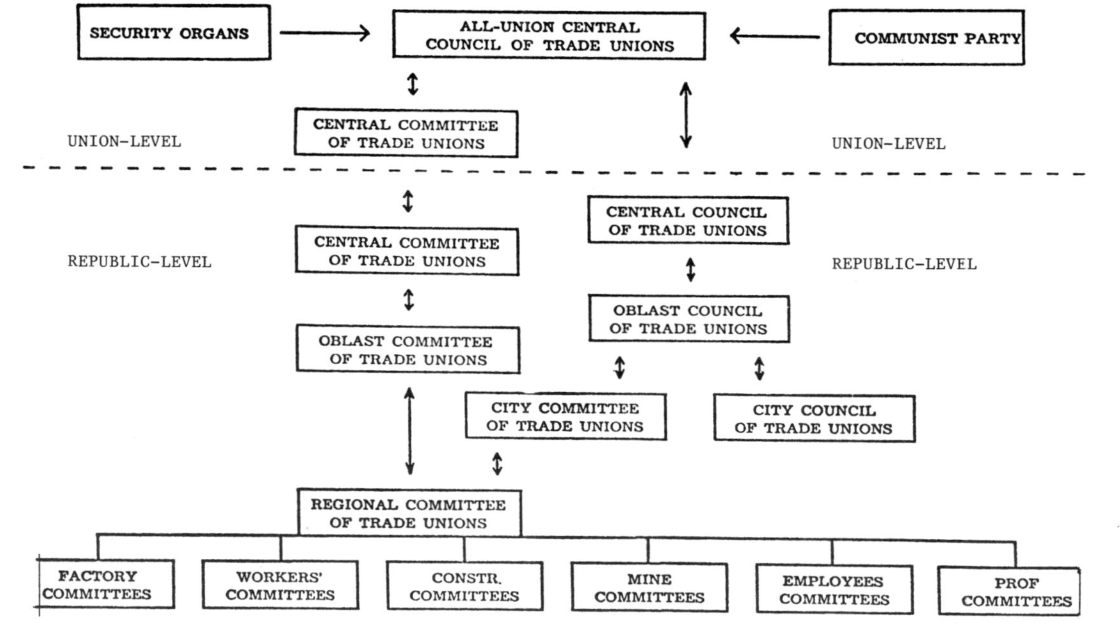

Chart 15

ORGANIZATION OF SOVIET TRADE UNIONS

MEMBERSHIP IN PUBLIC ORGANIZATIONS

Trade Unions	135,100,000
KOMSOMOL	42,500,000
Red Cross, Red Crescent Societies	117,000,000
Society of Inventors and Rationalizers	13,100,000
Scientific and Technical Societies	11,100,000
Union of Writers	9,000
Union of Artists	18,000
Union of Architects	17,000
Union of Filmmakers	6,000
Union of Composers	2,000
Union of Journalists	76,000

Chart 16

Chart 17

Sports Activities Sponsored By
Youth Organizations,
Trade Unions and Sports Clubs

Total number of clubs engaged in sports:	220,000
Total number of members:	52 million
Annual dues per member:	30 kopeks
Major national sports:	67

Of the latter:

Skiing:	4.8 million members
Track and Field:	6.7 million members
Volleyball:	5 7 million members
Soccer:	4.2 million members

Major Sport Societies (total of 38) include:

College Students:	"Spartak," "Burevestnik," and "Dynamo."
Military:	"Central Army Sports Club."
Vocational Students	"Labor Reserves."
Railroad Workers:	"Lokomotive."
Water Transport Workers:	"Vodnik."

Of course the unions cannot call a strike or take other measures such as slowdowns or picketing. The unions must consider themselves on the same side as management rather than in conflict with it. They have no authority over the base pay of workers since this area is regulated by the state.

The organization of Soviet labor unions is relatively simple. Everyone who works in the same establishment belongs to the same union. In a major plant this would include truckers, secretaries, lathe operators, chemists, janitors and others. If this happens to be a steel plant, all would belong to the metallurgy union, one of a total of 25 unions in the USSR. The union business is conducted by councils on the various geographic levels, e.g., city, district, SSR. The highest body is the Union Congress which meets every five years (most recently in 1987) to establish union policy for subordinate levels. The everyday business of the unions is conducted by the All-Union Central Council of Trade Unions, a body which is elected by the Congress.

The Women's Committee: This is primarily a front organization whose titular head is Valentina Tereshkova, the first woman astronaut. In reality the membership of this organization is relatively small, considering that it touts itself to be the leading society for the equality for women. Its real function is propaganda on the international scene, particularly in respect to African and Asian developing nations. Hundreds of young women from those areas are brought to the USSR and subsidized by the Women's Committee in the form of lengthy scholarships at Soviet institutions.

The Soviet Peace Fund is another front institution. Its leadership and members are never publicized. It purports its main function to be a collecting agency of funds from the common Soviet citizen. These funds are to be expended to further peace in the world. In reality, the funding is done by the Soviet State. In the past and present these funds have been expended to finance North Vietnam during the war, anti-Government forces in Chile, leftist anti-apartheid organizations in South Africa, freedom fighters in Mozambique and El Salvador, and other groups or organizations who are working to overthrow present governments and substitute pro-Soviet, socialist regimes in their place.

The Union of Red Cross and Red Crescent Societies of the USSR: In many respects, this large organization which boasts 91 million members has the same functions as similar organizations anywhere: to prevent disease; provide emergency food supplies; organize a blood donor program; search for lost relatives. The organization also conducts a program of assistance to foreign countries, primarily developmental areas in Asia and Africa. There are now more than 400,000 Red Cross (Red Crescent in Moslem areas) organizations throughout the country.

The Komsomol (Young Communist League): This youth organization is open to all persons between the ages of 14 and 28. Its main function is to serve as a breeding ground for the Party. It is, for this reason, under the firm supervision and leadership of the Party. In fact, the only normal way a young person may become a Party member is through the Komsomol. This is a relatively important organization, since most of the younger Soviet citizens in government, the arts and the sciences are members. In addition, virtually all members of the military not older than 28, all young factory workers, and all university and institute students belong. The major activity of the organization is political self-indoctrination. In addition, a great deal of time is spent on sports and youth festivals, on summer camping and on para-military training. This organization would also constitute an important strategic mobilization reservoir in case of war.

The Young Pioneers: This youth movement which has over 25 million members is for children between the ages of 10 to 15 The organization is administered and supervised by the Komsomol. Again, the primary purpose for this organization is political indoctrination. Nevertheless, it does have many positive points. It arranges a plethora of varied activities for the child which effectively diminishes juvenile delinquency. There is also a great deal of handicraft and job preparation, and gifted children are quickly identified and nurtured. The state financial support for youth activities is immense. The many, well supplied Pioneer Camps alone (more than 23 million children attended a camp during the summer of 1986) require great monetary outlay. The expenditure for young people's literature, to include Komsomol and Pioneer newspapers, is also tremendous. Two newspapers alone, the Komsomol and Pioneer versions of Pravda, have a combined circulation of well over 20 million.

The Union of Soviet Writers: This organization only has members who are recognized writers. To be a professional writer (in opposition to an amateur), one must belong to the Union All manuscripts are submitted to the Union by its members, for publication in one of the literary journals or in bound form. If the membership approves of its ideological contents, it is published; if not, it isn't. If a member is expelled from the Union (e.g. Pasternak and Solzhenitsyn) he will never be able to publish again. In other words, this organization has an iron grip on literature. Exactly the same commentary may be made about the Union of Artists, the Union of Cinematographers and the Union of Composers who also have iron control over their respective fields.

The Union of Journalists, the Union of Architects and the Medical Societies are just a few other examples of professional organizations. All have their own publications. Some belong to international organizations.

READINGS

Brown, Emily C. Soviet Trade Unions and Labor Relations. Cambridge: Harvard University Press, 1966.

Fisher, Ralph T. Pattern for Soviet Youth: A Study of the Congress of the Komsomol, 1918-1954. New York: Columbia University Press, 1959.

Fundamental Labor Legislation of the USSR and the Union Republics. Moscow: Novosti, 1975.

Kahan, Arcadius and Ruble, Blair, (eds.) Industrial Labor in the U.S.S.R. New York: Pergamon Press, 1979.

Kassof, Allen. The Soviet Youth Program. Cambridge: Harvard University Press, 1965.

Lazarenko, I. Labor Remuneration, Labor Incentive Funds and Soviet Trade Unions. Moscow: Novosti Press, 1972.

McAnley, Mary. Labour Disputes in Soviet Russia. London: Oxford University Press, 1969.

Odom, William E. The Soviet Volunteers. Princeton: Princeton University Press, 1973.

Reshetov, P. and Skurlatov, V. Soviet Youth. Moscow: Progress, 1977.

Skilling, Gordon and Griffiths, Franklyn (eds.) Interest Groups in Soviet Politics. Princeton: Princeton University Press, 1973.

VIII. The Armed Forces

The Soviet Union has universal military conscription which requires that all Soviet males, regardless of nationality or social status, undergo military service. They must spend either two years in the ground forces or three years in the navy. In special cases only one year is required of those who have a specialty which is in great demand on the civilian plane.

There are a total of approximately 4.8 million men in the armed forces. There are five branches of service as follows:

The Land Forces: This is the largest subdivision. At the present time the USSR has approximately 140 divisions of which fewer than half are combat ready. Twenty-two of the latter are in East Germany and nine in Afghanistan. More than fifty additional divisions are reduced in strength but can be brought up to full strength very quickly, within approximately two weeks. The remainder are skeleton divisions which would require at least six weeks to become combat ready. As in all other modern armies, the land forces are divided into infantry (including airborne), artillery and armor. In addition there are air defense, missile (medium-range and tactical), engineer, signal and other units.

The Air Force: Approximately 5,000 combat-ready aircraft are maintained. Its mission is the same as that of any other air force.

The Navy: The priority for the past several years has gone to building up a large submarine fleet (there are over 400 in operation). Many are missile-bearing and nuclear powered. The Soviet surface navy is also increasing.

The Strategic Rocket Force: Soviet military priority has been to establish superiority in the field of intercontinental ballistic missiles. Their warheads considerably outnumber those in the United States. They also have numerous short and intermediate range missiles in place targeted against European NATO bases.

The Air Defense Force: The purpose of this force is to repel aerial attack. The force has radar installations and other electronic surveillance mechanisms It is equipped with surface-to-air missile installations and supersonic fighter-interceptor aircraft

If one reads Soviet figures on military expenditures one is led to believe that they are minimal compared with those of the United States. The disparaty may be attributed to the secresy of the USSR and the difficulty of pinning down the real military expenditures. According to American military experts, Soviet military outlays grew from 50 million rubles in 1970 to 154 billion in 1983 and are expected to exceed 180 billion in 1987 — an annual growth rate of approximately 8.5 percent. In fact, these are only minimum estimates since Soviet data on total military spending do not include civil defense, military pensions, and several other important items.

In the procurement realm Soviet expenditures rose from about 18 billion in 1970 to about 86 billion in 1983 and are certain to exceed 100 billion in 1987. This represents an annual rate of increase of about 11.9 percent. The reason for this sizeable increase is the introduction of high technology into Soviet weapons systems.

The military share of the Soviet GNP rose from about 12 percent in 1970 to about 18 percent in 1980 and is expected to exceed 21 percent in 1987.

The disparity between real and published figures may be explained as follows:

a. Most of the ministries charged with production (e.g. light industry; heavy industry; construction, etc.) write off major military equipment costs to another field of expenditure. This covers the cost of many new weapons in the research stage.

b. Research and development is, to a large part, carried out by Academy of Sciences research organizations which do not appear in military budgets.

c. Military training is often conducted out of funds allocated for education.

d. Soviet enlisted men are paid a pittance - just a little pocket money. Military personnel wages, in general, are surprisingly lower in the USSR than in the US.

e. Purchases of equipment from the production-combines by the military are done at cut-rate prices. In other words, the military pays only approximately one-fourth of the price which another purchaser would have to pay.

Nevertheless, because of the abominable state of the Soviet economy, there are definite indications that the high expenditures for the military are hurting the USSR. Added to this are the heavy costs of supplying Cuba, Syria, Vietnam and other puppet regimes. The occupation of Afghanistan was also quite costly not only in money but also in prestige. It showed that more than 100,000 Soviet military cannot overcome a sparsely populated, backward nation.

In actuality, the military itself has little decision-making authority. Such power rests with the Party's nebulous Defense Council which is allegedly composed of the Secretary General CPSU; Minister of Defense; Foreign Minister; Chairman, Council of Ministers; Chief of Staff; Minister of Defense Industry; and head of the KGB. This group has similar functions to our National Security Council.

The ultimate power which the military has in the Party has had its ups and downs during the past two decades. It did play a significant part in the removal from office of Khrushchev after the Cuban missile fiasco. Until 1976 it was represented in the Politburo by Marshall Grechko, a respected professional soldier (Marshall of the Army) and Minister of Defense of the USSR. After his death, however, he was replaced by the present Minister of Defense, D. Ustinov, a more than seventy-year-old civil engineer. At this writing, the minister is Marshal Sokolov who isn't even a full member of the Politburo. There are numerous versions of what this means for the military. Perhaps this signifies tighter control of the civilian arm over the military.

Chart 18
The Armed Forces

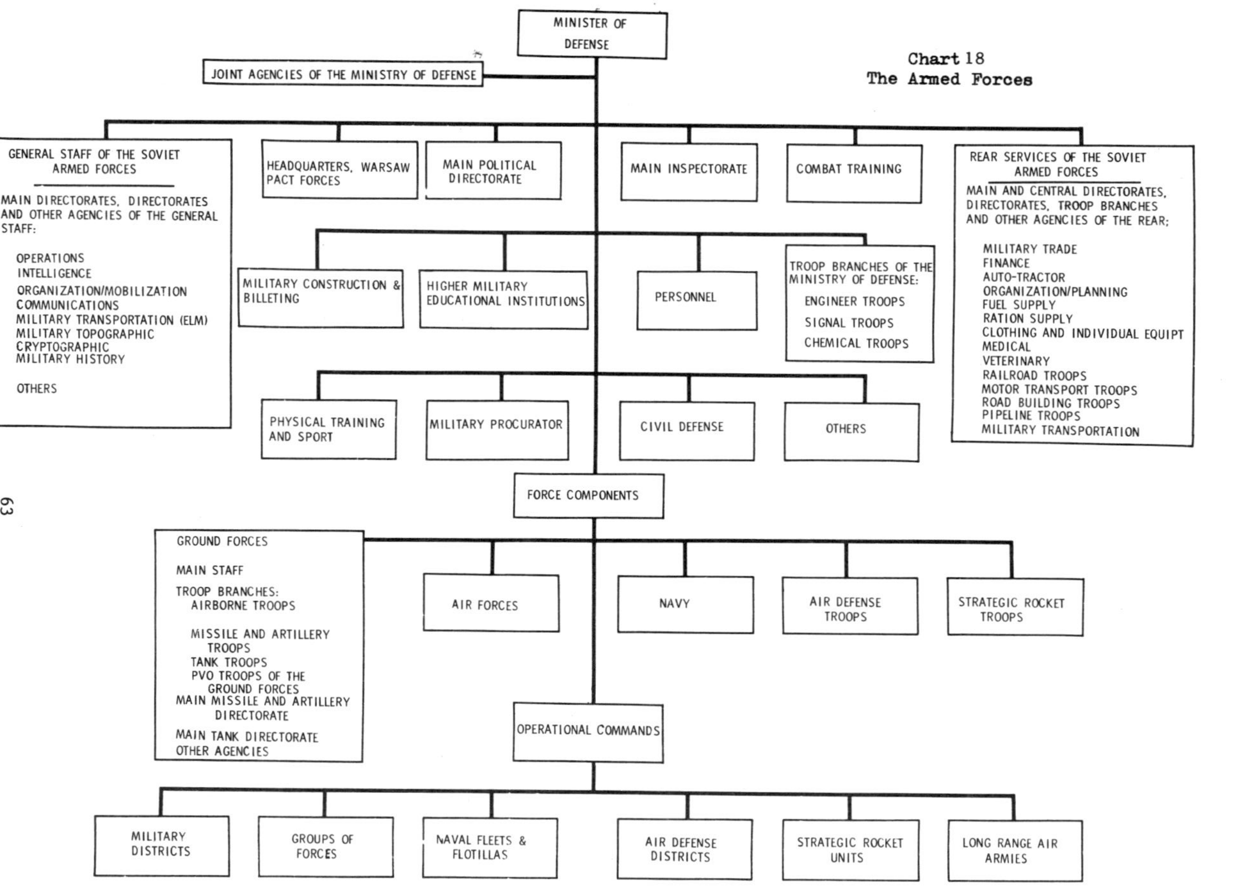

The ultimate battle for power, of course, remains in the Central Committee. Although the military has only 1% of the population, it has approximately 9% of the seats on the Central Committee There, it consists of an extremely cohesive clique, is virtually always of one mind, and comprises a significant voting bloc on that body. Most recently this military group has joined into a marriage of convenience with the economic "managers" or technocrats. These two groups have a great deal in common: They are generally younger than the other members; they are extremely efficient by Soviet standards; they normally have a better education; they all have an organization of some sort backing them up; they consider the present second level party leadership to be archaeic and ripe for a change. Representation and function-allocation at the 1986 Party Congress shows the military emerging even stronger than before.

It must be pointed out that this ideological struggle being waged by the military on national level is in no way intended by them to weaken the Party structure within the military. This structure is the military's internal control mechanism and they could ill afford to lose it. Specifically, there is one party functionary assigned to all units that are company-size and larger This individual who is called the political deputy and is an outgrowth from the World War II commissar system, is charged with political training. All political deputies are members of the Chief Political Administration. Its chief is the first deputy to the Minister of Defense At any given time there are more than 80,000 such political deputies in the armed forces. They are all career military officers and may be transferred from political work to straight military duties. By the same token, outstanding line officers may be assigned as political deputies. For all intents and purposes, this officer is in charge of the party structure of whatever unit he may be assigned to. The duties of the political deputy include such varied responsibilities as unit morale, unit entertainment, unit censorship, political indoctrination through daily lectures, propaganda, and, most importantly, he acts as the Party and the Komsomol chairman All promotions, including that of the unit commander, require his recommendation. He is, beyond a doubt, a highly influential individual in the unit.

Party membership is quite high in the military. Approximately 98% of all officers belong to the Party. Even among senior enlisted men the percentage is nearly that high. In conformance with the principles of "territorial production," this means that members of the military occupy a proportionate number of seats in the Party organization of every territory which has a significant number of military units stationed upon it. In other words, because of the relatively high percentage of Party membership in the armed forces units of any given area, a larger-than-warranted percentage of the Party representatives will be military. The same is true when elections take place for various levels of deputies. Nevertheless, the local populace does not seem to resent this. In fact, the military appears to be a well integrated segment of society which involves itself in all the social, political and cultural activities of the respective geographic regions. The general populace is encouraged to become closely knit with the military. The most common way of achieving this objective is to join the Voluntary Society for Cooperation with the Army, Navy and Air Force, an organization which apparently has approximately 42 million members (although membership figures are a well-guarded secret). The Party, Komsomol and Labor Unions cooperate with and support this organization to the fullest extent. There are branches in factories, schools, collective farms and universities. The Society is charged with training in military skills and providing instruction in civil defense. Army officers involve themselves by giving courses in the use of weapons, parachute jumping and forced marches.

Young men are well prepared for the military by the time they are drafted. Starting with the fifth grade, they take lessons in civil defense. Starting with the ninth grade they are exposed to compulsory military training. If they attend universities, their curriculum requires courses in military training. They are also encouraged to participate in actual reserve unit exercises. Once they complete their studies they are inducted as officers if they have completed their training cycles. If they have not, they may be inducted as enlisted men.

Most Recent Innovations

In 1985 the Soviet Union changed its military draft law to open the way for women to serve in the armed forces. The amendment was decreed by the Presidium of the Supreme Soviet and published in its official bulletin. It appeared to reflect the growing concern over the declining population growth which is likely to make it increasingly difficult to maintain the 4.8 million current strength of the armed forces later in the decade.

The new decree provides for draft registration of women with "medical and other specialized training." Such women between the ages of 19 and 40 could be required to undergo military training and be "accepted on a voluntary basis into active military service."

According to western estimates, the USSR would have to recruit 85 percent of all 18-year-old males in 1987 to maintain its forces at their present levels. An alternative would be to lengthen the period of conscription beyond the two-year minimum — an unpopular move. In previous years university students could defer their service until graduation. But, in an effort to cope with the problem, all deferments have been drastically cut. It is projected that net gains to the working population which averaged 2 7 million a year in the last decade will shrink to about 300,000 in 1987, with most of the gains coming from the Moslem republics.

It is unclear whether the military will make special efforts to induce women to join. The armed forces employ women now, but they are paid regular civilian salaries. The new regulation seems designed to place more women into important jobs such as communications and computers to offset the influx of non-Russians has hampered the efficiency of the armed forces. This is particularly reflected in official complaints that many new recruits do not speak good Russian, the only language used by the military.

Since his appointment as General Secretary, Gorbachev has beefed up the "Special Service Forces" (SPEZNAZ) whose mission is to kidnap or assassinate the key leaders of the NATO countries in the hours before a Soviet blitzkrieg is launched against Western Europe. The GRU now has more than 20 such SPEZNAZ companies. Each one consists of 115 personnel, all of them professional soldiers, linguists, and expertly trained commandoes. Their infiltration techniques are part of an audacious Soviet strategy for a lightening-fast, non-nuclear victory over NATO troops. The clandestine SPEZNAZ missions would be followed up by regular armed forces in lightly armed, highly mobile units called "Operational Maneuver Groups."

READINGS

Bonds, Ray. Russian Military Power. New York: Salamander, 1980.
Collins, John M. U.S.-Soviet Military Balance. New York: McGraw-Hill, 1980.
Collins, Joseph J. The Soviet Invasion of Afghanistan. Lexington: D.C. Heath, 1985.
Erickson, John et. al. Soviet Ground Forces: An Operational Assessment. Boulder: Westview, 1986.
Gardner, Michel. A History of the Soviet Army. New York: Praeger, 1966.
Garthoff, Raymond L. Soviet Military Policy. New York: Praeger, 1966.
Herrick, Robert Waring. Soviet Naval Strategy. Annapolis: United States Naval Institute, 1968.
Jones, Ellen. Red Army and Society: A Sociology of the Soviet Military. Winchester: Allen & Unwin, 1986.
Kolkowicz, Roman. The Soviet Military and the Communist Party. Princeton: Princeton University Press, 1967.
Kolkowicz, Roman and Mickiewicz, Ellen (eds.) The Soviet Calculus of Nuclear War. Lexington: D.C. Heath, 1986.
Nadysev, M. A. et.al. Russian-English Military and Technical Dictionary. Moscow: Military Publishing House of the USSR Ministry of Defense, 1975.
Petrov, Iu. P. Stroitel'stvo politorganov, partiinykh i komsomolskikh organizatsii armii i flota (1918-1968). Moscow: Voennoe izdatel'stvo, 1968.
Politotdely. Moscow: Voennoe izdatel'stvo, 1967.
Scott, Harriet F. and William F. The Armed Forces of the USSR. Boulder: Westview, 1979.
Scott, Kintner and Harriet F. The Nuclear Revolution in Soviet Military Affairs. Norman: University of Oklahoma Press, 1968.
Sokolovsky, Marshall. Military Strategy and Soviet Doctrine and Concepts. London: Pall Mall Press, 1963.
Soviet Aerospace Almanach 1982. Special Issue Air Force, March, 1982.
Soviet Military Power. US Department of Defense, 1981.
The Military Balance 1981-1982. London: The International Institute for Strategic Studies, 1981.
The Soviet Military Technological Challenge. Washington, D.C.: Georgetown University Center for Strategic Studies, 1967.
U.S. Government Printing Office. Soviet Military Power. Annual.
Wegener, Edward. The Soviet Naval Offensive. Annapolis: Naval Institute Press, 1975.

IX. Intelligence

The KGB (State Security Organization) is by far the most powerful and most important intelligence organization in the Soviet Union. Ostensibly, since it is by definition an arm created for the protection of the State, it is under the direct supervision of the Council of Ministers. In reality, all activities of the KGB come directly under Party supervision. The policy for KGB operations is established by the Politburo; the actual day-to-day supervision of the KGB, primarily to make certain that the organization does not become powerful enough to challenge the power of the Party, is exercised by the Administrative Organs Department of the Central Committee. Their watchdog-function is especially important since the Chairman of the KGB is himself a member of the Politburo.

The Chairman has a board of governors, or Collegium, to assist him in establishing operational procedures for the organization. There is also a Party Secretariat at that level, which personifies a second chain of control by the Party. There are four Chief Directorates which encompass the top operational levels These Chief Directorates are the First, the Second, the Fifth and the Border Guards. There are no Third and Fourth Chief Directorates. The total strength of the KGB is approximately 450,000 men and women, about 360,000 of whom are in the Border Guards. The mission of the Chief Directorates is as follows:

a. The First Chief Directorate: This office manages most of the intelligence activity carried on by the Soviet Union in foreign countries. It is, in turn, divided into the following Directorates:

1. The Illegals Directorate: This organization recruits, trains and assigns KGB agents to operate clandestinely, i.e., illegally, under false identities, in foreign countries. Most of these operations are being conducted in the United States, Western Europe and Communist China.

2. The Scientific and Technical Directorate: This Directorate is charged with the collection of scientific data by all means, illegally or legally, on nuclear and space research and on scientific data of strategic value in all foreign countries. This office has a rather large analysis section which uses the expertise of the top men of science in the USSR.

3 The Planning and Analysis Directorate: This is the smallest Directorate. Its mission is to collect operational data based on now defunct operations, and to develop techniques which may be useful in future operations. This ineffectual office is staffed primarily with personnel who are either inefficient or too old to be used in another capacity.

4. The Information Service: This office disseminates the routine intelligence which has been collected by the First Chief Directorate subordinate elements (except for Scientific and Technological information) to those who have a need-to-know. It publishes intelligence bulletins for the upper echelons of the Party and government, and also undértakes the compilation of studies when ordered.

5 The Disinformation Department: Through this office false information is disseminated which will have a tendency to disrupt the orderly activities of potential enemy nations, or at least to influence their strategic decisions. It also serves as an internal affairs department for the entire KGB and spends a great deal of time covering up mistakes by other departments.

6. The Executive Action Department: This department is charged with kidnapping, sabotage, political assassinations and any other acts of violence as ordered. It also places its agents with Soviet embassies all over the world with the mission of forming networks of agents who, when ordered, can create total internal chaos in population centers of a nation with whom the Soviet Union may be engaged in a war.

7. The Geographic Departments: Most of the KGB agents who collect intelligence information abroad, belong to one of these departments. All activities in a foreign area which do not fall within the purview of the Executive Action Department are conducted by these departments. These departments are expanded or reduced as demanded by the political situation, e g., the Middle East. They are designated as follows:

Department 1: North America
Department 2: Latin America
Department 3: Great Britain, Skandinavia, Australia and New Zealand.
Department 4: West Germany and Austria.
Department 5: Spain, Portugal, France, Italy, Holland, Belgium, Ireland and Luxembourg.
Department 6: China, Korea and Vietnam.
Department 7: The rest of Asia.
Department 8: The Balkan Peninsula, the Middle East.
Department 9: The English-speaking nations of Africa.
Department 10: All other African nations.

8. The Eleventh Department: Liaison and cooperation with the intelligence services of the satellites. In reality, the KGB exercises nearly complete control over them. Occasionally it recruits residents of these satellites without the knowledge of the indigenous services

9. The Cover Organs Department: This office places KGB operatives into Soviet groups which travel abroad, e.g., newspapermen, students, trade missions.

10 The Thirteenth Department: Responsible for cyphers and codes and all means and methods of communication with operatives who have been placed in deep cover abroad.

11. The Fourteenth Department: Responsible for technical devices.

12. The Fifteenth Department: File repository and central registry for all current operations conducted by the First Chief Directorate.

13. The Sixteenth Department: Personnel affairs.

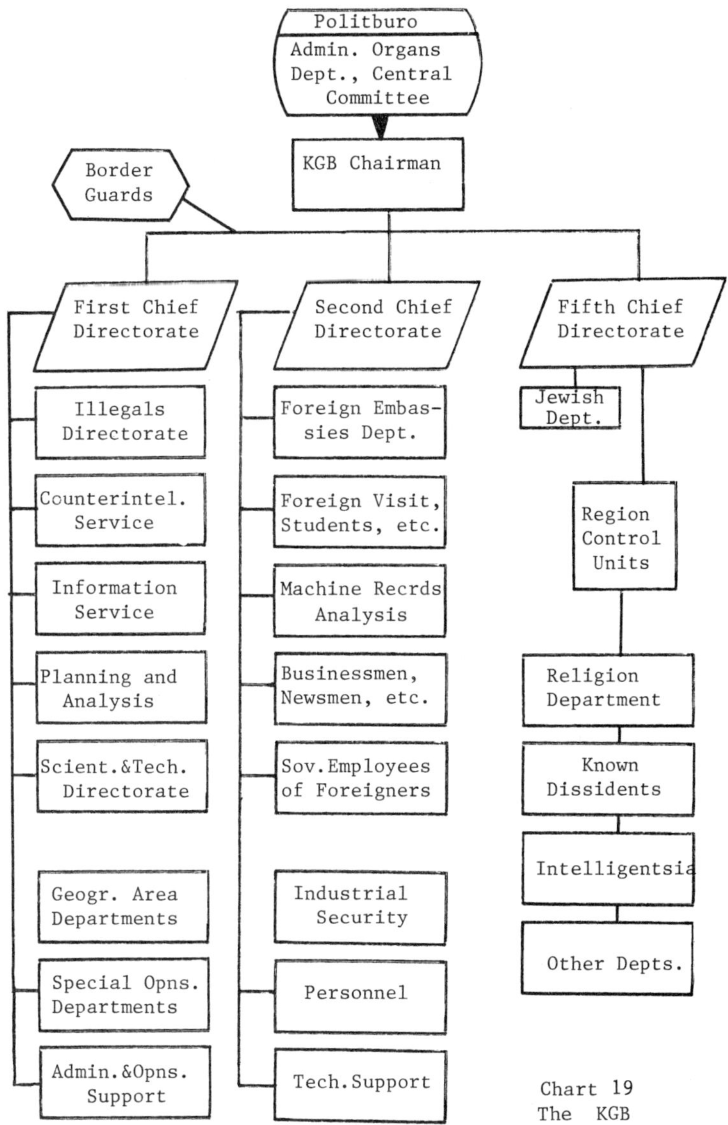

Chart 19
The KGB

b. The Second Chief Directorate: This chief directorate, which is the smallest in size, is responsible for all activities connected with foreigners within the borders of the Soviet Union It is divided into the following departments:

1. Six Geographic Departments which have the mission of surveilling and possibly recruiting foreign embassy personnel (this has become increasingly difficult since Soviet personnel have been withdrawn from the U.S. Embassy in 1986); detecting and neutralizing intelligence operations conducted out of foreign embassies; establishing and maintaining dossiers on all Soviet citizens who have contact with foreign embassy personnel; recruitment of foreign embassy personnel for intelligence activities in third countries; and close surveillance of foreign business representatives, foreign exchange groups and tourists. The departments are as follows:

Department 1:	North and South America.
Department 2:	Members of the British Commonwealth.
Department 3:	Scandinavia, West Germany and Austria.
Department 4:	All other West European countries.
Department 5:	All non-European developed nations.
Department 6:	All non-European underdeveloped nations.

2. Department 7: Surveillance and recruitment of foreign tourists.

3. Department 8: Operates the computers for the Chief Directorate through which the whereabouts of any foreigner in the USSR may be ascertained immediately.

4. Department 9: Surveillance and recruitment of foreign exchange students and faculty.

5 Department 10: Surveillance and recruitment of foreign journalists.

6. Department 11: Regulates and approves all travel abroad by Soviet citizens.

7. The Technical Support Group: Charged with surreptitious entry and listening devices in buildings occupied by foreign embassies or trade missions.

8. There are a number of other smaller subdivisions of this Chief Directorate which have domestic missions including the detection of black marketeering, graft in government offices and other economic sabotage

c. The Fifth Chief Directorate: This Chief Directorate was created in 1969 to establish firm control over all segments of Soviet population and to detect and stamp out dissidence. It has taken over much of the domestic mission which was previously assigned to the Second Chief Directorate. Its organizational composition is still not solidified and many changes are taking place. In general, contrary to the other two Chief Directorates, the Fifth does not have a central office for each phase of operations, but delegates the authority for operations to regional subdivisions. The reason is, that each geographic region has its own, peculiar minorities and its individual problems. Each region therefore has its own departments which may not be duplicated in other regions, for example, the RSFSR may have a problem peculiar to Tartars, while the Ukraine is preoccupied with a large Roman Catholic population. In general, however, one may say that each region has departments in the following target areas:

Intelligentsia.
Youth.
Sects.
Nationalities.
Religious leaders.
Known dissidents.

There appears to be a separate Department for Jews at the Chief Directorate level. This was brought about by the militant dissidence in this group and their desire to leave the USSR. It is also connected with the focus of world attention on the plight of the Jews in the Soviet Union.

d. The Chief Directorate for Border Guards: This is a rather large elite army and navy with the latest equipment and the best trained personnel. Its mission is to secure the Soviet borders both ways, i.e., to prevent Soviet citizens from leaving the country and to catch infiltrators from the outside. This military unit is totally subordinated to the KGB and may be used as a private army by it.

e. There are rumors of a new Eighth Chief Directorate for Codes and Cryptography, which also concerns itself with electronic surveillance, but these rumors are not completely substantiated. This new Chief Directorate is allegedly a derivative of the Communications Directorate listed under paragraph f. 4. below.

f. There are additional Directorates and Departments assigned to the KGB Headquarters which do not fit into any of the categories circumscribed by the Chief Directorates. Among them are:

1. The Personnel Directorate: All manpower needs of the KGB world wide are considered here, as is all recruitment and training.

2. The Administrative Directorate: Housekeeping chores primarily connected with building facilities, housing, etc.

3. Technical Operations Directorate: Develops and produces technical devices other than communications equipment, e.g., poisons, gases, false documentation, secret inks, etc.

4. The Communications Directorate: Codes and cyphers; interception of foreign transmissions; electronic surveillance.

5 The Guards Directorate: This is the personal protection unit for the leaders of the Soviet Union.

6. The Special Investigations Department: This unit investigates potential penetration of the KGB by foreign intelligence, uncovers treasonous acts and assesses the damage done by defectors.

7. The Physical Security Department: This department assures that the premises of the KGB are secure from physical penetration. It conducts constant security inspections.

8. The Department of Finances: This department is charged with all fiscal matters. This includes the payrolls of KGB officers and informants and expenditures for equipment. The budget of the KGB is unknown.

9. The Department for Files and Archives: Although files on ongoing operations are kept by the Chief Directorates, this is the central location with short card file material which informs on where the complete files may be found. This department also contains the files of past operations going back to the beginning of the Soviet State. Also on file here are dossiers on all agents and informants, Soviets who have traveled abroad or who have relatives abroad, and known dissidents.

The KGB is the coordinating agency for all intelligence operations. One of the agencies it coordinates is the GRU (Main Intelligence Headquarters) of the Ministry of Defense This unit conducts intelligence operations on a world-wide basis and operates in much the same fashion as the First Chief Directorate. It is charged with the collection of military information, but occasionally does surface valuable intelligence of a non-military nature. If such a source is developed by the GRU, the KGB has the power to step in and take the operation over. During the past several years, however, the GRU has increased its power and has developed many foreign operations more valuable than those of the KGB. Another office which conducts intelligence within the USSR is the Ministry of Internal Affairs; in most cases, if anything of real intelligence value of a non-local nature is uncovered, it is turned over to the KGB. The top echelons of the Party organization may, of course, involve themselves in international political intrigue of an intelligence nature without even notifying the KGB.

The KGB is an extremely powerful organization which is dreaded by most Soviets. They have the power of arrest, a power which is denied to its Western counterparts. The heavy knock on the door at 2 a.m. is not exclusively fictional. Although the rights of the citizen are allegedly protected by the Constitution which make arrests and searches illegal without warrants, the KGB never feels compelled to abide by these restrictions.

Until recently, only whispered rumors were audible about the KGB. The Soviet citizen desperately avoided mentioning these initials out loud, simply out of fear. It was also a fact that the KGB could do no wrong and that any conflict between a private citizen and that organization was certain to end in disaster for the individual. Lately, however, there has been a perceptible change in the treatment of the KGB. There has been an all-out effort to humanize it in the eyes of the citizenry. For this reason, numerous television programs and films now fictionalize the efforts of the KGB in their fight to protect their homeland. The members of the organization are depicted as decent, clean-cut patriots who often give their lives for their just cause. Even more importantly, the major press organs have been given authority to expose injustices caused by the "over-zealousness" of some operatives, in which innocent citizens have been adversely affected. In some cases KGB officials have been removed from office as a result of investigations into such excesses. This is truly an innovation.

READINGS

Barron, John. KGB. New York: Bantam, 1974.

Barron, John. KGB Today: The Hidden Hand. New York: Berkley Books, 1985.

Bittman, Ladislav. The KGB and Soviet Disinformation: An Insider's View. New York: Pergammon-Brassey, 1985.

Dallin, David I. Soviet Espionage. New Haven: Yale University Press, 1955.

Dolgun, Alexander. Alexander Dolgun's Story: An American in the GULAG. New York: Knopf, 1975.

Ginsburg, Eugenia. Within the Whirlwind. New York: Harcourt Brace Jovanovich, 1981.

Goren, Roberta. The Soviet Union and Terrorism. Winchester: Allen & Unwin, 1984.

Myagkov, Aleksei. Inside the KGB. Richmond: Foreign Affairs Publishing Co., 1975.

The Penkovsky Papers. New York: Avon Books, 1965.

Rositzke, Harry. The KGB: The Eyes of Russia. New York: Doubleday, 1981.

Seth, Ronald. Unmasked! The Story of Soviet Espionage. New York: Hawthorne Books, 1965.

Shultz, Richard H. and Godson, Ray. Dezinformatsia: Active Measures in Soviet Strategy. New York: Pergammon-Brassey, 1984.

X. International Relations

Soviet foreign policy is based purely on national interests, i.e., on political and economic considerations which are favorable to the USSR and would strengthen its position as a world power. There is no doubt that the USSR wants to establish its legitimacy in the family of nations. Nevertheless, in cases where the question is whether to be loved or to gain another piece of ground, the decision will invariably be the latter.

Although the foundations of this foreign policy remain firm, the individual application will differ in each case. The following are examples of the Soviet posture vis a vis some of the major protagonists and antagonists:

The "Soviet Bloc": Included herein are Czechoslovakia, Hungary, East Germany (GDR), Romania, Bulgaria and Poland. These countries are also united in a mutual defense pact (Warsaw pact) and an economic treaty (COMECON). Although, on paper, all of these partners enjoy the same rights and privileges, in reality the USSR wants to be more than a leader - it wants to be the absolute master of the bloc. It may appear to the outsider that the individual countries are being given quite a wide leeway for independent action. For example, Romania appears to be the captain of its own fate at times. But this is really not the case.

At this writing, the situation in Poland is far from resolved. The Jaruzelski government was forced to impose severe measures in order to prevent a direct incursion into Poland by the Soviets. "Solidarity" cannot be permitted to function as a major force outside Communist Party control, especially since it once enlisted more than a third of the total population and the major portion of the industrial working force of Poland. The fact that the new labor union was poorly organized, grew too quickly and contained opposing factions also contributed to its demise. Despite the courage of the "Solidarity" leaders, giving in to their demands would have meant total disruption of the already chaotic economy and a complete restructuring of the political system. This could not be tolerated. It is expected that opposition in Poland will continue on a much less flagrant level. Of extreme importance is the fact that such opposition, in order to exist, must have the active support of the Church. For this reason, the Church has been under propaganda attack, although it is not expected that this will be successful among the extremely devout Polish Catholics.

In general, it must be understood that in all cases where fundamental political national interests are concerned, the USSR will not hesitate to take direct action. World condemnation will not be a deterrent if the Warsaw Pact or COMECON are endangered. The Soviet Union will continue to take direct military action, as it did in Hungary, Czechoslovakia and Afghanistan.

The Soviet Union needs its satellites for a number of reasons: They are excellent sources of manufactured items which the USSR finds difficult to produce itself; they constitute a captive market for Soviet products; they create a buffer zone around the west flank of the Soviet Union which makes them less vulnerable to military incursions and to western intelligence operations; and it avoids borders with nations which are ideologically opposed to the USSR, thereby keeping the Soviet citizenry from dangerous exposure.

There is little love lost between the Soviets and the Poles, Czechs and Hungarians. The Bulgarians are the most docile and also the most backward, economically and culturally. The East Germans are the only real Stalinists left, but they are Germans nevertheless and not trusted by the Soviets. After all, they killed more than 20 million Soviets during World War II. The Rumanians, although they show a courageous face to the rest of the world, are quite restrictive in their own country and are fully cooperative with Soviet instructions. Besides these outright satellites, the USSR also has strong spheres of political and economic influence in Mongolia, North Korea and Vietnam, a fact which causes a considerable amount of ill will with the Chinese People's Republic

China: The basic conflict here is ideological. The Soviets consider the Chinese to be upstarts who dare to teach the teacher and who are jealous of the economic successes of the USSR. The Chinese feel that the Soviets have been traitors to Marxism, have turned into opportunists who will even cooperate with an arch enemy for a momentary gain, and are trying to encroach upon Chinese spheres of influence. Contrary to western belief, the Soviets are not afraid of the Chinese at this time, since they feel that it will take China at least half a century more to attain any respectable economic and strategic power. They are, however, uncomfortable with the balance of power arrangements between the PRC and the United States. China, because of the pressure of an ever increasing population, must expand. The only two directions are northward, into the Mongolian area, or southward, into Southeast Asia. Both areas are Soviet spheres of influence. The Chinese rightfully feel that they are being blocked. The Soviets feel that they are the only nation which can show the rest of the world the path to true socialism. The Chinese feel that Asia is their own rightful missionary sphere. Although several attempts towards a rapprochement between the USSR and China have been made in recent years, none has succeeded. There is no reason to believe that there will be any drastic improvement in the near future.

Western Europe: The major program of the Soviet Union is to weaken the North Atlantic Treaty Organization. The only way this is possible is to subvert members of this alliance and of any other western pact. In Italy, the Communists have made steady gains and are now taking part in the central government for the first time in history. Nevertheless, there are strong indications that the Communist Party of Italy, although partly loyal to the USSR, is much more independent than the Soviet Union would like it to be. The Party in France constantly reminds the USSR that it is older than the Soviet Party and therefore enjoys a special position. After the death of Franco, the USSR was hoping for a strong communist bloc in the national parliament of Spain. In actuality, although the Communist Party is quite strong, they have given notice to the USSR that they will plot their own course and will not subordinate themselves. More or less the same is true for Portugal. Yugoslavia is ambivalent: On the one hand it professes to be the true socialist state in Europe, on the other hand Yugoslavs are notorious for their desire to accumulate personal wealth. At any given time, there are literally millions of Yugoslavs employed in capitalist countries as "guest workers," i.e., with the intention of returning to their homeland after completion of a labor contract. Most importantly, Tito and his successors have constantly stressed the doctrine of national communism in opposition to international communism directed out of the Kremlin. This is a dangerous Trotzkyite ideological precedent which has periodically resulted in extreme enmity between the two countries. At the present, the USSR is doing its best to bring Yugoslavia back into the fold. By the same token, Yugoslavia does not wish to antagonize the USSR. When the Soviets invaded Czechoslovakia 1968, many Yugoslavs were afraid that their country was next in line. Yugoslavia also borders on Albania, the only European country which had aligned itself ideologically with the Chinese against the Soviet Union, but has severed this tie and is now a free radical communist agent. West Germany is a key country because of its great industrial strength. Although it is hated by the Soviets for obvious reasons, there have lately been series of clear attempts to be conciliatory. The Soviet Union hopes with some justification, that promises of economic ties which would open eastern markets to the GFR would cause the latter to turn its back to US political interests. They are also applauding a new wave of anti-Americanism and pacifism in Western Europe, brought about by the placement of US ballistic missiles on Western European soil. The gas pipeline will also continue to have great economic impact.

The Middle East: This area has cost the Soviets a great deal of money and material during the past several decades. Although countries such as Syria and Lybia remain friendly, the vast majority of Arab nations including Saudi Arabia, Egypt (to a lesser degree under Mubarak), Jordan and the Sudan, have taken a series of anti-Soviet steps. It is to the great benefit of the USSR to cause as much unrest in that part of the world as possible, since the oil supply to the West would thereby be disrupted. They therefore support the Palestinians and fan the flame of discontent against Israel, the one enemy against whom different Arab nation might unite. Peace in the area would constitute a severe political loss to the Soviets. This is why they are extremely unhappy about the series of accords between Egypt and Israel. As far as Turkey is concerned, the Turks and the Russians have been traditional enemies for centuries and there is little in present day relations that would alter that relationship. A major portion of the border area on the Soviet side belongs to Armenia. Many thousands of Armenians were slaughtered by the Turks earlier this century, and the Armenians have not forgotten. Nevertheless, several relatively insignificant commercial treaties between the two countries have been closed recently. The turmoil in Iran is more complicated to analyze. On the one hand, the USSR is quite happy that this important oil producer and strategically located land is no longer in the camp of the United States. On the other hand, they are not at all comfortable with the Moslem fundamentalism which the mullahs are trying to export, considering that there are about 35 million Moslems in the USSR. They are happy with the embarrassment caused by Iran to the United States and with the fluctuations of the oil market. They also like the instability in the region caused by the differences with Iraq. By the same token they must prepare for the eventuality of a change of government in Iran and are therefore carefully nurturing the communist factions in Iran and helping them to plan for an eventual take-over, despite recent Soviet overtures to the fundamentalists. In 1987 an Iranian delegation visited the USSR for the first time in order to hold secret negotiations. It is rumored that the Iranians will give the USSR a number of concessions.

Latin America: Cuba's importance to the Soviet Union should not be underestimated. First of all, since the Soviet citizen consumes more than double the sugar of his American counterpart, the Cuban sugar crop is of great help in meeting this demand. Secondly, since the Soviets feel strategically surrounded by the West, this is one opportunity to establish a strategic position on the doorstep of the major adversary. Thirdly, they can use Cubans as mercenaries in other areas of the world such as Africa. There is no doubt that they will continue to try to expand military installations on the island again - if not missiles, then submarine docks, as soon as a likely opportunity arises. Cuba is also an excellent center for the subversion of other Latin American countries. The objective is to cut off the source of raw materials to the US, to deprive the US of markets, and to involve the US in military actions similar to Vietnam. Nicaragua is also quite likely to become a Soviet colony on the American mainland to be used not only as a center of subversion but also to house Soviet military installations.

The United States: We are still held in awe by the Soviets. They are fully aware that we have considerably greater economic strength than they. They feel, however, that we are declining while their star is in the ascendency. Therefore they wish to gain as much time as possible, continue entering into treaties which do not hurt them, continue to subvert governments on the periphery, in other words, go as far as possible without risking armed conflict. In this manner, slowly but surely, they will win the economic war world-wide, which will result in the economic isolation of the United States and will turn it into a second-rate power. At the present time they know that they cannot compete with the United States in economic projects in developmental areas. This is the foremost method to gain new markets and possibly new political alliances. Such actions would be much too expensive for the Soviet economy. However subversion is much cheaper and just as effective. Unrest, instability and disruptive terrorism are difficult to fight and open the door to change from allegiance to the western camp, to neutrality and then to the Soviet camp. It is to the great benefit of the USSR to subsidize radical movements in the west, be they radical left or radical right. There are strong indications that terrorist movements in many areas of the world have financing and training threads which lead to Moscow.

Africa: The major purpose of the USSR is to remove western influence from strategic and wealthy areas. For this reason the Soviets have traditionally supported subversion in key areas such as the Republic of South Africa under the guise of anti-colonialism, anti-apartheid and self-determination by the majority. In reality the Soviets wish to replace the West in control of natural resources and markets. They have no real altruistic desires to help the black against the white no matter how much they support African revolutionaries with funds and Cuban surrogates. Anyone who has ever been to the RSFSR or the Ukraine, or has ever spoken with black students who have studied at a Russian University will be fully aware of the discrimination and racism to which these students have been exposed in the European part of the Soviet Union. After all, they treat their own national minorities badly, why should they behave differently towards the black African?

READINGS

Arbatov, G. Soviet - American Relations: Progress and Problems. Moscow: Novosti Press, 1976.

Archer, Jules. The Russians and the Americans. New York: Hawthorn Books, 1975.

Boichenko, Victor. Foreign Tourism in the USSR. Moscow: Novosti Press, undated.

Brzezinski, Z. K. The Soviet Bloc. Cambridge: Harvard University Press, 1960.

Declaration of the Meeting of Communist Parties of Latin America and the Caribbean, Havana, June 1975. Moscow: Novosti Press, 1975.

Gittings, John. Survey of the Sino-Soviet Dispute. New York: Oxford University Press, 1968.

Goldman, Marshall I. Soviet Foreign Aid. New York: Praeger, 1967.

Gribanov, M. Security for Europe. Moscow: Novosti Press, 1972.

Hayter, Sir William. Russia and the World: A Study of Soviet Foreign Policy. New York: Taplinger Pub., 1970.

Horelick, Arnold L. and Rush, Myron. Strategic Power and Soviet Foreign Policy. Chicago: University of Chicago Press, 1966.

In the Interests of All the People. Moscow: Novosti Press, 1972.

Isenberg, Irwin. The Russian-Chinese Rift: Its Impact on World Affairs. New York: H. W. Wilson, 1966.

Kaser, Michael. Comecon: Integration Problems of the Planned Economies. London: Oxford University Press, 1967.

Kulski, Wladyslaw. The Soviet Union in World Affairs: A Documented Analysis, 1964-1972. Syracuse: Syracuse University Press, 1973.

Laqueur, Walter Z. Russia and Germany: A Century of Conflict. Boston: Little, Brown, 1965.

Lenczowski, George. Soviet Advances in the Middle East. Washington: American Enterprise Institute for Public Policy Research, 1972.

Mackintosh, J. Malcolm. The Evolution of the Warsaw Pact. London: Institute for Strategic Studies, Adelphi Papers No. 58, June, 1969.

Mackintosh, J. Malcolm. Strategy and Tactics in Soviet Foreign Policy. New York: Oxford University Press, 1963.

McLane, Charles B. Soviet-Asian Relations. New York: Columbia University Press, 1973.

Menon, Rajan. Soviet Power and the Third World. New Haven: Yale University Press, 1986.

Moreton, Edwina and Segal, Gerald. Soviet Strategy Toward Western Europe. Winchester: Allen & Unwin, 1984.

Nation, R. Craig and Kauppi, Mark V. (eds.) The Soviet Impact in Africa. Lexington: D.C. Heath, 1984.

Oswald, Joseph C. (ed.) Soviet Image of Contemporary Latin America. Austin: University of Texas Press, 1970.

Papp, Daniel S. Soviet Perceptions of the Developing World in the 1980s. Lexington: D.C. Heath, 1985.

Paterson, Thomas G. Soviet-American Confrontation. Baltimore: Johns Hopkins University Press, 1973.

Patolichev, Nikolai. Foreign Trade. Moscow: Novosti Press, undated.

Rakhmaninov, Yuri. Security and Cooperation for Europe. Moscow: Novosti Press, 1973.

Schneierson, Vic (trans.) Soviet Foreign Policy -- A Brief Review. Moscow: Progress Publishers, 1967.

Sivachev, Nikolai V. and Yakovlev, Nikolai N. Russia and the United States. Chicago: University of Chicago, 1979.

Sonnenfeld, Helmut. Soviet Style in International Politics. Washington, DC: The Washington Institute for Values in Public Policy, 1985.

Terry, Sarah M. (ed.) Soviet Power in Eastern Europe. New Haven: Yale University Press, 1983.

Tomashevsky, Dmitri. On the Peaceful Co-Existence of States. Moscow: Novosti Press, 1973.

Ulam, Adam B. Expansion and Coexistence: the History of Soviet Foreign Policy, 1917-1967. New York: Praeger, 1968.

USSR-USA: Cooperation for Mutual Benefit. Moscow: Novosti Press, 1973.

What Peking Keeps Silent About. Moscow: Novosti Press, 1972.

Wiles, P. J. D. Communist International Economics. Oxford: Basil Blackwell, 1969.

Wolfe, Thomas W. Soviet Power and Europe 1945-1970. Baltimore: Johns Hopkins, 1970.

Yefremov, Alexander. A Basis for Lasting Peace in Europe (Problems of European Security and Cooperation.) Moscow: Novosti Press, 1973.

XI. Economic Planning

The basic planning period in the USSR is five years. The first Five-Year-Plan lasted from 1928 to 1932 and was initiated as one of the first acts of Stalin as the major tool for collectivization. The twelfth Five-Year Plan commenced in 1986 and will run through 1990. Not all Five-Year-Plans run for five years. There have been several which lasted for only four years, when the quotas were fulfilled a year earlier. It was also possible for a plan to run for eight years, for instance when the period was interrupted by World War II. Although there have been many changes during the fifty years of planning, it is still an absolute fact that the overall plan is divised by the Party and is under total, central control.

The theme of a Five-Year-Plan originates in the minds of the Politburo with consultation of various sub-committees within the Central Committee. This may happen right after the extant Five-Year-Plan goes into effect Planning is a never ending process. The Party leadership devises guidelines of where the economy of the country is to be headed in the future. This depends on several considerations, e.g., international politics, internal shortages, primary needs, lessons learned from the presently in-force Five-Year-Plan, etc. The Party may think, for instance, that relations with the United States are going to become increasingly strained, so that an increase of military spending will be necessary; or, that further curtailment of consumer items may cause popular unrest and that the food industry should therefore be supported more strongly; or, as has happened on several occasions, that land reclamation and resettlement projects in Siberia be stressed; or, more specifically, that one sector of industry should receive greater subsidy than others. Still, these thoughts are primarily of a general nature and to be used as guidelines for the governmental agency charged with translating these politically determined objectives into a set of planning targets.

The governmental agency which probably consumes more paper than all agencies combined and which probably is charged with more painstaking work than any other, is the State Planning Committee (or Commission) which is generally referred to as "Gosplan." This agency is subordinated to the Council of Ministers and has representation throughout the nation, down to the district level. Upon receiving the embryonic plan from the Party, Gosplan asks all levels of government, all geographic areas, all industrial combines, all trade unions and numerous other organizations for maximum input. There are actually millions of people involved in this process. Every area of the economy down to the most minute detail has to be taken into consideration. Nothing can be overlooked, since if there is a gap, there are no private entrepreneurs to fill it. This phase is unbelievably complex. For example, let us consider that the Party has determined that a considerable increase in oil tankers will be necessary. Gosplan would then be charged with not only planning and consulting with the shipbuilding industry, but all the industries which even remotely contribute to the final product, e.g., the forestry industry, ferrous metals, non-ferrous metals, plastics, fuel, glass, mining, fine instruments, insulation, etc., down to the smallest screw. It would also have to determine where the additional labor force could be obtained, e.g., from another industry with a diminished priority, or from trade schools to be built for this purpose. This is just one single end-product. When this process is multiplied by a million, one can imagine the tremendous complexity. This is even more mind-boggling when one

Chart 20
Targets and Results
1980 - 1985

	Guidelines targets approved by the 26th Congress	Actual fulfilment
Average monthly wages of factory and office workers. 1985 in per cent of 1980	113-116	113
Average monthly payment for the work of collective farmers, 1985 in per cent of 1980	120-122	129
Social consumption funds, 1985 in per cent of 1980	120	125
Housing completed in 1981-1985, million square metres overall	530-540	552
Pre-school facilities completed in 1981-1985, million places	2.5	2.9
Completed general schools in 1981-1985, million places	4.3	5.2
Hospital beds, 1985 in per cent of 1980	108-110	108.7
Specialists trained by institutions of higher learning and specialised secondary schools in 1981-1985, million	10	10.5

Chart 21
Comparative Growth
11th - 12th Five-Year-Plans

	Increment in absolute terms, billion roubles		Average annual growth rate, per cent	
	1985 against 1980	1990 against 1985 envisaged in the draft Guidelines	11th five-year plan	12th five-year plan envisaged in the draft Guidelines
National income used for consumption and accumulation	71	96-111	3.1	3.5-4 0
Industrial output	135	169-194	3.7	3.9-4.4
of which means of production (group A)	99	123-142	3.6	3.7-4.2
consumer goods (group B)	36	46-52	3.9	4.1-4.6
Agricultural output (average annual output growth against the preceding five-year plan, in prices for 1983)	11	28-32	1.1	2.7-3.0
Retail trade turnover	46	59-73	3.1	3.4-4.0
Volume of paid services to the population	9.8	13.7-18.2	5.0	5.4-7.0

Chart 21 (cont.)

	Total for 1981-1985, billion roubles	Absolute growth for 1981-1985 as against 1976-1980, billion roubles	Growth of total volume in 1981-1985 as against 1976-1980, per cent
National income, share used for consumption and accumulation	2,398	353	117
Industrial output	3,778	628	120
Apricultural output (in 1983 prices)	1,010	53	106
Freight turnover of all modes of tranbsport (trillion ton-kilometres)	37.1	5.7	118
Installed basic assets	815	147	122
Capital investment	842	125	117
Retail trade turnover	1m466	226	118

realizes that the entire process is not fully computerized and that literally tens of thousands of people sit there with pencil and paper and an abacus figuring out these minute details. This is the foremost reason why the Soviets are trying so desperately to attain access to our advanced computer technology. It is also easy to see that a relatively small error or oversight can, and often does, retard an entire process by months.

After about 18 months of intensive work, Gosplan is ready to submit a draft plan. The plan is divided into the same areas as the fields of responsibility of the national-level ministries, e.g., heavy industry, light industry, defense industry, foreign trade, education, agriculture, etc. The Council of Ministers then approves the draft and sends it to the Central Committee/Politburo. These bodies then suggest changes. After these changes have been incorporated, the final plan is presented to the Party Congress (which meets every five years) for final approval. After the plan has been approved, it is returned to the Council of Ministers, and in turn to Gosplan, for implementation.

This is certainly not where the work of Gosplan ends. A Five-Year-Plan may be a nice thing to have, but it is virtually impossible to plan fully five years in advance and take many yet unknown factors into consideration. Therefore, for all intents and purposes, the Five-Year-Plan is divided in a series of one-year-plans. Each of the latter is based on experience factors obtained during the immediately preceeding one-year-plan. The work of Gosplan therefore never ceases.

The advantages and disadvantages on a planned economy vis a vis a free economy have been argued for decades, and it is not up to us to resolve the argument. We must, nevertheless, be aware of both sides. The major advantages of the Soviet system include the following:

a. The entire economy may be geared to the foreign and domestic political policy.

b. It is quickly responsive to specific needs, e.g., an entire economic area may be purged ruthlessly and new major projects may be initiated without a lengthy process of litigation. The leadership is centralized and indisputable.

c. The economy is geared to the availability of natural resources and therefore allows for the imposing of conservation methods without question.

d. Personnel needs are adjusted with a stroke of the pen, e.g., if there are too many workers in Kiev and not enough in Frunze, the system will correct the problem without major difficulty.

e. Central price fixing virtually eliminates inflation.

f. Instead of allowing the production of frivolous and useless items so common in the West, the State may insist on concentration in fields where proven shortages exist, not where the most profit may be earned.

g. The system prevents over-production.

There are also many shortcomings in the system. The major disadvantages include the following:

a. In such a highly complex system, no matter how good the planners may be, gross errors will appear. It is quite usual, for example, to make simple oversights, such as establishing a quota for a machinery plant and overlooking that spare parts must also be produced. Or, as is frequently the case, establishing a timetable for the construction of housing, without a fitting timetable for the elevator manufacturer or the tile supplier. Shortages are therefore quite common.

b. The system requires a tremendously large planning force and a great deal of supervision. It is no wonder, therefore, that people are assigned supervisory or planning duties in areas with which they are totally unfamiliar.

c. It is extremely dangerous for the directorship in a production area to permit that area to produce less than the set quota. By the same token, it is highly lucrative if the area exceeds its quota. The directorship will therefore do its best to overproduce and to reap the profits of significant monetary bonuses for themselves and all their workers. One way of accomplishing this, is by severely underestimating their production capacity during their initial input towards the preliminary plan, thereby seeing to it that the quota is set lower than it logically should be Another common development is for the directorship to see to it that the quota is not exceeded too greatly, for fear that next year's quota will be appropriately raised. This causes conscious under-production.

d. Since every means of production is tied in with the entire production picture, there is a great deal of rigidity and little flexibility since a change in one production area would necessitate a change in an entire chain of other production areas.

e. The system encourages hoarding. For example, a plant producing generators is constantly in need of copper for its wiring. Copper is a valuable commodity. The copper-producing industry has to be prodded constantly to keep up the necessary production. The generator plant managers will do everything they can to assure themselves that they will have enough copper to fulfill their quota. During periods of affluence, they will hoard excess supplies for leaner years. Often they will enter into an arrangement (bribery or exchange of favors) with the copper producers to assure an adequate supply during lean periods. Sometimes, when two different areas are vieing for the same materials, the competitor with most to offer will succeed. It is estimated that approximately 15% of all the rolling stock in the USSR, at any given time, is transporting "black" materials. Industrial managers are deathly afraid of not fulfilling their quotas, since that could very well mean that they would be replaced, and will do anything illegal to avoid it.

f. The system sometimes indiscriminately shifts areas of concentration, even during critical phases of development. This severely hampers product improvement. Sometimes entire areas of production lie fallow in order to support other areas. This not only results in a great loss of productivity, but causes serious imbalances in numerous production areas. When neglected areas are reactivated, most of the preparatory work has to start at the very beginning again.

Despite all these problems, the Soviet economy is generally healthier now than it has been before. Production is increasing significantly in many fields. Production methods are improving, personnel are better trained and new areas of production are being opened. Alas, this is not a result of the planning methods, but rather in spite of them. The planning process continues to be highly inefficient and defective. In 1986, in the course of recapitulating the results of the just completed Five-Year-Plan, it was determined that there were significant shortfalls in both industry and agriculture. This is due, in part, to the planning process itself. This process cannot be eliminated since it constitutes one of the pillars of the Soviet system. Nevertheless, the new breed of Soviet economists is strongly pushing for streamlining the planning process, allowing a degree of competition and self-determination within the Soviet production system, therefore making the economy of the USSR more efficient.

The most recent innovations suggested by Gorbachev and partly put into effect in 1987 include the following:

a. Since the plant managers do not want to produce as much as they are capable of producing for fear that next year's quota will be appropriately raised, it has been proposed that there be no quota adjustments within any Five-Year-Plan already in effect.

b. In line with Gorbachev's emphasis on eliminating shoddy workmanship, i.e., quality control, inferior products should no longer count towards fulfillment of quotas. For this reason, quality control inspectors are to be hired for all production areas.

c. In consonance with production incentives, workers may be paid an annual bonus as high as half of their annual wages.

d. The production of spare parts is normally not taken into full account in quotas system. Therefore it is quite common to produce many fewer spare parts than are needed. This, in turn, causes cannibalism of machinery and other wasteful practices. Under a new system special emphasis is to be placed on spare parts production for full quota credit.

e. Most importantly, Gorbachev feels that Gosplan has been a deterrent to Soviet production rather than a catalyst thereof. As a good communist he agrees that control of the economy must always be in the hands of the Party. Nevertheless not everything should be planned, since the overlooking of one small screw may hold up the production of an entire ship. He feels that there should be some autonomy in the individual production area which would enable them to complete their mission without having to rely on someone else's whim for every little item. He also feels that Gosplan has gotten much too large and inefficient to take the USSR into the 21st century, and that there is nothing wrong in adopting a few capitalist production practices as long as the basic adherence to Marxian economic principles is not raped.

Chart 22
Percentage Increments
12th Five-Year Plan

	Increment for five years (per cent)		Growth (+). fall (-) of increment rates
	1981-1985	1986-1990 as envisaged in draft Guidelines	
I. Results of Production			
National income share used for consumption and accumulation	17	19-22	+2 to 5
Industrial output	20	21-24	+1 to 4
Agricultural output (average annual)	6	14-16	+8 to 10
II. Basic Resources			
Number of people employed in material production	2.3	0.5	-1.8
Fixed production assets	37	30	-7
Production of instruments of labour	17	15	-2

READINGS

Bergson, A. The Economics of Soviet Planning. New Haven: Yale University Press, 1964.

Bor, Mikhail. Aims and Methods of Soviet Planning. New York: International Publishers, 1967.

Campbell, Robert. Soviet Economic Power. Boston, Houghton Mifflin, 1966.

Conolly, Violet. Beyond the Urals: Economic Development in Soviet Asia. London: Oxford University Press, 1967.

Feiwell, G. R. (ed.) New Currents in Soviet-type Economics: A Reader. Scranton: International Textbook Co., 1968

Felker, J. L. Soviet Economic Controversies. Cambridge: MIT Press, 1966.

Finder, Joseph. Red Carpet. New York: Holt, Rinehart & Winston, 1983.

Holzman, F. D. Readings on the Soviet Economy. Chicago: Rand McNally, 1962.

Kaser, Michael (ed.) Economic Development for Eastern Europe. New York: St. Martin's Press, 1968.

____. Soviet Economics. New York: McGraw-Hill, 1970.

Katz, Abraham. The Politics of Economic Reform in the Soviet Union. New York: Praeger, 1972.

Korop, Pyotr. USSR: Looking at an Economic Map. Moscxow: Novosti, 1985.

Lempert, Leo, (trans.) Soviet Planning: Principles and Techniques. Moscow: Progress, 1972.

Maddison, A. Economic Growth in Japan and the USSR. London: Allen and Unwin, 1969.

Nove, Alec. The Soviet Economic System. 3rd Ed. Winchester: Allen & Unwin, 1986.

Ryzhkov, Nikolai. Guidelines for the Economic and Social Development of the USSR for 1986-1990 and for the period ending 2000.

Spulber, Nicholas. The Soviet Economy, Principles, Problems. New York: Norton, 1969.

Spulber, Nicholas. Socialist Management and Planning. Bloomington: Indiana University Press, 1971.

Treml, Vladimir G. (ed.) The Development of the Soviet Economy. New York: Praeger, 1968.

Wellisz, S. The Economics of the Soviet Bloc. New York: McGraw Hill, 1964.

Wilczynski, J. The Economics of Socialism. Chicago: Aldine Publishers, 1972.

Zaleski, E. Planning Reforms in the Soviet Union. Chapel Hill: University of North Carolina Press, 1967

XII. Industry

Contrary to popular opinion, the Soviet citizen is fully aware that his industrial output lags far behind that of the United States. The motto "to catch up to and surpass America" is still in wide use even on Party circulars. Before we become too smug, let us consider one thing: We have had a century and a half to develop our industry. Before the Russian Revolution there was virtually no industry in the country. For all intents and purposes it did not start until after the Civil War, in the 1920's. Industrial development was interrupted by World War II when most of the Soviet plants were destroyed by the Germans. In actuality then, the USSR has had less than fifty years to build up an industrial complex second only to ours. They are rightfully proud of their achievement now that their industrial output has reached 725 billion rubles in 1985.

Everything is going far from smoothly, however There are too many persons involved in the decision-making process who are thoroughly unfamiliar with efficient industrial management. This is quite obvious considering the shortcomings in the coordination of production. It is not uncommon, for example, to produce relatively sophisticated machinery in accordance with the Five Year Plan quota, and to forget, totally, to plan for spare parts. It is relatively common for a plant to receive a quota for the manufacture of a finished product, while a raw-material plant which is to supply it, has a quota to furnish less than half of the raw materials needed. It is just as common that a plant may be deluged with many more materials than it can possibly use. This is, of course, conducive to black marketeering. On the more visible plane, it is quite commonly the case that a brand new building may be constructed in Leningrad or Kiev and would then have to stand empty for a year waiting for the elevator industry to catch up on its quota. This is one reason why a foreigner may be surprised by seeing shoddy forty-year-old elevators from demolished buildings, which do not fit and rattle around in the shaft, installed in sparkling, multi-million-ruble skyscrapers

One of the main causes of this mismanagement is the fact that, until quite recently, the pertinent ministries were directly responsible for coordinating the production of all the individual plants within their jurisdiction. This was very inefficiently handled since the ministries in Moscow were totally unaware of local problems and idiosyncracies. At the present time a new system of management is being introduced and is expected to be complete nation-wide in the late 1980s. Under this so-called "three stage system" the two stages (ministry to enterprise) are being replaced by three stages (ministry to Industrial Association to enterprise). Under this innovation, they are creating Industrial Associations which will be charged with producing a finished product by controlling the entire process beginning with research, design, and raw materials, through the final manufacturing phase. Approximately 2,600 such associations have already been established. There is some similarity between this system and the major trusts which were created in the United States in the early twentieth century. The boards of directors of such associations and those of a major corporation in the United States resemble each other greatly.

Chart 23

Energy Tables

a. Electricity:

Output of Electric Power in Billions of Kilowatt-Hours

1970	1975	1980	1985
741,000	1,039,000	1,295,000	1,550-1,660.000

Types of Stations	1975	1980	1985
Nuclear	2.0	5.6	14.2
Hydroelectric	12.1	14.2	14.8
Thermal	85.9	80.2	71

b. Gas:

Output of Natural Gas in Millions of Cubic Meters

1970	1975	1980	1981	1985
198,000	289,000	435,000	458,000	600-640,000

Gas Pipelines

	1970	1980	1985
Length in Kilometers	68,000	130,000	180,000
Capacity of Pumping Stations	3.5	18.0	43.0
	(in millions of Kilowatts)		

Chart 23
Energy Tables (cont)

c. Coal:

Output of Coal in Millions of Tons

Year	Quantity	Increase (tonnage)	Increase (percentage)
1960	510		
1965	578	68	13
1970	624	46	8
1975	701	77	12
1980	716	15	2
1985	770-800	54-68	7-11

d. Oil:

Changes in Annual Oil Production of Major Oil Producing Regions in Millions of Tons

Region	1970	1986
Tyumen	31.4	323.5
Tataria	100.4	57.1
Bashkiria	40.4	38.8
Kuibyshev	34.9	23.1
Komi ASSR	5.6	19.4
Azerbaidzhan	20.2	14.8
Mangyshlak	10.4	14.8
Perm	16.1	13.9
Orenburg	7.4	11.0
Tomsk	none	10.8

Total Energy Production (Overview)

Type of Energy	1940	1960	1978	1986
Electricity (in Billions Kilowatt Hours)	48.6	292	1,202	1,295
Oil (in Millions of Tons)	31.1	148	572	720
Gas (in Billions of Cubic Meters)	3.2	45.3	372	435
Coal (in Millions of Tons)	166.0	510.0	724.0	765.0

Some of the industries will remain under the two step system, i.e., under the centralized control of the ministries. These are primarily strategic and military industries, including all aircraft, ships and nuclear systems.

Another major new development in the industrial system is a clearly noticeable shift to the east. The USSR is immeasurably wealthy in raw materials and vast sources of power which have yet to be exploited. Under the present Five Year Plan, 92% of the increased production of coal; 78% of the increase in copper; and 50% of the increase in paper products will be provided by newly developed eastern regions. The new exploration of oil and natural gas sources in the east are expected to bring similar results. At the same time, the industrial production in already developed western areas is also expected to increase. A short discussion of some of the major industries would be appropriate at this point:

The Iron and Steel Industry: In 1986 the USSR accounted for approximately 20% of the world's steel production by producing approximately 162 million tons. The Soviet Union has 310 steel and iron plants, the largest of which (in order of size) are Magnitogorsk, Krivoi Rog, Zhdanov, Nizhnii Tagil, Cherepovets and Cheliabinsk. New eastern plants include those in Novokuznetsk and Karaganda.

The Automotive Industry: The vast majority of vehicles on the road are government owned. It is still relatively rare for a private person to own a car unless he has some political pull, has an income far above the average, and has waited for the privilege of purchasing one for a very long time, up to two years. The cost of cars is prohibitive, ranging from $9,000 to $25,000. There is a great shortage despite a dramatic increase of production caused primarily by the construction of the Fiat plant. Although the capacity of the Fiat plant (called the Volzhskii Plant in Togliatti) is supposed to be 660,000 cars a year, the actual production is considerably lower because of inefficiency in production methods and supplies In 1986 the USSR produced a total of 2.6 million motor vehicles including over 800,000 trucks. In addition, about 590,000 tractors and combines were produced.

The Chemical Industry: This is one of the branches of Soviet industry which leaves room for a great deal of improvement, despite the fact that it is second only to the United States in size. The quality control leaves much to be desired. In 1986 the production of chemical fiber was over 1.2 million tons, and plastics and synthetic resins 3.5 million tons. There were 65 million automobile tires produced that year. The mineral fertilizer produced in 1986 (102 million tons) is not nearly sufficient to cover the demand (approximately 170 million tons annually).

The Timber Industry: The USSR is the largest producer of timber in the world and possesses more than 25% of the world's total reserves. Nevertheless, due to faulty planning and inefficiency, there was a paper shortage in 1986.

The Power and Fuel Industry: Few visitors to the USSR can get away without being shown at least one hydroelectric power station. The pride in electricity goes back to the period of Lenin who foresaw the future need of power and planned the electrigication of the entire nation. In 1986 the Soviet Union produced 1.32 billion kwh of electricity. There are 54 power stations with a capacity of over one million kw each. Thermal power stations are currently being constructed near the Ekibastuz coal deposits in Kazakhstan and Kansk-Achinsk coal fields in Siberia.

There are large nuclear power stations already in operation in Leningrad, Novovoronezhskaia and Kola. Most of the USSR is covered by a power grid in which 650 atomic, thermal and hydroelectric stations produce three-fourths of all the electric energy of the nation. The coal production has also increased greatly, to the level of 770 million tons in 1986. There has been a similarly dramatic increase in the production of oil, to the level of 620 million tons in 1986, although demand has now caught up to supply. The USSR has the largest deposits of natural gas in the world (approximately 19 billion cubic meters). It is estimated that after exploration has been completed, the USSR's reserve will probably come to about 100 billion cubic meters. Gas is being extracted from Southeastern and Western Ukrain, Western Siberia, Northern Caucasus, the Volga area, Transcaucasia, Turkmenia and Uzbekistan. During the tenth Five Year Plan 35,000 kiolmeters of pipelines have been completed. The USSR supplies gas to all its satellites, plus Austria, Yugoslavia, West Germany, Finland, Italy, France and Japan. The United States is also seriously considering the purchase of Soviet gas sometime in the future.

Light Industry: Under Soviet terminology this includes the following consumer items, among other branches:

Textiles: There is still a considerable shortage of good quality materials although the USSR, in 1986, produced 7.4 billion square meters of cotton fabrics; 820 million square meters of woolen fabrics; 800 million square meters of linen facrics; and 1.9 billion square meters of silk fabrics. All good clothing is prohibitively expensive. Much is imported from Poland, Hungary, Czechoslovakia and East Germany.

Shoes: There is a great shortage of shoes in the USSR. The ones that are available are very poorly made (except for those that have been imported) and extremely expensive. In 1986 the USSR produced 805 million pairs.

Furs: Only the Soviet elite wears expensive furs. The rest are exported, mostly to Western Europe, for hard currency.

Recent Developments

Everyone is well aware of the meltdown of the Chernobyl reactor in 1986. This accident had a tremendous psychological effect on the Soviet population which, at this writing, is still quite visible. It is not only that over 100,000 people were relocated and fled the area on their own, it is also the great economic havoc the incident created for many months. Not only were a number of foodstuffs very difficult to obtain, but the entire supply system from the south to the north was disrupted. The population always had a dread fear of nuclear war and this incident reinforced their horror. It was amazing to the population, however, that the Soviet government discussed the mishap so openly in all the media. This was the first big sampling of "glasnost" which was later reinforced by the publicized trial of those who were responsible for the laxity of safety measures. Although people still talk about Chernobyl, the fear is now mostly gone. The Soviets realize that they cannot cope with their energy needs without nuclear power and have accepted the reactivation of the Chernobyl plant and the construction of numerous similar plants. One great worry they still have is caused by the fact that there are quite a number of similar nuclear power plants in the middle of major cities, including Moscow. The potential effects of meltdown there, boggle the mind.

Another recent development is Gorbachev's insistence that individual production plant managers have an increased involvement with plans for expansion, quality control, rationalization, modernization, and other decisions affecting production at their installations. He believes that the managers on the ground often know a great deal more than some minister on USSR or SSR level. For this reason he has proposed that an increased portion of the profits of a plant be returned to the plant directly. Of course, continuation of this new method will depend on the degree of success of failure by plants to become more efficient and productive. One negative experience starting in 1987 has been the bankrupcy of several plants brought about by the mismanagement of enterprises which had been afforded a greater degree of independence.

Another deviation from exclusive nationalization of all means of production, distribution and services is a series of announcements by Gorbachev in 1987 that some forms of private enterprise should now be permitted. Many of his suggestions follow the Hungarian model. For example, it is a fact that the services of mechanics, plumbers, carpenters and other craftsmen are very difficult to obtain. At the present time, the best way of getting such services is through craftsmen who "moonlight" illegally. Gorbachev has made it legal for a group of craftsmen who work at regular jobs to band together into a service center wherefrom they could sell their services in the evenings or during their time off from regular work. In addition, the possibility is being investigated on the legal opening of small daytime enterprises including arts and crafts stores and small eating establishments which would be owned and operated by private individuals. Gorbachev feels that national productivity could thereby be raised significantly. The one caveat is, that none of these private endeavors are permitted to hire employees.

Estimates by U.S. intelligence agencies concerning the state of the Soviet economy in general in 1987 include the information that the rate of expansion of the economy under Gorbachev has doubled and that this rate will accellerate considerably in the foreseeable future.

READINGS

Ames, E. Soviet Economic Progress. Homewood: Irwin Publ., 1966.

Bogatko, Sergei. Kama Auto Works Comes of Age. Moscow: Novosti Press, 1976.

Cahan, Arcadius and Ruble, Glair, (eds.) Industrial Labor in the U.S.S.R. New York: Pergamon Press, 1979.

Campbell, Robert W. Accounting in Soviet Planning and Management. London: OXford University Press, 1963.

Conquest, Robert (ed) Industrial Workers in the USSR. New York: Praeger, 1967.

Chart 24

AVERAGE DAILY OUTPUT
1987

Electric Power (million kwh)	4,500
Oil, incl. gas condensate (thous. tons)	1,690
Natural Gas (million cubic meters)	1,750
Coal (thousand tons)	1.950
Steel (thousand tons)	430
Iron Ore (thousand tons)	680
Tractors (units)	1,580
Textiles (million square meters)	33
Leather Footware (thousand pairs)	2,100
Television Sets (thousands)	26
Watches (thousands)	185

READINGS (continued)

Feiwel, George R. The Soviet Quest for Economic Efficiency. New York: Praeger, 1967.

Goldman, Marshall I. Soviet Marketing. London: Macmillan, 1963.

Gumpel. W. Das Verkehrswesen Osteuropas. Cologne: Verlag Wissenschaft und Politik, 1967.

Hough, Jerry F. The Soviet Prefects: The Local Party Organs in Industrial Decision-Making. Cambridge: Harvard University Press, 1969.

Lane, David and O'Dell, Felicity. The Soviet Industrial Worker. New York: St. Martin's Press, 1978.

Mangushev, Kamil. Power Industry. Moscow: Novosti, 1985.

Osipov, G. V. (ed.) Industry and Labour in the USSR. London: Tavistock, 1966.

Richman, Barry M. Soviet Management. Englewood Cliffs: Prentice-Hall, 1965.

The Soviet Financial System: Structure, Operation, abd Statistics. Washington: Dept. of Commerce, 1968.

USSR Industry. Moscow: Novosti Press, 1976.

Westwood, J. N. Soviet Railways Today. London: Ian Allan, 1963.

XIII. Agriculture

This area of the national economy has been a political sorespot for decades. Numerous officials, even including the minister of agriculture and a member of the Politburo, have lost their positions because of the failure of the agricultural areas to feed the country. There are numerous reasons why this is such a weak area:

a. Although the Soviet Union is immense in size, most of the country is covered with forests, mountains, lakes, deserts and other natural barriers to exploitation. Therefore, only about twenty percent of the land is arable, i.e., considerably less than in the United States.

b. Even the arable lands have severe problems. For instance, while there is too much moisture in the soil in Belorussia and parts of the RSFSR which requires expensive draining operations, there is not enough moisture in parts of the Ukraine and in the Asian republics, which requires costly irrigation projects.

c. During the past decade the USSR has been hit by a series of crop failures brought about by adverse weather conditions.

d. Farming methods are outdated.

e. There is insufficient production of fertilizers.

f. There is insufficient production of farm machinery.

g. The planning and administration are inefficient. Unreasonable demands are levied upon some areas while other areas are permitted to lie fallow. There is too great an overhead in administrators. Numerous officials who do not understand farming are involved in the chain of command which establishes quotas.

h. The Soviet peasant feels no personal involvement with what he is doing, since the piece of land he is working on does not belong to him. His proceeds, whether he works hard or not, are approximately the same. He would much rather spend his effort cultivating his own little plot of land.

i. There is a great deal of theft of tools and fertilizers for the benefit of private plots.

It is difficult to discuss agriculture without mentioning the large grain shipments from the U.S. to the USSR. These shipments occurred during years of crop failure when the grain production dropped to approximnately 160 million tons a year. One thing must be kept in mind, however. The Soviets produce more wheat than the United States. The shortages come about because of the Soviet diet, which requires a great deal more grain than ours. The same is true for potatoes of which the USSR is the largest producer in the world. Harvests in 1978 and 1979 were abominable and created considerable shortages in feed grain. This, in turn, created shortages in meat and animal products in the early 1980's.

Approximately 606 million hectares of the USSR may be used for agricultural production. Of this amount, 226 million are plowable land. Approximately 30 million hectares of desert land have been reclaimed through irrigation, of which 10 million hectares were improved during the period of the Tenth Five-Year-Plan alone (1976-80).

According to the law, land in the USSR cannot belong to anyone except to the state. The permission to use a specific parcel of land may be bestowed for a specified period or for perpetual use, depending which type of agricultural production is involved.

There are three means of agricultural production in the Soviet Union:

a. The Collective Farm (Kolkhoz): the average Kolkhoz has approximately 6,500 hectares of land (1 hectare = 2.47 acres). There are approximately 600 families living on it. Although the ground belongs to the State, all the property on it belongs to the members of the Kolkhoz. This includes houses, farm machinery and means of transport. Usually a Kolkhoz has a diversified crop and also raises livestock. It has self-government and decides at general meetings how much of a commodity the farm will produce in the coming year, how much it will sell to the State, what capital outlays are required, and how much each individual farmer can expect to earn this year. Of course, these decisions are not made completely independently. The entire economy functions on the basis of a five-year-plan which, in turn, contains five one-year-plans. This means, that the Kolkhoz must close a five-year contract with the State based on a planned quota which more or less commits the Kolkhoz to sell to the State a certain amount of produce for a certain amount of money. The beginning of each year, the Kolkhoz signs an additional contract which is more specific although it is based on the five-year contract. This annual contract promises to deliver a definite amount of produce to the State, within the current year. Should the Kolkhoz produce more than it planned, it can sell the excess to the State at a somewhat higher price, or it can sell the overage on the open market at a considerable profit. The excess profits are distributed among the members of the collective farm, minus operational expenses and new equipment costs. Should it be a bad harvest, below that promised to the State, then the members of the Kolkhoz will receive relatively little for their year's work and will undergo a period of sometimes devastating deprivation despite the minimum compensation law which was recently extended to include collective farmers.

New means are constantly sought to improve production. The one most strongly advocated by the State, is the cooperation of several Kolkhozes of an area in enterprises which may be too costly for a single Kolkhoz (e.g. mechanized milking; slaughter houses; sophisticated farm machinery, etc.) Such Councils of Collective Farms are now being established from the rural level to the Republic level. There is even an all-Union Council of Kolkhozes which is strongly supported by both the Government and the Party. In fact, these councils do not only include senior members of the Kolkhozes, but also government officials, Party functionaries, and directors of State Farms. Decisions, therefore, end up being made by the Party and Government rather than by the segment of the population to be ultimately affected. It is definitely the intent of the State to eliminate as many Kolkhozes as possible and turn them into Sovkhozes. Once a number of Kolkhozes unite their production processes, the State may say that the resulting cooperative is too large for a Kolkhoz and would be much more efficient as a Sovkhoz. The

Chart 25
Farm Production
1986

	Million Tons
Raw Cotton	8.7
Sugar Beet	85.9
Sunflower	4.7
Potatoes	88.2
Other Vegetables	30.7
Grain	240.0
Meat	16.9
Milk	99.2
Eggs (billion)	78.0
Wool (thousand tons)	471.0

Livestock
1986

	Million Head
Cattle	122
Pigs	79
Sheep and Goats	150

members of the Kolkhoz then dutifully vote to abolish themselves. Thousands of Kolkhozes are being dissolved all over the country every year. There are only 28,000 left.

The standard of living and educational level on a collective farm are relatively low, as is Party membership. Since they are considered to be self-employed, they often do not join trade unions. It is therefore quite unusual for a Kolkhoz member to be able to travel to an attractive vacation site. Many young people therefore leave the Kolkhoz when they have the chance and either go to work in a Sovkhoz or change their occupations.

b. The State Farm (Sovkhoz): The State Farms are normally at least three times the size of a Kolkhoz and have triple the population. Contrary to collective farms, they normally specialize in one product, e.g., grain, animal husbandry, vegetables, or poultry breeding. They are much more highly mechanized than the tractor-starved Kolkhozes. All the property on the Sovkhoz belongs to the State. Farmers are paid a straight salary which in no way is dependent upon the size of the harvest. In an especially good year, bonuses are paid. The Sovkhoz worker, as an employee of the State, does belong to a trade union. There is also strong Party representation in his Sovkhoz, and there is a much greater opportunity for education and advancement. They are also eligible for pensions under the national social security system. They have much more support from the State than Kolkhozes. In fact, there is a Ministry of State Farms in each of the 15 Republics. The director of a State Farm is also a State-appointed official who has total authority in the Sovkhoz. Decisions are made by him, personally, not by any council.

Because of the shortage of arable land, there is a major land reclamation drive to turn virgin and fallow soil into productive land. Whenever a sizeable tract is reclaimed, it is normally formed into a Sovkhoz. In addition, their numbers are being constantly augmented by the metamorphosis of Kolkhozes into Sovkhozes. There are about 18,500 State Farms in the land. By 1988 Sovkhozes are expected to outproduce Kolkhozes for the first time in history.

c. Personal Plots: All members of both collective farms and state farms are permitted to work a small parcel of land (1/2 acre to 1 1/4 acres depending on the region and the quality of land) for their own purposes. They may also raise a small number of livestock. It is a sad commentary for the Soviets to have to admit that fully 30% of all the vegetables, fruits, milk, eggs and meat products, originate on these very carefully manicured, postage stamp size plots. In 1986 these plots fed and produced 15 million cows, 13 million pigs, 32 million sheep and goats and hundreds of millions of poultry alone. It seems to point out that the capitalistic system, even in miniature, even on Soviet land, produces much more than the socialist system. The owners of these plots may use the produce themselves, may sell it to the State, or, virtually all of them do this, may sell it on the open farmer's market in urban centers. Not only is the quantity of the produce much greater, but the quality is far superior to that of similar produce produced by both Sovkhozes and Kolkhozes. The Soviets would like nothing better than to abolish this significant remainder of capitalism, however they are in sore need of the food they produce. This is why they are continuing to encourage this form of agricultural

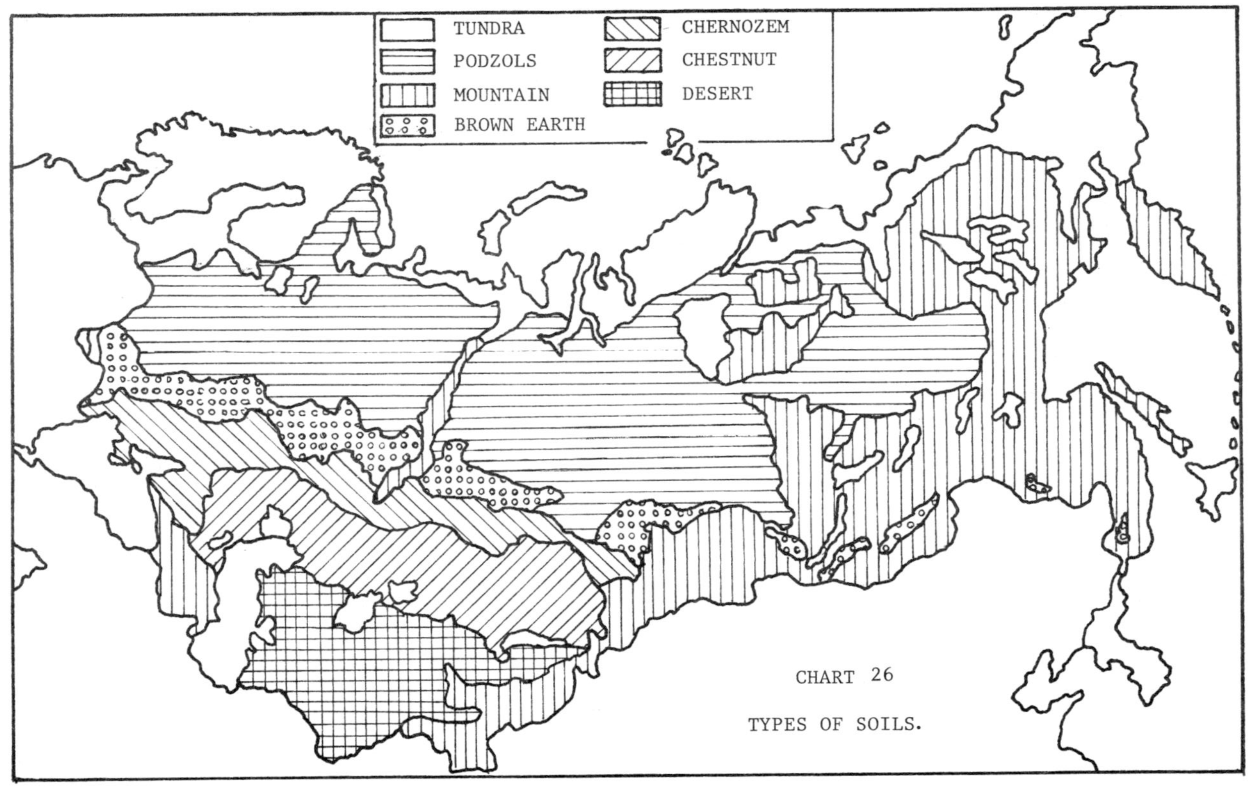

CHART 26

TYPES OF SOILS.

Chart 27

Machine Attachments for Each Tractor Produced in the USSR

Type of Attachment	Total Number of Attachments
Attachment for loading, unloading and ditching work	18
Attachment for transporting various loads	14
Attachment for tilling prior to sowing	29
Attachment for sowing a variety of crops	28
Attachment for fertilizer, herbicide and pesticide application	24
Attachment for planting and inter-row tilling	31
Attachment for harvesting crops	57
Attachment for fodder production and the mechanisation of livestock raising	45
Total attachments for each heavy tractor:	246

Farm Machinery Produced and To Be Produced

Type of Machinery	1975	1980	1986
Tractors (incl. the 7hp "Rioni" for orchards and gardens and the 300hp K-701 heavy wheel tractor)	552,000	580-600,000	620,000
Grain Harvester Combines (incl. the Niva, Kolos, Sibiriak and the 6-row sugar-beet harvester)	85,000	125,000	141,000

production. The private plot has even become vogue in urban areas, since city dwellers may request the allocation of land outside the city to grow agricultural produce.

READINGS

Abramov, Fyodor. The New Life: A Day on a Collective Farm. New York: Grove Press. 1963.

Hahn, Werner. The Politics of Soviet Agriculture 1960-1970. Baltimore: Johns Hopkins University Press, 1972.

Johnson, D.G. and Brooks, K.M. Prospects for Russian Agriculture in the 1980. Bloomington: Indiana University Press, 1983.

Karcz, Jerzy (ed.) Soviet and East European Agriculture. Berkeley: University of California Press, 1967.

Laird, Roy D. (ed.) Soviet Agriculture: The Permanent Crisis. New York: Praeger, 1965.

Lewin, Moshe. Russian Peasants and Soviet Power: A Study of Collectivization. London: Allen and Unwin, 1968.

Potichnyj, Peter J. Soviet Agricultural Trade Unions. Toronto: University of Toronto Press, 1972.

Strauss, Erich. Soviet Agriculture in Perspective. New York: Praeger, 1969.

Ussovsky, B. N. et.al. Comprehensive Russian-English Agricultural Dictionary. New York: Pergamon Press, 1967.

Voskresensky, Lev. Farming. Moscow: Novosti, 1985.

XIV. Housing

The housing situation is continuing to be one of the severest problem in the Soviet Union The shortage of housing is primarily due to the following factors:

a. During the Revolution and the Civil War a great number of dwellings were destroyed. This occurred at a time when the construction industry was still virtually non-existent.

b. During the ensuing years there was a concerted effort towards urbanization. A traditionally agrarian country was asked to change into a predominantly industrial, urban nation.

c. During World War II vast housing areas were destroyed by the Germans.

d. Although the population is leveling off towards zero growth at the present time, there was a considerable increase during the post-war years.

e. A very considerable number of older houses had to be torn down and had to be replaced.

f. Despite many improvements in recent years, the construction industry is still inefficient. Many new buildings show severe defects soon after they are built and deteriorate relatively quickly.

g. Although a great deal of emphasis has been placed on new housing construction by the government, there were other areas which received priority. In addition, the existing building industry was not sufficiently developed to keep up an accellerated pace.

To paint a clearer picture of the housing shortage, it is necessary to describe the housing presently available:

a. Old apartment buildings in urban areas, which are large complexes built around a courtyard. The construction is quite solid and these homes are not being razed. Several generations of the same family have grown up in them. In fact, the entire building is like a closely knit family. Soviets are loathe to move out even if offered newer quarters; it would be like leaving home. Of course, Soviets are not anywhere nearly as mobile as Americans. These apartments have few modern conveniences. Many do not even have hot water!

b. There is even older, more inconvenient housing in many large cities. Smaller houses which used to quarter one noble family are sub-divided into space for four families. Of course there is only one kitchen which is very poorly equipped. This means that four women are trying to prepare supper for their families on the same small stove at the same time. It is therefore understandable that a good part of the cases heard by the People's Courts involve physical assault among women. These houses have a communal toilet. There is no bath in most of the older houses, so that the tradition of Russian commercial bathhouses still persists.

Chart 28

Housing
1981-85

Construction in millions of Square Meters of Useful Floor Space	553
Paid By State Investment (Total Square Meters of Useful Floor Space)	497
Number of Apartments Built (millions)	10.4
Number of square meters allocated to each inhabitant	14.5
Percentage of Public Housing Units With:	
Water piping	92.1
Sewage	89.5
Central Heating	88.9
Gas	79.2
Hot Water	72.2
Bathrooms	82.3

c. There are newer apartments in tall apartment buildings many of which were built during the Khrushchev era. In fact, entire districts composed of such buildings in several major cities are named "Khrushchevka." Each apartment has its own toilet and bath. Most have a small balcony. They are generally poorly built and major problems arise very quickly, e.g., the central heating or the plumbing does not work, cracks appear in the walls and ceilings, and, invariably, the elevators are out of commission a good part of the time. The most recently built housing, though of better quality, has many of the same construction defects.

d. In rural housing, there is quite a big difference between an apartment project for a well-supported Sovkhoz in the RSFSR (these are mostly three-story buildings with individual apartments which furnish adequate comfort), and a remost Kolkhoz where the housing looks like something out of the middle ages, with absolutely no modern conveniences, no inside plumbing; but nearly all do have electricity.

In the 1980s the floorspace assigned to each resident reached a little more than 12 square meters in urban areas. This is ridiculously little according to American standards, but quite an improvement compared with the Soviet past. Nevertheless it will take many more years until the housing needs of the nation are adequately met, especially since capital outlay for housing is being curtailed.

The cost of rental is possibly the lowest in the world. The average apartment rents for approximately 6-9 rubles a month. Utilities are just as reasonable:

Gas - 16 kopeks (1 ruble - 100 kopeks) per family member, per month.

Electricity - 4 kopeks per kilowatt-hour.

Hot Water - 29 kopeks per month for each family member.

Central heating - 5 kopeks per month per square meter of floor space.

Telephone - 2 1/2 rubles per month for unlimited calls.

The total expense for rent and utilities approximates 4 1/2 percent of the average family income. The total contribution by the tenant covers only approximately 20% of the cost. The rest is paid by the State.

The allocation of quarters is conducted by the housing authority of the local Soviet of People's Deputies. This office is petitioned for housing by:

Families whose old residences have been demolished.
Families which have grown beyond the size which could still be maintained in their old quarters.
Newlyweds.
Workers who have been transferred from other locations, and their families.
Persons who have been promoted into prestige positions and need quarters suitable for entertainment.
Persons who have been demoted and have been told to vacate their apartments.

The local housing authority is one of the principal localities for influence peddling and bribery. A plain, ordinary worker with nothing to offer will find himself in one of the older, geographically inconvenient, uncomfortable buildings. An assistant director at the opera (who can assure a steady flow of complimentary tickets) or a manager of an automotive distribution point (who may advance a name on the list for permission to purchase a car) will certainly receive special attention Occasionally, there are cases of outright bribery with relatively large sums of money. Ostensibly, housing is distributed fairly. In fact, there are even commissions composed of volunteers whose job it is to inspect the present housing of a new-housing applicant and to make recommendations to the housing authority. The labor unions are also asked for input when the case concerns the family of a member of the union. In reality, the housing authority may, and quite frequently does, reach decisions which are contradictory to these recommendations.

Wealthier members of society may opt to buy condominiums for their families. These are normally quite attractive, tall apartment buildings, although construction quality still leaves quite a bit to be desired. Soon after they are constructed, the concrete may crumble and expose sharp, upward-curving steel reinforcement rods; or, since there has been no allowance for breakage, there were insufficient marble tiles to finish the entrance hall and other materials had to be pieced together. Nevertheless, this is the best housing in the USSR (except for VIP housing in special apartment blocks). The purchaser has to pay 40% down (30% in remote areas) and finances the rest through a state loan at 2% annual interest. At the present time, approximately 7% of all new housing constructed in the Soviet Union falls into this category. The apartments remain the property of the purchaser forever, and are inherited by his children.

Finally, let us consider the individual house which may be used as a principal residence in a rural area, or as a summer home (dacha). Every Soviet citizen is entitled to built such a home if he can show need and the ability to keep up payments. He then receives a bank loan for twenty years at the rate of 2% annually. He also is given the use of a piece of land free of charge. There are certain restrictions:

a. The size and configuration of the structure may be limited by the local authorities.

b. Normally the house may not contain more than five rooms plus a kitchen and bathroom.

c. If the State needs the plot of land on which there is a private house, it may be demolished and the owner may be offered monetary reimbursement or a condominium of the same approximate value.

d. Private houses are inheritable. They may not, however, be sold to any party other than the State. Of course, this is true for all tangible property, since no such private enterprise is permissible.

During the past decade there has been a significant move towards urban renewal, especially in the larger cities. The intent is to move both industry and residential areas out of the cities. As new factories are being constructed, the normal procedure is to find major sites approximately fifteen kilometers outside the city. This serves to beautify the cities and also to diminish pollution. Normally, with the construction of major plants, there are also major housing projects built several kilometers away from the plant. Sometimes these projects are of a size and configuration of small cities. They contain their own schools, shops and recreation centers. In addition, both the plants and the housing areas are connected with each other and with the major adjacent cities by an adequate network of cheap and efficient public transportation. It is planned that within two to three decades the major cities will contain only government buildings, stores, mass organizations, cultural and amusement centers and parks, and housing for top-level functionaries either in the form of palatial old apartments or condominiums.

READINGS

Andrusz, Gregory D. Housing and Urban Development in the USSR. Albany: SUNY Press, 1984.

DiMaio, Alfred J. Soviet Urban Housing. New York: Praeger, 1974.

Hulicka, Karel and Irene M. Soviet Institutions: the Individual and Society. Boston: The Christopher Publishing House, 1967.

Inkeles, Alex and Geiger, Kurt (eds.) Soviet Society, a Book of Readings. Boston: Houghton Mifflin, 1961.

Nogee, Joseph L. (ed.) Man, State and Society in the Soviet Union. New York: Praeger, 1972.

USSR '87: Novosti Press Agency Year Book. Moscow: Novosti Press, 1987.

Whiting, Kenneth. The Soviet Union Today. New York: Praeger, 1966.

XV. Income and Living Standard

We have a tendency to compare our incomes with the Soviets and to come to the conclusion that we are considerably superior. Although our standard of living is appreciably higher than that of a Soviet citizen, we must not forget that the disparity has shrunk considerably during the past two decades. If the Soviets do attain the average income they are planning by the end of the twelfth Five-Year-Plan, they will have more than tripled the average income figure for 1950. Although this may also be true for the United States, there is one major difference: there has been relatively little inflation during this period in the Soviet Union, while in the United States inflation has eaten up the major portion of the income increase.

There is one more major difference between a salary of 180 rubles (270 dollars) and an American salary of 1,000 dollars a month. From $1,000 gross pay, we must deduct federal tax, state tax, local tax, sales tax, excise tax, property tax, medical insurance, dental insurance, education, interest payments, etc. In the USSR, only slightly more than 8 1/2% of the national budget revenues are derived from taxes. This results in the fact that individual income taxes range from .7% to an absolute maximum of 12%. Pensioners, students and invalids are totally exempt from tax, no matter what their incomes may be, as are families with numerous children. Only a nominal, very small, amount of tax is paid for the use of private plots. No taxes are levied on the agricultural produce of the plots. The owners of dachas (summer homes) pay a maximum tax of 20 rubles annually. Owners of small automobiles pay a maximum of 15 rubles annually for automobile tax.

In addition, there are no deductions for social security, health insurance, high interest rates, etc. Very importantly, the average total cost of living-quarters plus utilities is no more than 10 rubles a month. A comparison of gross incomes is therefore not very enlightening.

The average income for factory and office employees in 1987 was approximately 185 rubles a month. This does not include the farm workers whose earnings are appreciably lower. But this figure does not tell the full story. The bonuses which may be earned by a worker can be quite high. Bonuses may be received on a pro-rated basis if the entire plant overfulfills its economic quota; they may be granted individually for especially hard work; or they may be given for activities on free time, such an active work in the Party, in the trade union, or for attending evening or correspondence courses in the attempt to enrich one's knowledge.

As a sampling, it may be of interest to list some of the salaries for different occupations: (the following are approximations) (1 ruble = 100 kopeks = $1.65)

Professor - 550 rubles a month;
Senior engineer - 350 rubles a month;
Physician - 200 rubles a month;
Miner - 280 rubles a month;
Sovkhoz farmer - 145 rubles a month;
Schoolteacher - 180 rubles a month;

Sales person - 130 rubles a month;
Mechanic - 190 rubles a month;
Cleaning personnel - 95 rubles a month.

Obviously, a professor would live quite well while a salesperson would have to struggle. For this reason, in the vast majority of families, both the husband and the wife are forced to work in order to make ends meet. It also explains why so many Soviets are happy to engage in some form of political activity, since it enhances their chances of getting bonuses. For example, a mechanic who has been elected to the Supreme Soviet still draws his base pay as a mechanic, but he receives additional allowances for travel expenses, entertainment expense, he will get sizeable bonuses for extra-curricular activities and he will receive additional privileges which are translatable into money. He and his family will be able to live quite well.

A part of the national income of the USSR is set aside in the form of Public Consumption Funds. These funds are to be used to purchase benefits which are to be bestowed free of charge upon the public to increase the people's cultural level. Money may also be given for special purposes. Most of these funds are expended on pensions, education, culture, sanatoriums, nurseries, homes for the elderly, etc. It is estimated that these funds add 25 to 30% to the average family's real income.

Chart 29
Payments from Public Consumption Funds

	1940	1970	1978	1980	1986	1987
Annual Payments in Billion Rubles	4.6	24	105	119	147	153
Per Capita Allocation	24	263	404	434	527	527

During the past two decades there has been a concerted effort to increase the production of consumer items. According to the latest Soviet figures which appear to be somewhat inflated, there are at present 82 radios, 81 TV sets, 70 refrigerators and 71 washing machines per hundred families. The state of repair of most of these mostly primitive appliances, however, leaves much to be desired. Also to be remembered is the fact that the Soviets do not have a "throw away" mentality and that most of these appliances have been in operation for two or three decades.

Food production has also risen significantly. In 1986 the average Soviet citizen consumed 60 kg of meat; 305 liters of milk; 217 eggs; 45 kg of sugar; 88 kg of vegetables; 38 kg of fruit; and 19 kg of fish. Although this may not seem too much according to American standards, and although this food is not at all evenly distributed throughout the USSR, it is still quite high compared with most countries in the rest of the world, and with the USSR two decades ago. This trend is expected to continue despite recent severe shortages.

Basic staples are relatively cheap. They include such items as bread, cabbage, milk, processed cheese, apples of poor quality, potatoes and onions. Other foodstuffs in the luxury class are extremely expensive. A few examples are:

Eggs - 2 rubles a dozen;
Oranges - 1 ruble for five very small ones;
Lemons - 1/2 ruble each (imperative for tea);
Beef - 6 rubles a kilogram;
Cheese - (unprocessed) - 3 rubles a kilogram;
Wine - 4 rubles for a low-quality bottle.

The largest, single expense for the Soviet family is clothing. A man's suit, or an overcoat for a man or woman is approximately 150 rubles. A pair of shoes is at least 40 rubles and generally of poor quality. This has resulted in a large number of inefficient dry cleaning establishments which try to maintain clothing in usable shape for as long as possible. It is also a fact that virtually all women sew most of their own clothing and some of their husband's.

Other consumer items are available, but normally hard to get. All over the Soviet Union one may see long lines in front of stores. One normally gets in line without knowing exactly what is being sold, with the assurance that if it proves useless to the purchaser, he will always be able to get rid of it for a profit if it was worth lining up for. Rumors of special shipments to certain stores are constantly being spread, and people line up in front of the stores hoping to be able to buy hard to get rugs, drapes, watches, toiletries etc. Yet, the authorities can point with pride to the fact that virtually any item which falls into the normal consumer category is available somewhere at nearly all times. This claim is, however, misleading when we consider the system of sales in the USSR. Let us say, for example, that one would like to buy an umbrella. One stands in line at a department store at the umbrella counter and finally is able to ask the salesperson to be shown one of the three different styles normally being sold. The purchaser then decides on one, determines that it costs 10 rubles, and tells the salesperson that he will take it. The purchaser then gets into the long line in front of the area cash register and pays for a ten-ruble chit. He then again gets in line in front of the umbrella counter, then finally hands the chit to the salesperson and receives his purchase. This process takes a long time. During the time that it takes to buy one item in a Soviet department store, ten items could have been purchased in a similar store in the West. This puts a great damper on the economy, reduces the necessary production of consumer items and still permits the statement to be made that virtually everything is available in the USSR.

Important members of the society, this includes top Party officials, high government figures, important intellectual workers, artists, educators, scientists, find shopping a great deal easier There are a number of special, unmarked stores in all major cities at which the best, most hard to get items are sold at a very low price. Even many imported items from the West are available there. Of course, all Soviets know about these stores. One frequently hears the question whether such privileged segment of society may rightfully exist within a socialist system. The answer is yes. The Marxian concept defines production and consumption with the words, "From everyone according to his ability to everyone according to his need." Quite obviously, the Kolkhoz farmer or the plumber does not have the same needs as the government official or intellectual worker. His is not a representative function. He does not need a large personal library, or a place of retreat, or the intellectually stimulating social life of a professor; nor does he have to deal with the upper levels of society as an equal. However, if that plumber does experience such a personal desire, he can always aspire to it by becoming involved in extra-curricular work or by attempting to obtain a better education.

Contrary to popular belief, every Soviet likes money a great deal. He tries to live as well as possible on his income, and then to augment his income in order that he may be able to afford more. Unfortunately, since private enterprise is forbidden, the average citizen must find illegal ways of making ends meet. Soviets are extremely inventive in this respect. The following is just a sampling of some of the more common ploys to make extra money:

a. Moonlighting. This includes the plumber, carpenter or mechanic who provides services which are virtually impossible to obtain normally. It also includes the university student who tutors.

b. Theft of tools and materials from the place of work.

c. Misappropriating entire shipments of materials from one geographic location to another. It has been estimated that as much as 15 percent of the rolling stock in the USSR is carrying such illegal merchandize at any given time.

d. Selling personal goods on the black market which bring much more than if they were sold back to a government store. Just as an example, a translated novel by Steinbeck or Hemingway, or a Beatle record would bring ten or twenty times as much money on the black market than in a legal commission store.

e. Ticket scalping. People who have the time to stand in line for tickets to the Bolshoi or the Palace of Congresses may sell them for up to five times what they paid for them.

f. Special care and attention for services. Doctors fall into this category. Most physicians have a list of private patients whom they treat at home, individually, rather than in the production line of the polyclinic. This is also true for elective surgery such as plastic surgery.

g. Receiving illegal tips. Every taxi driver and most waiters will be only too happy to accept gratuities when offered.

h. Most store clerks who sell goods that have to be either measured or weighed and which do not have to go through cash registers - this includes most of the many small snack bars - pocket part of the proceeds.

i. Street vendors keep the change. For example, ice cream sold by such vendors does not cost 20 to 30 kopeks, but for some reason, 19 and 28 kopeks. These vendors claim never to have change, although their pockets may be bulging with it. This means, that on every sale they make one or two kopeks. Over the course of the day this may add up to an amount which will nearly double their legal income.

j. A great number of items are being smuggled back and forth across borders, e.g., to and from Finland. Such items, including cosmetics and panty hose, sell for a great deal of money. Tourists from the West are also offered high prices for clothing and other goods (100 rubles for a pair of Levi jeans, for example).

In general, the entire country is involved in some illegal enterprise. One observation one hears frequently is, that the USSR is a form of organized chaos. The average Soviet citizen likes the system because he has developed a million ways in which to circumvent it. He dreads the possibility of changes which would

Chart 30

Employment Structure By Percentage of Population

Urban Employment	65%
Rural Employment	35%
Industry and Construction Work	41%
Agriculture and Forestry	20%
Transport and Communications	10%
Trade, Catering and Supply	9%
Education, Health Service, Science and the Arts	18%
State and Public Institutions	2%
Housing Maintenance, Military Services and Other Fields	4%

\- - -

Total population of working age:	133 million
Total employed or attending educational institutions:	122 million

impose complete adherence to legality since this would cut his standard of living radically. Very few persons could live well and still stay completely on the right side of the law. By the same token, the State is well apprised of these transgressions and does little to counteract them. Once in a while a show trial is held for the commission of economic sabotage. In nearly all cases, however, the person being tried is politically out of favor from other reasons.

Gorbachev is well aware of the corruption in his country. He also realizes that, were he to attempt to eliminate all illegalities overnight, the economy of the Soviet union would be badly hurt. What he does want, is to attack corruption not at its lowest level, but at the highest. This will have a snowball effect, he feels, which will make it unattractive to steal and blackmarket. Illegalities will always occur in any society, but he feels uncomfortable when an entire economy is built on illegalities. By giving the worker both the incentives and opportunities to raise his standard of living through legal means, he wishes to eliminate the necessity for economic crimes.

To reiterate the introductory statements, however, it is absolutely true that the Soviet Union has made great strides in improving the standard of living of the citizens. The people can afford more and be more active in more fields than they ever could before in their history. There is every indication that this trend will continue in the future despite the economic problems which the Soviet Union may be experiencing.

READINGS

Bocca, Geoffrey. The Moscow Scene. New York: Stein and Day, 1976.

Cohen, Rabinowitch and Sharlet, (eds.) The Soviet Union Since Stalin. Bloomington: Indiana University, 1980.

Hanson, Philip. The Consumer in the Soviet Economy. Evanston: Northwestern University Press, 1968.

Herlemann, Host G. The Quality of Life in the Soviet Union. Boulder: Westview, 1986.

Kaiser, Robert G. Russia: The People and the Power. New York: Atheneum, 1976.

Kaiser, Robert G. Russia from the Inside. New York: Dutton, 1980.

Kirsch, Leonard J. Soviet Wages. Cambridge: MIT Press, 1972.

Labor Legislation in the USSR. Moscow: Novosti, 1972.

Mathews, Mervyn. Privilege in the Soviet Union. London: George Allen and Unwin, 1979.

Matthews, Mervyn. Poverty in the Soviet Union. Cambridge University Press, 1986.

Miller, Margaret. The Rise of the Russian Consumer. London: Institute of Economic Affairs, 1965.

Nettl, J. P. The =Soviet Achievement. New York: Harcourt Brace, 1967.

Pejovich, Svetozar. Life in the Soviet Union. Dallas: The Fisher Institute, 1979.

Treml, Vladimir G. Alcohol in the USSR. Duke University Press, 1982.

Volodarsky, Lev. How Soviet Pepple Live. Moscow: Novosti Press, 1971.

Wesson, Robert, (ed.) The Soviet Union: Looking to the 1980's. Stanford: Hoover Institution Press, 1980.

XVI. Health Care and Care for the Aged

All medical care in the Soviet Union is free for all residents in the USSR, including foreigners. Financing is built into the national budget and state allocations for public health are considerable. This figure is augmented by the amount expended by organizations such as the trade unions for hygiene and sanatoria.

If a Soviet citizen becomes ill and is still ambulatory, he goes to the nearest polyclinic (there are more than 37,000 of them), takes a number at the door which indicates what time he is to proceed to what room to see a doctor, sits down and waits. Most of these clinics are subordinated to hospitals and offer an adequate number of specializations such as ENT, surgery (minor), cardiology, obstetrics and gynecology, etc. These clinics are open six days a week. Doctors work six days a week, in alternating morning and evening shifts. Should a patient be too ill to go to a clinic, the doctor will, without question, make a housecall with the ambulance which is assigned to each polyclinic. Nearly all of these clinic doctors are women. Such an assignment is the lowest level which a doctor may receive. These physicians are very poorly paid and do not possess anywhere near the prestige which their counterparts enjoy in the West. There is little mystique connected with the medical profession; the doctor is simply a mechanic of the body and should therefore not receive more pay than a mechanic of the tractor. This is not true for the upper reaches of the profession, e.g., top surgeons, neurologists or cardiologists, who are very well paid and are invariably men.

Hospitals are abominable. Even in large cities, general hospitals are overcrowded, understaffed and evil smelling, noisy, not particularly clean institutions. In the USSR it appears that it is not the quality, but the quantity that counts. The country prides itself on its statistics, on the fact that there are now over three million hospital beds in the USSR, i.e., more per capita than in the United States. Specifically, there are 120 beds for every 10,000 people. Most of the hospitals are outdated buildings, many of them more than a century old. Although new, more modern, large hospitals are being built at the present time, it will take many years before an alleviation of the abysmal picture will be felt. Again, one should not condemn the country unjustly. The West has had a long standing medical tradition, centuries before Russia. In general, the Soviets have made great strides in the last two decades.

In the large cities there is at least one hospital (Moscow has two) which is outstanding by Soviet standards. This hospital exists only for the upper reaches of Soviet Society, e.g., party officials, members of the government, leading members of the intelligentsia, and Western foreigners. Even these hospitals leave much to be desired, although they are much cleaner, better staffed and less crowded. There are individual rooms which contain a sink and a toilet, but there is no privacy since the inside walls are made of glass. The food is horrible. Hospital food is notorious throughout the land. The basic staple, even for patients with severe intestinal disorders, is vermicelli and greasy meatballs. It should therefore be no surprise that the Soviet hospital patient has most of his food brought in to him by relatives and friends. Hospital stays are normally quite long, since Soviet hospitals do not like to release a patient until he is either completely recovered or dead. Convalescence at home with outside medical supervision is generally not permitted. It is easier to be admitted to a Soviet hospital than to be released.

There are nearly as many doctors as there are nurses. At the present time there are 1,189,000 doctors employed. Eighty-four medical colleges turn out 45,000 doctors annually. There are 35 doctors to every 10,000 population. The Soviets have initiated one excellent program: there are 15 medical refresher colleges and 28 refresher departments at medical colleges with specific specializations. A medical specialist must periodically attend refresher courses in order to remain current on innovations in his field. Approximately 100,000 doctors attend such courses each year.

Prescription drugs are free for in-patients, children, war veterans and those suffering from diabetes, rheumatism, cancer, tuberculosis and blood dieeases. Others pay a token amount (never more than 40 kopeks).

Some work is being done in preventive medicine, but not nearly enough. There are some dispensaries in larger cities which are primarily concerned with VD and tuberculosis, but there are none in the rural areas. Just the fact that tuberculosis is still such a great scourge which requires many specialized hospitals and a number of sanatoria, seems to indicate that preventive medicine in the Soviet Union has still a long way to go. Although there are now numerous "drying out" stations, little progress is made in eradicating the greatest social problem — alcoholism. In 1986 Gorbachev announced that the only way to curtail this problem was to curtail the production and sale of alcohol. He therefore ordered that stores which sell alcohol cut their hours of operation by more than half. This created the longest waiting lines in the history of the Soviet Union. The alcoholics made it a point to line up from early in the morning while the average working citizen could not afford standing in line all day. The alcoholic, then, still gets his alcohol while the average citizen must go without his glass of wine in the evening. Gorbachev has also ordered the closing of numerous vinyards in the Transcaucasus. He has run into a great deal of difficulty enforcing this order. Even in the North, in large cities, the habit of moonshining has again been revived, and numerous people have been caught and prosecuted. More importantly, many have lost their lives or have been blinded because of toxic alcohol. Not much seems to work to curtail alcoholism, not even the high price people have to pay for drink. Many Soviets object that they can no longer serve alcohol at official functions, nor can they buy champagne during theatre intermissions.

Medical research in general and the production and development of pharmaceuticals is also far behind the West but in the process of improving. Medical research is conducted not only at the universities and medical institutes, but also at over 300 research centers. There is also a Sanitary-Epidemiological Service which has over 5,000 disease monitoring stations with 50,000 employees. A great deal of their effort is directed toward curbing the use of toxic chemicals such as harmful insecticides and dyes.

There are 4,000 first aid stations in the USSR which answered more than 70 million calls in 1986. In remote or mountainous areas these stations are assigned aircraft, primarily helicopters. There are also medical stations at every major plant and at every nursery-kindergarten and school.

Although medical care is free, the more well-to-do segment of the Soviet population would rather pay and have better service. It is therefore not at all unusual for the better physicians to "moonlight" and give special, personal care to those who can afford it.

Chart 31

The Soviet Pension System

	1960	1970	1975	1980	1986
Number of pensioners (in millions)	21	40	45	49	54
Percentage of the total population	9.8	16.5	17.3	18.6	19.3
Expenditure on pensions (in billion rubles	7.1	16.2	24.3	31.2	34.3
Percentage of total outlays for social security and medical services	41.8	44.6	59.1	unavailable	

Number of homes for pensioners as of 1986:	1.600
Number of pensioners in these homes permanently:	322,000

Category of retirees who receive 50% of their old age pensions if they work beyond the age of retirement: Urban teachers; medical doctors and dentists; engineers and skilled technicians; skilled workers in construction, transport, communications, housing, and communal and service industries.

NOTE: These categories receive 75% of their pensions if they agree to work in the Urals, Siberia and the Far East).

The care of the aged falls under the social security system. The worker does not contribute to any retirement fund. Pensions are paid out of the national budget. At the present there are approximately 54 million pensioners in the USSR. The amount of the pension varies with the income the pensioner had before retiring. On the average, pensions are quite low despite the fact that most pension payments have nearly doubled during the past decade. The pension is insufficient to live on, which is why pensioners continue working.

Men may retire with a pension at the age of 60 after having worked a minimum of 25 years. Women may retire at age 55 after 20 years of work. This computation includes time in military service and years spent as a student above the intermediate level. In some professions, especially those which are detrimental to health (e.g., mining, chemical industry or timber felling), persons are eligible for retirement at an earlier age with fewer years of service, e.g., miners-age 50; female weavers-50; female radiologists and flight attendants-age 45. The lowest pension is 50% of the working wage; the highest pension is 100%. The higher the wage, the lower the pension percentage.

Until recently, members of a Kolkhoz were ineligible for retirement pensions. They now have full pension rights with all other citizens. The funds come out of the national budget without contributions by the Kolkhoz.

Nearly all pensioners who are physically able, continue working. This is an extremely attractive facet of the Soviet system. All citizens have the right to work, no matter what their age may be. There is ample employment available. Many old women, without specialty training, are used as cleaning personnel, street vendors and for other menial tasks. On the other hand, it is not unusual to find an 80-year-old professor or scientist still busy at his profession. Soviet research into geriatric problems which incorporated 40,000 case studies claims to prove that there is a distinct correlation between longevity and good mental and physical health, and continuing to work as long as one is physically and mentally able. White collar workers, if they decide to continue working, will continue to receive their regular pay, plus one half of their pension. If they work in a remote area such as Central Asia or Siberia, they receive 75% of their pensions. Those in agriculture will receive their full pensions. On the lower pay scale, this means doubling one's pay at the age of 55 or 60. Many elderly therefore act as the financial backers of young couples or of students trying to get through their university education.

Those aged who are incapable of working have a less attractive future. Many continue living in the cities, primarily in the homes of sons and daughters where they are charged with taking care of the children. They are the lucky ones. Those who have no younger relatives and are taking up vital apartment space, or those who are so incapacitated that they cannot any longer take care of themselves, are placed into homes for the aged. The number of such homes is highly inadequate, so that they are horribly overcrowded. Conditions are worse than in the hospitals, and considerably worse than in the worst old age homes in the United States. The State obviously feels that these persons no longer contribute to the benefit of the society and therefore should not drain the manpower and material wealth of the society they no longer serve. The same statement may be made about the treatment afforded to physically and mentally handicapped citizens. Visitors to Moscow and Leningrad may not have realized the fact that they extremely rarely saw amputees or blind persons, and virtually never a retarded child. Such people, if they cannot be integrated into society, are removed from view. Of course there are a number of exceptions to this rule which were created to show the humane inclinations of the Soviet system. There are some blind, crippled and deaf Soviets who have been nurtured through higher education, who are used as symbols and are highly propagandized.

READINGS

Davis, Christopher and Feshbach, Murray. Rising Infant Mortality in the USSR in the 1970's. United States Bureau of the Census, Series P-95, No. 74, 1980.

Eliseenkov, Iu. B., et. al. Russko-angliiskii meditsinskii slovar'. Moscow: Izd. "Russkii iazyk," 1975.

Field, Mark. Soviet Socialized Medicine. New York: The Free Press, 1967.

Fundamentals of Legislation of the USSR and the Union Republics on the Health Service. Moscow: Novosti, 1975.

Knaus, William A. Inside Russian Medicine. New York: Everest House, 1981.

Osborne, Robert J. Soviet Social Politics, Welfare, Equality and Community. Homewood: Dorsey Press, 1970.

Simirenko, Alex. Social Thought in the Soviet Union. Chicago: Quandrangle Books, 1969.

Soviet Medicine: A Fibliography of Bibliographies. Bethesda: U. S. Nation Institute of Health, 1973.

XVII. Education

Tremendous emphasis is placed on education in the Soviet Union. There is deep pride in the fact that illiteracy, which was so prevalent before the revolution, has been virtually completely eradicated. It is the dream of all parents that their children will attain a higher education, and parents will do anything, legal or otherwise, to realize this dream. From the point of view of the State, also, education has paramount importance for obvious reasons. The entire youth of the country becomes a captive audience for inductrination. In addition, as Lenin tritely stated in a sentence which is oft-repeated, "the future of the Soviet Union lies in its young people." Also, the mentality of the children themselves is such, that attending school and working for good grades is a positive act, while absenteeism from school is to be socially condemned.

THE NUMBER OF STUDENTS AND SCHOOLCHILDREN IN 1986
(in millions)

General education secondary schools	44.7
Specialized secondary schools	4.5
Vocational schools	4.1
Institutions of higher learning	5.3
Refresher courses	47.6
TOTAL:	109.2

Chart 32

The first contact with the Soviet system of education may come at the age of six months. The first institution is the <u>nursery</u> which attends small children on a daily basis until the age of three. It is primarly an organized baby sitting service which enables both parents to work a full day. Normally it is housed on the same premises as the kindergarten. In accordance with the law, there is a unified set of printed procedures for conducting the operations of the nurseries which are to be equally applied throughout the USSR. In actuality, the quality of the nurseries depends on the geographic area and on the relative wealth and ethnic makeup of the local population. There are a number of things which are quite different from similar institutions in the west. In the USSR, even at the most tender age, the element of social interaction is of supreme importance. They do have playpens for the children, but instead of having just one child in it, the playpens are larger and usually contain up to four children who learn to get along with each other. Also, instead of putting a playpen on the floor where the child sees only feet, the pen is raised to the eye-level of an adult. Especially in the Russian part of the USSR a great deal of attention is paid to the ability of children to withstand the extremely cold climate in the winter. Therefore, from the earliest age, children go through an

Educational Structure

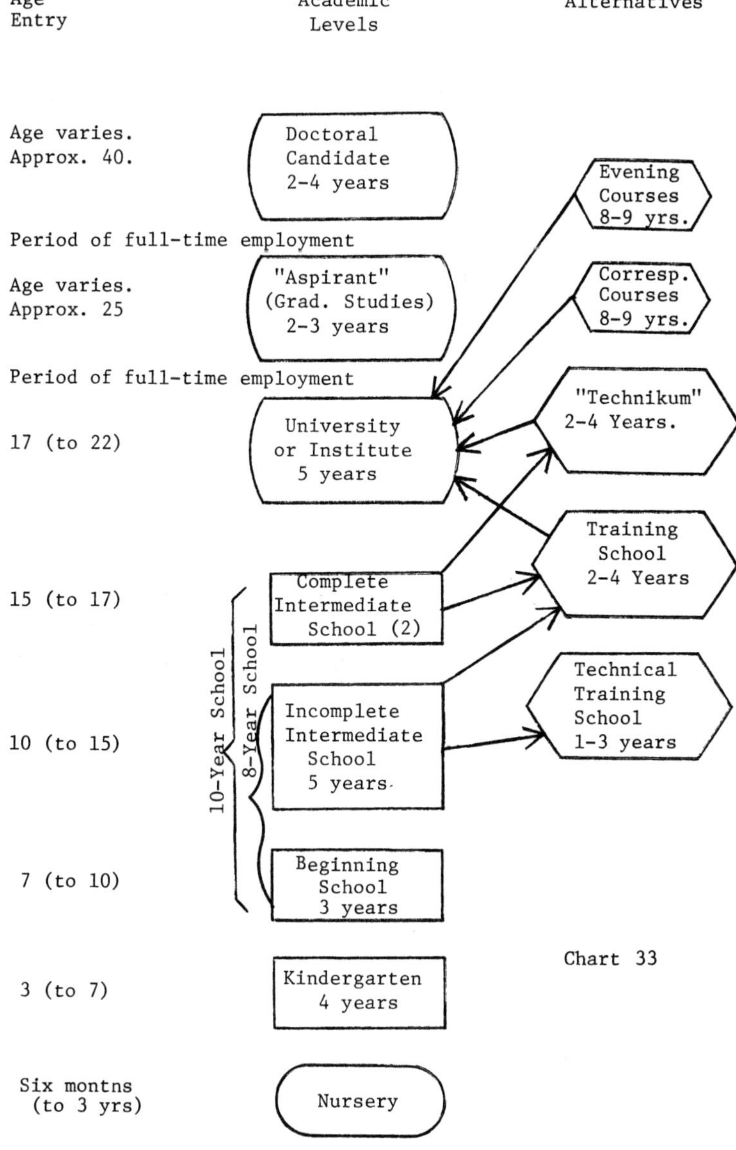

Chart 33

inuring process. They are bathed in progressively colder water and are left outside for progressively longer periods wearing progressively less clothing. This is a rather recent development which, according to Soviet research, has resulted in much healthier children. Parents try to avoid sending their children to a nursery because they consider it too impersonal and fear that their children will not get all the attention they require. For this reason, whenever the possibility exists, children of that tender age are attended by a grandmother or old aunt, someone who is on a pension and can devote all day to the children. Often such an elderly relative even moves in with the young couple to give the children the fullest attention. Couples often prefer this to the nursery, although the latter is extremely inexpensive

The next level of the educational system is the kindergarten which caters to pre-school children from the age of three to the age of seven. Frequently it shares its premises with the local nursery. It, also, is extremely inexpensive; the small fee depends on the family income. A considerably larger number of parents take advantage of this service, especially in urban areas where more than half of all children attend. The kindergarten also operates all day and frees both parents for full-time work. In fact, many of these facilities are attached to major plants and factories. On this level, children become acquainted with basic arithmetic and writing and accomplish the work which in American schools would take them through first grade. More importantly, this is where their original indoctrination into society begins The child is taught that it is a part of an organism rather than a separate individual, and that it must function in harmony with others. It must learn how to behave in society. Therefore, the severest form of punishment in the kindergarten is social ostracism, i.e., the silent treatment. This child is made to feel that, if it doesn't conform, society will force it to become an outsider. Another important seed which is implanted at this age is the work-ethic. If a child does especially well and behaves as it should, it is rewarded with permission to perform work. It is interesting to see the pride on the face of a four-year-old who is assigned to set the plates for the group at the daily lunch, the six-year-old who is permitted to serve it, or the five-year-old who is allowed to sweep and dust the playroom.

The Soviet pedagogical researchers are also convinced that the brains of small children are not sufficiently taxed and therefore have been conducting experiments in teaching them higher mathematics. According to the Soviets, the results have been surprisingly positive. They also feel that the artistic talents in children should be allowed to develop, not by placing great big chunks of crayon into their tiny hands, but slender brushes more suited to their grasp. Again, they claim excellent results because of this and frequently have exhibits of work by children which appears to be of a quality far beyond what would be expected.

One other important factor in both kindergartens and nurseries is the concept of "touching." Soviet pedagogues frequently refer to the United States and claim that American parents do not like to touch their children. Most personal touching is therefore in the realm of slapping and spanking. Children need touching and therefore will do bad things in order to be touched, even if it means a spanking. In Soviet kindergartens and nurseries the staff may be frequently observed hugging their wards.

The first level of schooling is called the beginning school. It lasts for three years, from the age of seven to age ten. The child then enters the incomplete middle school (also called eight-year-school) which is frequently located on the same premises. This is a five-year period, from the age of ten to age fifteen. The

Chart 34

Curriculum for Primary and Secondary Schools

Number of Hours per Week by Grade Level

Subject:	I	II	III	IV	V	VI	VII	VIII	IX	X
Russian language	12	10	10	6	6	3	3	2	2/0	-
Literature	-	-	-	2	2	2	2	3	4	3
Mathematics	6	6	6	6	6	6	6	6	5	5
History	-	-	-	2	2	2	2	3	4	3
Sociology	-	-	-	-	-	-	-	-	-	2
Nature studies	-	2	2	2	-	-	-	-	-	-
Geography	-	-	-	-	2	3	2	2	2	-
Biology	-	-	-	-	2	2	2	2	0/2	2
Physics	-	-	-	-	-	2	2	3	4	5
Astronomy	-	-	-	-	-	-	-	-	-	1
Technical drawing	-	-	-	-	-	1	1	1	-	-
Chemistry	-	-	-	-	-	-	2	2	3	3
Foreign language	-	-	-	-	4	3	3	2	2	2
Art	1	1	1	1	1	1	-	-	-	-
Music	1	1	1	1	1	1	1	-	-	-
Physical education	2	2	2	2	2	2	2	2	2	2
Military training	-	-	-	-	-	-	-	-	2	2

child then finds himself at a cross-road. He can switch to a vocational school or, if he has the academic ability, he can continue towards finishing the complete middle school (also called ten-year-school) This school, which is primarily in preparation for one of the forms of higher education, takes two years. The student is now seventeen.

Those children who have not completed their middle schooling, must nevertheless complete the national requirement for a total of ten years of education. They may accomplish this by attending one of three groups of trade schools:

a. The Technicum produces primarily technicians and highly skilled workers in a variety of fields through curricula which last from two to four years. Frequently they are called engineers, which is one reason why the Soviet figures on the number of engineers graduated each year is so highly inflated.

b. The Training School (uchilishche), produces medical and dental technicians, nurses, librarians and teachers on the beginning-school level.

c. The Technical Training School (professional'no-tekhnicheskoe uchilishche) teaches trades such as plumbing, carpentry, tailoring and mechanics.

Theoretically any graduate of the three professional schools listed may, if he is academically qualified, request admission to a school of higher education. In nearly all instances, however, graduates of these schools go directly into jobs.

All schools in the Soviet Union are free of charge. This is also true for a great many organized extra-curricular activities. Teachers are asked to identify, at an early age, those students who show a specific aptitude or a degree of learning ability which would make them likely candidates for higher education Special schools for such gifted children have been established in a number of cities. The most common schools of this type emphasize sciences and foreign languages. There are also some special schools for children with learning disabilities, but not nearly enough of them. Most mentally handicapped children, unless they are profoundly so, are retained in the mainstream of society and the school system.

Teachers normally establish their pace in accordance with the average and above average student. Little heed is paid to those children who are unable to keep up. Such children are frequently ridiculed aloud. There are frequent parent-teacher meetings which often end up in loud arguments, criticism and self-criticism. Parents frequently complain about the low grades their children receive and the heavy amount of homework. Although only about 5% of school children are not promoted, there is little grade inflation in the system.

The quality of education not only depends on the location (there is a great deal of difference between Turkestan and the RSFSR, and between rural and urban areas) but also on the individual school administrator. This is true despite the fact that all school curricula for the entire nation for all levels, have been standardized. Theoretically a child from a small town in Southwestern Ukraine may transfer to Kiev and just continue on at the same level of instruction. This is, of course, not really true.

Schooling is conducted in the majority language of the area in which the school is located. Every child, however, must also learn Russian as a foreign language. In the RSFSR, the major languages studied are English, French and German in that order.

The School Reform of 1985

A school reform bill was ratified by the Supreme Soviet of the USSR in late 1984. Its implementation commenced in 1985 As of this writing, implementation is far from complete. Major reforms include the following:

1. Primary and secondary education are to be extended by a year to total of 11 years (one more than the requirement in the United States). This new year will be initiated at the beginning of a child's education. At the present time, the age for entering a school is seven. Under the new law, every child will have to enter school at the age of six and join a "zero class," i.e., a class without a numerical grade designator. In this class the child will receive the basic knowledge of reading, writing and arithmetic so that more complex material may be covered immediately upon entering the first grade. In the fall of 1985 the first 1.4 million children entered these "zero classes."

2. Teachers salaries have been raised by 30 to 35 percent. This was primarily done to attract males to the profession.

3. Children are encouraged to concentrate on specific skills from a very early age. They are to choose an occupation which they think they will enjoy for the rest of their lives. Their taste may change in the future, but they will still retain a high level of skill in a secondary area which is bound to be useful to them.

4. Beginning in the fall of 1985, classes in computer fundamentals have been introduced in all secondary schools.

Computers

The leaders of the Soviet Union well realize that economic restructuring, increased efficiency in planning, and the ability to compete with the West will only be possible if computers are introduced throughout the nation. Nevertheless, they are well aware that computers are extremely dangerous tools. Those who have access to them, cannot be forced not to use them for anything besides their work. In addition, a computer and printer are a functioning press facility. With a computer and the necessary hookups one may communicate throughout the nation. Information exchange will no longer be as restricted as now. The leaders will lose control. They are therefore in a quandary as to what to do.

The solution they have chosen to this problem is one which will not work too well. First of all, they have severely restricted independent hands-on time for everyone. Even at Moscow University only a small minority of the faculty has ever sat behind a keyboard. At secondary schools, actual working time is highly limited. The rest of the time the computer is locked away. Very frequently there is only one computer to an entire school. Most importantly, printers are virtually unavailable. For this reason, word processing is nearly non-existent. This curbs the free exchange of information, but also prevents the students from seeing the results of their labor and causing them to lose interest.

READINGS

Ablin, Fred (ed.) Contemporary Soviet Education. New York: International Arts and Sciences Press, 1969.

Bereday, George and Pennar, Jaan (eds.) The Politics of Soviet Education. New York: Praeger, 1960.

Bronfenbrenner, Urie. Two Worlds of Childhood: U. S. and U.S.S.R. New York: Russell Sage Foundation, 1970.

DeWitt, N. Education and Professional Employment in the USSR. New York: National Science Foundation, 1962.

Eason, W. and Poignant, R. (eds.) Educational Planning in the USSR. Paris: International Institute for Educational Planning (UNESCO), 1968.

Fundamentals of the Legislation of the Union Republics on Public Education. Moscow: Novosti, 1975.

Jacoby, Susan. Inside Soviet Schools. New York: Hill and Wang, 1974

Learning a Trade in the Soviet Union. Moscow: Novosti Press, 1976

Morton, Miriam. Growing Up in the Soviet Union: From the Cradle to Coming of age. Moscow: Progress, 1982.

Public Education in the USSR 1971-1973. Moscow: USSR Ministry of Education, 1973.

Rosen, Seymour M. Education in the U.S.S.R.: Current Status of Higher Education. U.S. Department of Education. OE Publication No. 79-19140. Washington, D.C.: US Government Printing Office, 1980.

Rudman, Herbert. The School and State in the USSR. New York: Macmillan, 1967.

Shakhnazorov, G. Kh et. als. Social Science: A Textbook for Soviet Secondary Schools. Washington: US Dept. of Commerce, 1964.

XVIII. A Soviet University

The best illustration of the university system in the Soviet Union is the most important single university after which all others are patterned, namely, Moscow State University (MGU). It is MGU which is by far the most difficult institution of higher learning to which entry may be gained By the same token, a diploma from MGU virtually assures the recipient of a life of comfort and relative affluence and, contrary to popular belief, the Soviet citizen is extremely greedy for material wealth.

Let us stop for a moment and consider the student at MGU. At the present time there are approximately 23,000 full-time and 7,000 part-time students registered there To be admitted to full-time status, one has to vault two major hurdles: a. One has to qualify to pass from the eight-year-school into the academic ten-year-school at the age of fifteen (fewer than 10% qualify). b. One has to pass an extremely difficult and demoralizing battery of MGU entrance examinations (fewer than 10% pass) Cumulatively then, fewer than 1% of prospective applicants to MGU are finally accepted. Still, this is not the whole story yet if we consider specifically the process how a student may gain entrance to MGU, and what the non-academic prerequisites really are. First of all, MGU insists that approximately half of all students come from families of peasants and workers. In reality, this is a highly inflated figure. Approximately 15% would be closer to the truth since a number of positions are erroneously classified into worker/peasant categories for this purpose. For example, the party committee chairman of a State Farm - the lord and master over the lives of thousands of families - could hardly be considered a "peasant." By the same token, a member of the presidium of the labor union of a major industrial complex would not logically fit the description of a "worker." Let us also take into account that approximately two million low and mid-level legislative deputies and Party employees are still listed in their former occupational categories and are on leave of absence from them. The final result is, that the overwhelming majority of MGU students come from families of "cultural workers" (writers, musicians, teachers, actors, etc.); technical workers (e.g., doctors, engineers); and party and government functionaries. The workers and peasants are but a "token" minority. The same is true for the nationalities. All nationalities in the USSR are equal, but the Russians are more equal than all the others. In other words, one may occasionally run into a token Moldavian or Kazakh at MGU, but this is relatively rare If we consider the final selection process, this becomes clearer.

The prospective student has to take a number of written and oral examinations. Evaluation and grading of the results is at best a subjective process. When a student is denied admittance he is notified by form letter that he has failed to receive certain required grades (according to a five-point system) in certain subjects and is therefore considered unqualified. Those who are admitted are sent congratulatory letters which make no reference to the specific grades they received. It is therefore not unlikely that the offspring of a Politburo member would gain admittance even with a less-than-perfect score, especially since his grades would never be made public.

During the past several years the university has been literally swamped with applications from prospective students who wish to major in the social sciences Economics in particular seems to be most attractive This demand has resulted in significantly tight selection procedures in this discipline. On the other hand the number of applicants for the sciences, particularly physics and mathematics, has dwindled. It is common knowledge that these subjects are extremely difficult and demanding at MGU and the stories about student "burn-out" in these majors are quite common. For this reason, although the selectees for the social sciences and the humanities continue to require at the very minimum the grade 4 in all their subject examinations, the selection committees, for the first time, have had to review the students who have 3s in certain subjects for possible admission. Otherwise, the student admission quotas for the sciences could no longer be met This is worrying the faculty at MGU no end, since they constitute the epitome of elitism in education. The same problem manifests itself at all Soviet universities.

It is also common knowledge on the MGU campus that a Russian may "buy" a passing grade for 10,000 rubles, while a Jew, because of a quota system whose existence is constantly denied by the Soviet authorities, must pay 30,000 rubles to gain admittance.

After a student has been accepted, he is assigned free living quarters which, according to Soviet standards, are quite luxurious. He also receives a monthly stipend of between 40 and 45 rubles. He may receive additional money for academic achievement or for Komsomol and Party activism. This provision again discriminates against all those who are not ethnically and politically pure.

It is definitely not intended to imply that the MGU student is in any way inferior. Quite the contrary. The majority of MGU students are highly mature, deadly serious, clean-cut young men and women who, in general, are considerably superior in knowledge and motivation to their western counterparts It must be pointed out, however, that there are serious inequities in the system which insists that it is the most democratic and affords equal educational opportunity to all its citizens.

Additional flaws become quite apparent when one considers the administrative organization of the university. In the United States a state university has to satisfy the requirements placed upon it by the state government to which it is answerable. In the Soviet Union this is, of course, also true. However, in addition, there are a number of internal restrictions within MGU which an American university president does not have to face. The Rector of MGU can make very few decisions without the approval of the MGU Party Secretary and the Chairman of the MGU Labor Union and without at least consulting the Komsomol Secretary. But these are high-level considerations which do not concern us at the moment. Let us rather turn to the academic structure of MGU.

The university is divided into fifteen faculties and one institute as follows:

Faculty of Philosophy
Faculty of Psychology
Economics Faculty
Historical Faculty
Juridical Faculty
Philological Faculty
Faculty of Journalism
Institute of the Countries of Asia and Africa
Mechanical-Mathematical Faculty
Faculty of Computer Mathematics and Cybernetics

Physics Faculty
Chemistry Faculty
Biological Faculty
Faculty of Soil Science
Geological Faculty
Geographic Faculty

These sixteen subdivisions in turn contain a total of 272 departments, i.e., one for each logical sub-discipline. On the surface this seems to be a well-divised system which promises optimum efficiency. In reality, however, the subdivisions assure a rigid apparatus which allows for little flexibility and demands a doctrinaire approach. The first faculty on our list, the Faculty of Philosophy (of which Raisa Gorbacheve is a member), is an excellent example of the rigidity of the MGU approach, as the designations of its twelve numbered departments will testify. Most of them have little to do with the study of philosophy according to western standards:

1. Dialectic Materialism
2. Historical Materialism
3. Theory of Scientific Communism
4. Logic
5. History of Marxist-Leninist Philosophy
6. History of the Philosophy of the Peoples of the USSR
7. History of Foreign Philosophy
8. Theory and History of Atheism and Religion
9. Marxist-Leninist Aesthetics
10. Marxist-Leninist Ethics
11. Methods of Concrete Social Research
12. History of Socialist Teachings

Of course, the Faculty of Philosophy may be considered a bad example to choose, since it obviously lends itself to excessive ideological restrictions. However, the Faculties of History and of Journalism are nearly as bad. Certainly the faculties for the sciences are much more reasonably subdivided. Nevertheless, even the sciences place an undue amount of stress on Soviet achievements and Soviet locale. For example, geography concerns itself to an exaggerated degree with the physical and economic geography of the USSR and the socialist countries (3 Departments). We should also not overlook the fact that even those students who major in the sciences must attend, on a regular basis, numerous courses and lectures presented by the Faculty of Philosophy as part of their political indoctrination requirements towards their diplomas in any field.

At this point one may ask whether all the faculties are equally supported by the university The answer is a resounding <u>no</u>! Upon application to take the entrance examination the student is asked to note the faculty which he hopes to attend. In this respect, there is a strong similarity between the Soviet and the American systems in that the humanities clearly play "second fiddle" to the sciences. The students are definitely discouraged from applying for their fist preference, the Faculty of Philology, if they have exhibited a secondary aptitude for chemistry. By the same token, university funding for science projects is considerably more plentiful than for the liberal arts. One major difference between the Soviet system and ours is, that faculty pay is standardized no matter what the discipline may be. For example, the basic pay scales for a professor of physics or a professor of Spanish starts at 550 rubles a month, a very decent income by Soviet standards. This does not mean that both professors receive equal bonuses for any contributions they may have made beyond the call of duty. This is where the physics professor will come out far ahead

But there is one additional inequality between the faculties of MGU which has no bearing on traditional combat between the arts and the sciences, and which is clearly indicated by the physical location of these faculties. The main campus of MGU is located in the Lenin Hills, a considerable distance from the center of Moscow, on the other side of the Moskva River. The campus consists of an immense wedding-cake building with a cluster of other, newer buildings around it. Twelve academic subdivisions are located on this main campus. The other four are located in the heart of the city, directly opposite the Kremlin. It should be of interest to identify these four, and to search for the reasons for their special treatment. Incidentally, whenever an outsider inquires into this subject, he is told that the main campus is too small to house all 16 subdivisions, and that four were chosen at random from the ten faculties which did not require major laboratory facilities. The chosen four are:

The Juridical Faculty
The Faculty of Journalism
The Faculty of Psychology
The Institute of the Countries of Asia and Africa

Let us now consider the reasons for the special treatment of these faculties.

The Juridical Faculty was not created for the training of lawyers, although there are a relatively small number of attorneys in the USSR who function primarily in labor, housing and marital disputes. Contrary to American procedures, the main function of a law-school, and especially the one in MGU, is to turn out mid-level government officials commensurate to our GS 9 - GS 12, for all governmental agencies. There is no Faculty of Government and Politics. This is all included in the Juridical Faculty. In addition, it is the function of this faculty to select outstanding graduates for placement within the Procurator system which works closely with the Party leadership and has awesome powers to inspect and indict functionaries of the government from local to national level. The need for this faculty to be in constant physical proximity to the Soviet Government is obvious.

The same is true for the Faculty of Journalism. Since there is no such thing as a private, independent press in the Soviet Union, the newspapers and periodicals are purely mouthpieces of the Party or a government agency. It is clearly understandable that editors of leading newspapers and press establishments such as Pravda, Izvestia and Novosti Press are at the same time members of the Central Committee of the Communist Party. Errors in reporting, be they contextual or, even worse, ideological, cannot be tolerated in the news media. Although individual journalists may be from a variety of professional areas, there are a number of positions in the field of journalism which are closely guarded and held for those who have proven themselves both intellectually and politically worthy during their five-year period of training at MGU. Among these positions are those of foreign correspondent; editorial staff; distribution staff; and writers of any political commentary. If one considers that the only local, national and international news and its interpretation available to the Soviet public is the product of this journalistic monopoly, one can easily comprehend why the pertinent faculty of MGU must be located in the shadow of the Kremlin.

The reason for the special position of the Faculty of Psychology is less obvious. For the most part, the major fields of this discipline are approximately the same as ours, if we overlook undue exaggeration of "Work Psychology" and "Industrial Psychology" at MGU. The rather limited involvement of this faculty in "psychological warfare" which requires cooperation with the Ministry of Defense, is also no answer. One possible explanation is the fact that the clear line drawn in the United States between psychiatry and psychology is definitely not as clear in the Soviet Union. Psychologists play a greater clinical role in mental hospitals in the USSR than in America. When we consider the function of KGB mental institutions as a major weapon against dissenters, we begin to realize the special position of psychology. Still, this is only part of the answer. The real solution lies in the fact that a surprisingly large percentage of graduates receive their degrees in Social Psychology. They are trained in methods of population control and assigned to a regional or the central control office of the KGB in an ethnic, religious or social specialty. A good deal of their training is supervised by the Personnel and Administration Directorates of the KGB. The government considers control of the psyche of ultimate importance and insists on the proximity of the academic division responsible for its formulation.

The special position of the Institute for the Countries of Asia and Africa is much more easily comprehended. This is the research arm for the formulation and expression of governmental and Party policy on questions involving, for example, the Middle East, China, Afghanistan or Angola. This is also the training ground for diplomats and agents who will be working in these areas. Incidentally, this is the only discipline which requires a six-year study program rather than the normal five, the sixth year being a research assignment within the target country. This is probably the most expensive enterprise of MGU, since the departments of the Institute duplicate other departments already in existence under other faculties. For example, there are departments within the Institute which concern themselves primarily with history, geography and economics. Even more obviously it has departments which teach <u>all</u> African and Asian languages. Theoretically these languages should be taught by the Philological Faculty. The answer that the latter faculty does not have the mechanism for teaching these languages breaks down when we realize that the Institute also contains a department which teaches English, German, French, Dutch and Spanish. Quite obviously it is in the interest of the Soviet Government to separate this Institute completely from all other academic subdivisions, because of its highly sensitive political nature.

There is one additional MGU facility which merits separate consideration because of its peculiar nature, namely the Preparatory Office for Foreign Citizens which constituted a fully-fledged faculty until 1978. One thing which makes it unusual is, that it is the least propagated major subdivision of MGU. All descriptive literature concerning the university makes only fleeting reference to it. The location of the facility, or a roster of its members, appear to be rather well guarded secrets. Ostensibly, the major function of this branch is to see to it that all foreign students and exchange faculty are afforded the opportunity to learn a sufficient amount of Russian in order to cope with the lectures and seminars during their stay at MGU. Of course, a good part of this is true, but there is much more to the story. This office is also responsible for the introduction of these foreign students to the system of government, the economics, and the political and cultural philosophy on which the Soviet State is based Rather than being an introduction, this turns out to be an attempted indoctrination. One must keep in mind that many of these foreign students are from countries whose political posture is yet ill defined, and who are therefore quite impressionable. The Soviets have several years time to work on them and eventually recruit them. They do not have the same intelligence caveats as we do concerning activities within the academic community. The members of the Preparatory Office are not listed separately, since the teachers who convey the knowledge of the Russian language and culture are ostensibly all from the other faculties with specific expertise in these fields, e.g., the Faculties of Philology, History, Economics, etc. For the most part, this is so. However, the personnel specifically charged with the indoctrination of foreign students, intelligence spotting, assessment and recruitment among them, and observation or surveillance of potential trouble makers, are directly subordinated to the Department of Foreign Academic Personnel of the Second Chief Directorate of the KGB. These persons use their MGU status purely as a cover

The picture which has been painted may seem to be excessively dismal, especially for the non-science curricula at MGU. Physics, Chemistry, Mathematics and Geology seem to have the only faculties relatively immune from political manipulation of its basic instructional materials. Even Biology is still suffering the after-effects of Lysenko's warped genetics; Soil Science is tightly bound to the theory of State Farms and Collective Farms as the only viable form of land utilization for the future. Geography is not taught objectively, but as an adjunct to the idea of economic exploitation of the masses by western capitalism.

The major crimes, however, are committed within the faculties of the humanities. It is common knowledge that History has been rewriting the past so that it no longer bears any resemblance to fact; that Philosophy totally neglects to consider any ideas which effectively contradict Marxism-Leninism; that Philology does not discuss any great literature, foreign or domestic, which has been designated as dangerous by the censors. Yet the Soviets do continue to produce masterpieces in literature, art, criticism and historical analysis. How can such arrid soil produce such luxurious fruit? Undergraduate students rarely progress beyond this political drivel, since it is the only material to which they are ever exposed Their teachers must continue to deliver mass lectures which are politically pure. The graduate student, however, works very closely with his professor, sometimes on a one-to-one basis After the professor gets to know the individual <u>aspirant</u> for the M.A. or <u>kandidat</u> for the Ph.D. and starts to trust him, he can speak much more freely than in a group lecture In addition, graduate students do, upon occasion, have permission to read forbidden literature which is kept locked in special sections, away from general access. Thirdly, an increasing number of Soviet members of academe, both faculty and students, have had the opportunity to visit the West for lengthy periods of time Strange as it may seem, the real history of the Russian Civil War is much more easily accessible at the Hoover Library at Stanford University, than at the Lenin Library in Moscow. Finally, a very large amount of material is read illegally by the intelligentsia, i.e., smuggled in from abroad or handed around in manuscript form. It is virtually impossible, for example, to find anyone at MGU who has not read <u>Dr. Zhivago</u> or several of Solzhenitsyn's works.

To recapitulate, MGU is an institution possessed of great significance and great power which does affect the lives of all Soviet citizens. The student body is highly intelligent and seriously dedicated to the pursuit of the best education they are able to obtain in their chosen fields. The faculty contains numerous political hacks, but also some of the finest minds in the land The potential is there. MGU could easily become one of the finest institutions of learning in the world if its academic nature could be given preeminence over political restriction There is no indication, however, that anything will change in the foreseeable future.

READINGS

Moskovskii universitet. Moscow: Izdatel'stvo "Planeta," 1975.

Spravochnik dlia postupaiushchikh v moskovskii universitet. Moscow: Izd. Moskovskogo universiteta, 1982.

Taubman, William. The View from the Lenin Hills. New York: Coward-McCann, 1967.

Yelyutin, Vyacheslav. Higher Education. Moscow: Novosti Press, 1976.

XIX. Organized Science

Any discussion of this subject must begin with a consideration of the USSR Academy of Sciences which is by far the most important, most prestigious body in the nation. The title of "academician" is rarely bestowed and carries with it a lifetime of respect and a luxurious standard of living. At the present time the Academy has a total of 700 members and corresponding members, plus 70 foreign members. The number is intentionally kept low. This group, with the exception of a small handfull of political hacks, constitutes the cream of the crop in the Soviet scientific and academic world. The Academy has a President and a Presidium which directs the activities of four primary areas of science:

The Section of Physical-Technical and Mathematical Sciences contains the following departments: Mathematics; nuclear physics; general physics and astronomy; mechanics and control processes; and physical-technical problems of power engineering.

The Section of Chemical-Technological and Biological Sciences contains the following departments: Physiology; general biology; general and technical chemistry; physical chemistry and the technology of inorganic materials; and biochemistry, biophysics and the chemistry of physiologically active compounds.

The Section of Geosciences contains the following departments: Geology, geophysics and geochemistry; and oceanology; physics of the atmosphere and geography.

The Section of Social Sciences contains the following departments: Economics; history, philosophy and law; and literature and language.

The major objectives of the Academy, according to its written mission, are, "the development of fundamental research, the search for basically new possibilities of achieving technological progress, and the comprehensive application of scientific achievements." The organization is used as a think-tank, as the major research tool, and is frequently given direct instructions from the Party. It normally has to react to the scientific needs of the country and has little time for independent research on theoretical topics with little possibility of immediate application.

To facilitate research, the Academy has more than 250 research centers (e.g., institutes, observatories, laboratories) and a combined staff of over 41,000 scientific workers. It also possesses approximately 180 libraries. The Academy publishes voluminously in the "Nauka" Publishing House under the label "Akademiia Nauk SSSR." The published material is usually of a very high quality. The Academy also plays a leading part in the organization "Znanie" (Knowledge), the largest and most important scientific, educational and intellectual organization in the USSR. Znanie has over 142,000 primary organizations throughout the country, with a total membership approaching 3 million. It has at its disposal its own publishing house, central lecture agency, museums, planetariums, libraries, etc. It publishes not only books, but several monthly periodicals on various fields of science, with annual sales of over 100 million copies. The major function of the organization is educating the public in various fields of scientific research. For this reason, much of the time of Znanie members is taken up with lectures, both in auditoria and over the public media. In 1986, approximately 24 million lectures throughout the country were given by members of the organization.

There are other, similar organizations functioning under the guidance of the trade unions. Specifically, there are 23 scientific-technical societies which are organized by branches of industry and have a total membership of more than seven million. Each publishes journals specifically related to its own field of science Another organization in the same category is the "Society of Inventors and Innovators" with a membership of nearly 8 million. The purpose of the society is to further inventions and more efficient production methods. It, also, publishes a monthly journal.

The most significant innovation in the Soviet sphere of science was the establishing of a branch of the USSR Academy of Sciences in Siberia, specifically near Novosibirsk, where a new city, "Akademgorodok," was constructed for this purpose. This city now contains twenty research institutes and controls thirty others in Irkutsk, Krasnoiarsk, Tomsk and other Siberian population centers. At the present time this branch of the Academy employs 62 national academicians, i.e , nearly one-tenth of its membership. The center is continuing to grow and is extending into more remote East Siberian areas and into Yakutia and Buriatia. In Akademgorodok the most important fields of research are nuclear physics; mathematics; mechanics; mining; and geology. In Irkutsk research is conducted on the ionosphere, the earth's crust, mathematics, limnology and organic chemistry. Krasnoiarsk is the nations leading center on forestry and wood products.

Some western observers look upon this relatively recent development as the concerted effort of the Soviet Union to decentralize its scientific establishment in order to make it less vulnerable strategically. Akademgorodok is considered to be an experiment which has proven successful and will most probably be duplicated in several other areas in the USSR in the not-too-distant future

Each Union Republic has its own Academy of Sciences which works under the guidance of the USSR Academy of Sciences. Many of the members of the latter were selected because of their cumulative achievements in the former. Some of the contributions of the SSR Academies are listed below:

The Ukraine: Research on nuclear physics and solid physics is being conducted in three main institutes controlled by the SSR Academy. Here theories on deformed nuclei, on electron accellerators, on nuclear properties and on transformations were developed. At the Institute of Cybernetics, the first Soviet minicomputer was developed.

Belorussia: The Physics Institute of the SSR Academy is the leading center for quantum electronics, spectroscopy and luminescense. The Institute of Solid State Physics is doing important work on semiconductors and magnetic materials.

Georgia: This Academy is concerned with multi-purpose utilization of atomic energy.

Moldavia: Research is being conducted in quantum electronics, industrial cybernetics and engineering sciences.

Kazakhstan: Much work is being done on the exploration and exploitation of natural resources by leading geologists and geophysicists. This is also a primary research center for metallurgy.

Armenia: This SSR Academy is the leader in astronomy.

Azerbaidzhan: This is the leading center for oil exploration and for research into by-products of oil.

Estonia: The Academy in this SSR has made contributions in chemistry and in scientific methods for the utilization of shale and natural gas.

Uzbekistan: Research in textile fibers, e.g., cotton, hemp and silk.

Kirgizia: Research in agricultural methods and animal husbandry.

Turkmenia: Work is being done in the fields of desert studies, soil erosion and soil reclamation.

The scientific arm of the USSR is capable of accomplishing a great deal in areas which receive the full backing of the State. It is the State which determines which areas are to be stressed and are to receive the manpower, brainpower and funds. This means that other areas may be bled dry in order to support a strategically important area. Mostly it is the consumer area which will suffer in favor of a bigger rocket, a better bomb or a faster submarine. Although the potential is definitely there, the Soviet Union cannot compete with the United States in the scientific field. Although some of the achievements of Soviet science are definitely impressive, it must be remembered that they have been attained through great cost to the economy and that other fields, of similar long range importance, have been neglected. It should also be remembered that the Soviets were not signatories to the international copyright laws until 1973 and were free to adopt anything invented in the west with impunity. In addition, many of the Soviet innovations were accomplished with the help of satellite scientists, primarily Polish, Czech and East German. There is no doubt, however, that there are first class minds among the Soviet scientists and that they could make giant strides once the Soviets accept a long-range view of science which would permit independent research. At the present time they find it more convenient not to spend time and funds in research which has already been successfully concluded in the west. They prefer to conduct industrial espionage and to recruit unscrupulous western businessmen who keep them supplied with sensitive materials. The recently exposed illegal dealings in microchips are an excellent example.

Chart 35

Science Statistics

	1940	1965	1970	1977	1978	1980	1987
Research Scientists (In Millions)	0.1	0.7	0.9	1.3	1.3	1.4	1.6
State Expenditures on Science	0.3	6.9	11.7	18.3	19.3	21.1	24.7

READINGS

Alford, M. H. T. and V. L. Russian-English Scientific Technical Dictionary 2 vols. 2nd ed New York: Pergamon Press, 1974

Bromley, Yu. Soviet Ethnology and Anthropology Today. The Hague: Mouton, 1974

Callaham, Ludmilla Ignatiev. Russian-English Technical and Chemical Dictionary. New York: John Wiley & Sons, 1947.

Chernuchin, I. English-Russian Technical Dictionary. New York: International Universities Press, undated.

Emin, Irving. Russian-English Physics Dictionary. New York: John Wiley & Sons, 1963.

Fischer, George (ed.) Science and Ideology in Soviet Society. New York: Atherton Press, 1968.

Kneen, Peter. Soviet Scientists and the State. Albany: SUNY Press, 1984.

McLeish, John. Soviet Psychology. London: Methuen, 1975.

Ostrovitianov, K. V. (ed) Istoriia Akademii nauk SSSR. Moscow: Izd. Akademii Nauk, 1958.

Shtepa, K. Russian Historians and the Soviet State. New Brunswick: Rutgers University Press, 1962.

Soviet Psychology: a Symposium. New York: Philosophical Library, 1961.

The State of Soviet Science. Cambridge: M.I.T. Press, 1965.

USSR Science. Moscow: Novosti Press, 1976.

Zimmerman, M. G. Russian-English Scientific and Technical Dictionary. Moscow: Mir Publishers, undated.

XX. Printed and Media Propaganda

The Soviet Union prides itself on not only having the highest literacy rate in the world, but also the largest readership in the world. The vast majority of Soviet citizens actually do read voraciously. The printed word has much more significance there than in the United States.

In support of this statement is the fact that over 170 million copies of 8,000 newspapers are sold. This would mean that if not every adult buys a newspaper each, at least every family has one. This is due to several factors. First of all, there is a real thirst to know what is going on in the USSR and in the rest of the world. Unfortunately, the Russian addage that there "is no truth in Pravda and no news in Izvestia" is quite correct. Pravda (which means "truth") is the organ of the Central Committee of the Communist Party; Izvestia (which means "news") is published by the government. One major frustration is, that after reading both skimpy papers of eight pages each, one knows little more about what is going on than before reading them. There is relatively good reporting on sporting events and on TV and radio programming. Also, there is a daily playbill of the theater and musical events. Otherwise, the rest of the paper is filled with pure propaganda: so-and-so receiving the Lenin Prize; this or that plant over-fulfilling its quota; a pronouncement by Gorbachev or another Politburo member; a twisted account of social conditions in the West; an unhumorous political cartoon. The Soviet reads everything, nevertheless, since there is nothing else being offered. Also, the citizen must know what the Party line of the day is, in order that he may react in the correct manner when certain subjects or persons come up for discussion. Political journals are just as tasteless and are read for the same reasons. Technical and cultural journals are a different matter. Although they do contain considerable propaganda material, they are nevertheless informative and interesting. There are even some reasonably good humorous magazines such as Krokodil which even poke fun at some Soviet institutions, of course, with the blessings of the Party. All in all, there are 6,800 different periodicals with a total circulation of 155 million copies.

The main portion of our discussion must, however, be relegated to books. At the present time, there are 800 books for every 100 persons in the USSR - the highest ratio in the world. There are 229 major publishing houses, the largest being: Nauka; Mysl'; Mir; Russkii rabochii; Iskusstvo; Molodaia gvardia; Ekonomika; Prosveshchenie; Politizdat; Progress; Detskaia literatura; Novosti; and Sovietskaia entsyklopediia. Fully 25% of all the books published in the world, are produced in the Soviet Union. Every year more than 85,000 new titles in a total edition of two billion copies are produced.

Books are printed in 46 standard languages which existed before the Russian Revolution, plus 43 languages of smaller minorities which had no literary language prior to 1917. Books are also printed in 56 foreign languages, primarily by Progress and Novosti publishers. One-third of all books printed are fiction. The Soviet readership is especially starved for this material. Fiction is printed in large editions, rarely smaller than 100,000 copies. Often books in this category come out in series which require subscriptions. The Soviets frequently mention the fact that they recently announced a series called Library of World Literature, whose 200 volumes were to incorporate the best works of world literature from the classics to the contemporary period. Although the edition was to consist of 300,000 copies of

Chart 36

Principal National Newspapers and Periodicals

Newspapers (daily):

Pravda 10.6 million copies
Izvestia 9.1 million copies
Trud (Labor) 8.5 million copies
Sel'skaia zhizn' (Farmer's Life) 7.6 million copies
Komsomolskaia pravda 10 million copies
Pionerskaia pravda 10 million copies

Newspaper (weekly):

Za rubezhom (Foreign Press Review) 1 million copies

Periodicals:

Kommunist (Theoretical journal of the Central Committee)
Ogonëk (Socio-political, literary)
Novy mir (literary)
Znamia (literary)
Oktiabr (literary)
Inostrannaia literatura (foreign literature)
Nauka i zhizn' (Science and Life)
Nauka i religiia(Science and Religion)
Murzilka (juvenile)
Pioner (juvenile)
Smena (juvenile)
Iunost' (juvenile)
Tekhnika molodëzhi (juvenile)
Krokodil (humorous-satirical)

each volume, subscriptions had to be closed five days after the series was announced. There is no reason to doubt the veracity of this claim.

The Soviets also publish large editions of western works translated into Russian, e.g. Steinbeck, Hemingway, Gide, Sartre, Mann, etc. These works can never be seen on the shelves of any of the large, numerous bookstores since they are bought out by the public as soon as they are unpacked. Second-hand books cost approximately the same as new ones. They are sold by the owner to a bookstore and then put into the second hand section. It is illegal for an owner to sell directly to another person, since this would be private enterprise. Nevertheless, there is an active black market in books being conducted by courageous younger people in front of bookstores. Many books that are unavailable in the USSR for political reasons are either circulated in manuscript or in copies smuggled across the border. It is virtually impossible, for example, to meet a university student who has not read several forbidden Russian and foreign authors.

A large percentage of the non-fiction texts consist of technical and scientific books, or books on work experience written by the workers themselves, e.g., cooks, tractor drivers, nurses, farmers, etc. Another large production area are children's books. In 1986, approximately 2,600 new titles in editions totalling 280 million copies were produced in this category. The books with the largest edition figures, however, are in the spheres of politics. Party and government leaders such as Gorbachev and other Politburo members are constantly publishing books on communist theory, Marxist philosophy or governmental procedures. An important work by a member of the Politburo will come out in an edition of 15 million, since every party functionary, every library and every book stall will have to have at least one copy, if only for display purposes.

To encourage the immense readership, there are presently 360,000 libraries in the country, housing more than 3 1/2 billion volumes. It is estimated that more than 180 million citizens use these libraries on a regular basis. Libraries are open to all and free of charge. This is not the case with the two largest libraries in the country, the Lenin Library in Moscow (27 million items) and the Saltykov-Shehedrin Library in Leningrad (17 million items). It is extremely difficult to attain the right to use them; even one who has the right, cannot have access to the stacks and cannot request to see books which are locked away in special sections. A person attempting to do research on Trotzkii, for example, would find it virtually impossible to obtain research material. Smaller libraries, especially in rural areas, also have the function of a meeting place for lectures and for discussions with writers who are much more accessible to the Soviet general public than writers in the West.

Speaking in general, Soviets love books. This love is greatly encouraged by the State. The best form of encouragement is the fact that books are extremely cheap compared with similar editions in the West. The end of 1974 an All-Union Society of Bibliophiles was founded and immediately attracted several million members.

Another prevalent vehicle for printed propaganda is the political poster. The most striking impression a foreign visitor receives when entering any type of Soviet institution or public association is the plethora of multi-colored political posters Favorite subjects are Lenin in various poses; Gorbachev; the fulfillment of the present Five Year Plan; the achievements of Soviet economy; and agitation and propaganda posters which are supposed to stir the population to greater social activity. These posters are plentiful and extremely cheap.

Radio and television are much more limited in their programming than in the United States. There are four television channels and three radio stations in the Moscow-Leningrad area Most of the programming is primarily in the following categories:

Newscasts which are mostly concerned with domestic issues;
Highly biased descriptions of foreign areas;
Excellent classical music programs from major stages;
A great deal of foreign music including modern jazz;
Tips on handicrafts and gardening;
Poetry readings and literary discussions by the leading figures in the field of literature;
Other intellectual discussion on history, politics and the arts, of course from a very one-sided point of view;
Films, both foreign and domestic;
Health and hygiene;
Children's programming of a didactic nature;
Speeches by leading Party and government figures.

READINGS

Birkos, Alexander S. and Tambs, Lewis A. eds. Academic Writer's Guide to Periodicals: East European and Slavic Studies. Kent State University Press, 1973.

Bogoliuybov, K. M. Sovietskie zhurnaly. Moscow: Izd. polit. lit., 1958.

Finder, Joseph. Red Carpet. New York: Holt, Rinehart & Winston, 1983.

Dewhirst, Martin. The Soviet Censorship. Metuchen: Scarecrow Press, 1973.

Govorov, A. A. Iztoriia knizhnoi torgovli v SSSR. Moscow: Kniga, 1976.

Gorkhoff, Boris I. Publishing in the USSR. Indiana University Press, 1959.

Hazan, Baruch. Soviet Impregnational Propaganda. Ann Arbor: Ardis, 1982.

Hopkins, Mark W. Mass Media in the Soviet Union. New York: Pegasus, 1970

XXI. Belles Lettres and Depictive Arts

It would be impossible to discuss Soviet art intelligently without an understanding of the principles of Socialist Realism. This doctrine has pervaded all of the arts, including literature, since the early Stalin days. It has also been a great source of problems due to the various interpretations it has been given The problem becomes quite obvious when one tries to pinpoint what a socialist painting or a socialist piece of music could possibly be. It is easier to understand how a socio-economic doctrine can be expressed in literature; but how can it be depicted in a painting or be heard in a symphony? Obviously, only through irrational value judgements. Let us analyze the term Socialist Realism. According to the Soviets, the doctrine must have three components:

a. National Spirit (narodnost): It should convey the spirit of the nationality which produces it. This means, that a composer in Armenia should reflect local color rather than ape an Italian, German or American popular style.

b. Party Spirit (partiinost): A piece of literature or art may not conflict in content with Party pronouncements, but must rather support them.

c. Ideology (ideinost): Art cannot serve itself, i.e , there may not be "art for art's sake "

On the face of it, these components may seem to be quite reasonable. In reality, they can be impossibly complex. For example, what does National Spirit really mean? Does it restrict an Armenian composer from using a popular Ukrainian folk tune as a leitmotiv in a composition? or a Rumanian tune? or a tune of the "suppressed" people of Trinidad? Where does it all end? At the present time young Russian composers are working with jazz, swing and rock. Obviously this cannot fit into acceptable parameters. Yet, it is being done and is being quietly condoned by the authorities.

It is easy to see how a portrait of Gorbachev would pay lip service to the Party Spirit in art. But would this same portrait be acceptable if it were painted in an impressionist manner? Would a painting be acceptable if it clearly showed the birthmark on Gorbachev's forehead?

Every work of art must have Ideology. This means, that all paintings, literature and music must be didactic. Does this mean that there may not be any art purely for sensual enjoyment and amusement?

The answer to all these questions is quite simple: The individual Soviet artist does not have to worry about what is ideologically pure and in the national and Party spirit. This interpretation is up to the authorities. It is therefore not at all uncommon that a work of art which is considered to be a fine example of Socialist Realism one year, may be strongly attacked as a dangerous distortion the next and vice versa. The determination of what is Socialist Realism and what is not, is in the eye of the determiner.

Even more interesting, is a discussion of what is meant by "realism." The first thing which comes to mind here, is the style in which the work of art was accomplished Quite obviously, cubism, impressionism, expressionism, surrealism and most other "isms" are not realistic and would therefore have to be excluded from approval; but are they? The major galleries in the USSR are full of excellent examples of such styles, and the artists are celebrated throughout the land. Under Krushchev, and certainly under Stalin, such art would never have been permitted But besides style, the other basic component of realism is the content. Does the socialist type of realism tell the artist that he must present things as they really are? May he paint the hard lot of the Kolkhoz resident in Central Asia, or the luxurious life of a Soviet industrial director, or a sex orgy, just because these things exist somewhere in the Soviet Union? Obviously not. Since art must be didactic and must teach only good things, the theme of what is to be displayed realistically must be restricted. By the same token, even with an approved theme, the artist should not concern himself with "what is" but with "what should be" and "what will be " There must be an optimistic note which holds promise for a better future combined with pride in past and present achievements, in all of art. Again, the initial determination of these factors lies with the writers, artists and composers unions, and ultimately with the Party leadership.

Considering all the restrictions under which the Soviets have had to live all their lives, it is amazing that literature, art and music have reached such heights in the USSR. One may conjecture that it is this very adversity which produces great art; on the other hand, one may wonder what great works are lost because they are suppressed

Belles lettres have always held a special fascination for the Russian. It is difficult for us to imagine that much of prime time television and radio is taken up by poetry readings or readings of chapters from a new novel. By the same token, tickets to public readings in person by authors from some of their works are immediately sold out. This type of literature is not only a means of enjoyment and relaxation - it is far more than this. It constitutes the political arena where the more important questions are considered It is quite indicative that literature is listed under the "Social Sciences" in the Academy of Sciences. It is, of course, impossible to comment on a philosophical point in a literary work, in a manner which may be construed as derogatory and sacriligious by the State. It is, however, possible to put such words into the mouth of a fictional anti-hero, even if his pronouncements are later debunked. This type of "Aesopic Language" is a two-century-old tradition in Russia. Literature, therefore, is used to bring out points of view which cannot be verbalized in any other manner. By the same token literary criticism may also discuss the philosophical merits, or their lack, of any piece of literary work, without committing itself. Objectivity is a dirty word in the Soviet jargon since everyone has the duty to be subjective, but literary criticism can, at times, transgress against this law. It is on the literary stage that ideological battles have been fought most recently. The fate of writers such as Pasternak, Tertz, Solzhenitsyn and others is quite well known in the West. This is the reason why the Soviet government keeps such a tight rein on this medium and will permit an absolute minimum of deviation. The main watchdog to accomplish this, is the Writer's Union. Thus, many outstanding writers cannot be successful because of their political convictions and belief in freedom of expression, and end up "writing for the drawer," as the Russian expression goes, hoping for a better day when the manuscript may be brought into the light. In the meantime Party hacks, albeit with some talent, continue to receive the highest literary award, the Lenin Prize, for example:

S. Smirnov. <u>The Brest Fortress.</u>
M. Svetlov. <u>The Verses of Recent Years.</u>
N. Tikhonov. <u>Six Columns.</u>
S. Mikhalkov. <u>Collected Verses for Children.</u>
G. Guliam. <u>Colected Poetry.</u>
M. Shaginian. <u>The Lenin Tetralogy.</u>
I. Melezh. <u>Men in the Marshes and Breath of a Thunderstorm.</u>
A. Barto. <u>Flowers in the Winter Forest.</u>
K. Simonov. <u>Those Alive and Those Dead.</u>
J. Avizius. <u>Lost Paradise.</u>
G. Markov. <u>Siberia.</u>

There are, however, other writers who are attempting to be more true to their art. Many of them have been forced to flee to the west or were expelled from the USSR. Some of the best in this category include Alexandr Solzhenitsyn, Joseph Brodsky, Andrei Siniavskii, Edvard Limonov, Vasilii Aksenov, Vladimir Voinovich and Aleksandr Sokolov. Other fine writers such as Iuri Trifonov and Vasilii Shukshin are dead. It might be helpful, however, to discuss some of these writers and to attempt to characterize the past few decades of Soviet literature

With the death of Stalin in 1953 and the beginning of the "Thaw" period, there was a great deal of optimism among the ranks of the writers. The banality of the past began to give way before the innovative spirit of the day. Experimentation in poetry, which had lain dormant since the late twenties, was revived. Lyricism in general was now acceptable. New methods in style and structure of short stories were introduced. The only genre which saw little progress was the novel, despite magnificent beginnings in works such as Pasternak's <u>Dr. Zhivago.</u> But even the other forms were, and continue to be, restricted in their freedom to question political ideology. The relative permissiveness of the post-Stalin years and of the present, then, remains extremely selective

Aleksandr Solzhenitsyn: His early short novel, <u>One Day in the Life of Ivan Denisovich</u> contains much of the seed of nearly all his writings thereafter, virtually all of which are autobiographical. His social criticism is scathing, his observations profound, and his compassion with the afflicted is truly humane. His major novels are <u>Cancer Ward</u>, <u>The First Circle</u> and <u>August 1914</u>. His nonfictional writings such as <u>Gulag Archipelago</u> and <u>The Oak and the Calf</u> are not as intellectually honest as his novels. He intends, in the words of Andrei Sakharov, to eliminate the present social system and to substitute for it a system of equal inequity by reinstituting the authority of the Russian Orthodox Church. His most recent short essays and speeches are flagrantly didactic and one-sided.

Iurii Trifonov: He is a short story writer although his first major work was a novel, <u>The Students.</u> He published extensively in the literary journal <u>Novyi mir</u> and was a rather close collaborator of Aleksandr Tvardovsky. Trifonov writes about the well educated urban dweller and the multi-faceted problems, e.g., egoism, infidelity, family conflicts and psychological pressures, which face him daily. His is the clear and direct language of the city intelligentsia. His main works include the novels <u>The Old Man</u>, <u>Impatience</u>, <u>Thirst Quenching</u>; and the short stories "Vera and

Zoika," "A Summer Noon," "The Exchange," "Another Life," "A Spring for Picking Mushrooms" and "The House of the Embankment." Several of his stories were adapted for the stage. He died unexpectedly in Moscow in 1981 at the age of 55

Chingiz Aitmatov: This highly talented author writes in both Russian and his native Kirgizian. He is often characterized as a writer who centers on acute dramatic collisions and profound personal conflicts. Although the setting is normally in Central Asia, the themes are universal: The conflict between good and evil; the contrast between insignificant man and the grandeur of nature; the ethics of adults vs. the young. There is a great deal Rousseauan and Tolstoyan in his approach. Among his best stories and novellas are: "White Rain," "The Rivals," "Difficult Crossing," "Face to Face," "Dzhamilia," "The Eye of the Camel," "Farewell, Gulsary!" "The White Steamship," "Early Cranes," and "Spotted Dog Running Along the Seashore." He has also been extremely successful with a play which he co-authored.

Iurii Kazakov: This Muscovite writer became known as the representative of the younger generation. He was in trouble with the authorities from the very beginning of his career for depicting negative heroes and insufficient social commitment. His genre is virtually exclusively the short story written in colloquial Moscow language and deceptively easy to read. His prose is rich in sensory impressions and lyricism. His characters are complex, often sensitive, other times insensitive to their environment. Collections of his short stories were published under the titles: At the White Sea; Pigeon-Blue and Green; Manka; On the Road; and At the Station, which are also the titles of some of his best stories. Others are "Adam and Eve," "The Outsider," "A Couple in December," "Autumn in the Oak Forest" and "The Smell of Bread." There is also a cycle of stories set in the locale of peasant fishing villages in the north which include "Pomorka," "Nestor and Kir," "We Are Not Strangers," "The Secrets of Nikishkin," "Going to Town" and "Old Men."

Valentin Rasputin: A listing of Soviet prose writers would be incomplete without including at least one representative of "village prose." This is a tradition which was carried by many of the foremost Soviet writers, including Mikhail Sholokhov, Boris Pilniak, Leonid Leonov, Andrei Platonov, Aleksandr Tvardovskii, Fedor Abramov, Vasilii Belov, Vasilii Shukshin, Yurii Kursanov, Vladimir Soloukhin and Viktor Likhosonov. During the past decade this "village prose" has been on the wane and has taken a secondary position to prose in the urban setting. Rasputin, until recently, was the most successful of these writers and was frequently lauded by the authorities. His plots are usually set in remote Siberian villages and his heroes are simple peasants. He first appeared on the scene in the late 1960's when his first collection of short stories, A Man of This World and his first short novel, Money for Mariia were published. Although he was not a prolific writer he did publish a number of short novels and stories during subsequent years, enough to gain him a great deal of recognition. His strong points include the use of language which is precise and poetic; his narrative is smooth; the use of symbolism and dreams; and careful character development. Among his most recent and best stories is "Saying good-bye to Matera" in which a family leaves the village to come to the city. Rasputin was strongly attacked for this tale since it seems to indict the destruction of the village in the name of technological and social progress which the author views as no progress at all. This is more than just nostalgia. It is a forecast of the deterioration of man's state as a natural and noble being

Evgenii Evtushenko: This is the most flamboyant and most internationally well known Soviet poet. He is equally famous as a performer of his own poetry and as a writer of it. His poetry readings in which he declaims his work with passion and theatrics in the style of Mayakovsky have fascinated audiences worldwide. He has a great deal of self-assurance and believes himself to be the most important poet of his age. He loves to travel to the west, to live well - even luxuriously - to expose himself to new impulses, and to act the part of a poseur. He is given to exaggerations and purple prose. Nevertheless, he is also a fine and sensitive lyric poet and a romantic. His work may range from brilliantly courageous attacks against discriminatory practices in the Soviet Union ("Baby Yar"), to self-aggrandizement (A Precocious Autobiography), to his longest and weakest, rather pompous and pretentious poem, The Bratsk Hydroelectric Station. His brilliance is uneven. Fortunately he is still growing and it is hoped that the lyricism and religious imagery in his poetry will emerge victorious.

Andrei Voznesenskii: On the surface he has a lot of similarity to Evtushenko. Both were born in 1933 and both appeared on the scene simultaneously. In fact, they are close friends. Both have adopted the style of Mayakovsky and both share the same high degree of adulation in the USSR. Here the similarity ends Voznesenskii has an engineering background which is quite obvious in his poetry. His imagery is crisp and brisk. He is fascinated with sound and rhythm of language and, at times, becomes fascinated with his own technical ingenuity. Yet, he is much more modest and private than his friend, and frequently confesses that he is but a lowly disciple of Boris Pasternak This makes him an extremely attractive figure to his audience. Although he was a scientist, he is devoted to art in all its forms and incorporates music, painting and architecture in the themes of his work. He has consistently been courageous in supporting the victims of arbitrary repression by the state and has therefore, on a number of occasions, fallen out of favor.

Bela Akhmadulina: A poet of the same period who, in fact, was once married to Evtushenko. She was later married to the writers Iurii Nagibin and Gennadi Mamlin. She is highly romantic and personal, and refuses to participate in any political involvement. Her lyrics are delicate and melodious. She can switch from a joyful celebration of life to the deepest despair. Often she becomes introspective and somber - even neurotic. Her long poem "Chills and Fever" is an example. Her love lyrics are often exhuberant, e.g., "At Night." Frequently she searches for the meaning of creative inspiration, e.g., in her long poem Fairytale About the Rain. Since she is quite courageous in supporting causes frowned upon by the state, it is hoped that this highly talented woman will be allowed to continue to develop in her art.

Of course the writers listed above are but a few of the many worth mentioning. Many have been left out, though they deserve a better fate Nevertheless it is hoped that the eight listed, provide a good cross-section of the older writers in Soviet literature today.

Writers of 1987

The following are writers of several generations who are active today and appear to have at least the partial support of the Party:

Viktor Astafiev is a member of the older generation His background as a World War II hero comes him in good stead. He writes primarily long short stories, (his best include "A Civilian," "Chusavoi Worker," "King of Fish," and "A Last Farewell," and film scenarios (e.g., the recently released autobiographical Born Twice).

Viktoria Tokareva is particularly in demand She turns out a large number of short stories, most of them auto-biographical, about her life as a young girl in Moscow. She has also, quite successfully, written a number of film scenarios She is not a writer of particular depth, though quite entertaining, and a bit of a pompous Party hack.

Aimee Beekman, a good Estonian writer, is particularly frequently discussed because of her latest novel (1986), The Race, which is an impressive tale of human survival. Other works include "The Hour of the Equinox," "The Barrel Organ," "Thistle," "The Muffled Bells," "An Alternative," and "The Thicket."

Nina Bichuia has published several novels and collections of short stories. Her style is clear and crisp. Many of her works are for children. Her books for adults include Greater Celandine, The Highest Mountain of All, and the most recent (1986) Benefit Performance.

Vladimir Gusev is both a writer of short stories and novels, and an interesting literary critic. His work includes the long short stories "The Sun" and "The Legend of the Blue Hussar" (about Mikhail Lunin). His books include The Horizons of Freedom about Simon Bolivar and his latest, Days, published in 1986.

Vladimir Karnaukhov is a young writer who published his first novel, A Time for Parting, in 1986. It is about family conflict, triangles, and other emotional situations, and has received most more publicity than normally expected of a first work.

Vladimir Kolykhalov is one of the Siberian writers who has a sizable following. His latest collection of stories (1986) is The Kudrinsk Chronicle. Earlier works of this prolific writer include the novel Wild Sprouts and the following collections of essays and stories: July Frosts, A Traveler's Diary, The Cricket, and on Old Paths.

Feliks Krivin writes short stories and aphorisms and is an extremely popular writer. His collections include The Frivolous Archimedes, The Hyacinth Islands, Princess Grammar, or Descendants of the Ancient Verb, and his most recent one (1986), The Inventor of Immortality.

Viktor Likhosonov is also quite popular. His collections of lyrical stories include Happy Moments, Clear Eyes, The Elegy, When Shall We See Each Other?, and his most recent historical novel Our Little Paris.

Vatslav Mikhalskii has successfully published a number of collections including The Marksman, The Wind That Bears All Away, The Small World, and the most recent (1986) Selected Works. He has also published the novel Secret Favors

Valerii Osipov is also very well known He has published a large number of collections of short stories and novels, mainly concerned with Northern Siberia. His works include The Secret of the Siberian Platform, Accelleration, Pursuing the Horizon, I Am Looking for My Childhood, and his most recent (1986) A Name on the Map. Lately he has worked on historical books devoted to the memory of Lenin.

Anatolii Shavkuta is one of Moscow's most popular writers. His latest collection of short stories (1986) is For the Sake of Beauty. Previous collections include Such Different People, Snowstorm in Riazan, and The Old Master's Stories

Leonid Zorin is the best known writer on this list. His most recent work (1986), The Wander, contains the title novel plus a long story, "The Farewell March." Zorin is a writer of some talent but of uneven product. He is best known for his plays which include "A Warsaw Melody," "The Good Souls," "The Royal Hunt," "Man and Woman," and "Coronation "

In recent years the genre of science, detective and adventure fiction has grown tremendously. Such books are quite cheap and are printed in very large editions — the literature of the common man. This is a listing of the best known writers and their most recent works: Arkadii Adamov (Inspector Losev and The Search is On); Pavel Bagriak (The Blue People); Anatolii Bezuglov (Beasts of Prey and Public Procurator); Mikhail Culaki (Book of Joy, Book of Sorrow); Ruslan Kireev (Fire Fly); Oleg Korabelnikov (And the Doors Will Fling Open); Leonid Mlechin (An Old Man in a Black Kimono); Aleksandr Nasibov (Atoll Starfish); Vasilii Ardamatskii (The First Assignment); Kir Bulychev (Agent CF and Thirteen-Year Flight); Olga Larionova (The Sea Sonata); Viktor Pronin (Without Regaining Consciousness); Leonid Slovin (Backward Trace); Arkadii and Georgii Vainer (Remedy for Fear); and Aleksandr Zhitinskii (A Watch with Variants).

SOVIET PUBLICATION OF AMERICAN LITERATURE AND THE PUBLISHING INDUSTRY IN THE USSR

At present, there are several major publishing houses in Moscow that deal with translations of foreign literature. The most important are 1) the prestigious Publishing House of Literature, 2) the Publishing House of Fiction, which prints only pre-World War II classics, 3) Progress, the main publisher of foreign non-fiction, 4) Rainbow, which is responsible for post-World War II literature, and 5) Young Guard, the publishing house of the Komsomol—the Soviet youth organization Komsomol is the only Soviet organization besides Pravda that has its own printing press, which means it can turn out a great deal of material very quickly. The Soviet Union also maintains several specialized publishing houses for sports books and professional materials, etc.

The normal schedule for book publication in the Soviet Union proceeds along several well-defined stages and takes about three years. After an outline is accepted for publication by a particular publishing house, approximately a year is spent writing the manuscript. Next, all books go through a "year of editorial preparation." At this stage, the book is copyedited and undergoes final review, and if approved, it will not be rejected later. Finally, the book is printed during the "year of publication." Most books are published in one large production run. There are no serial printings, and if an additional printing is necessary, the new copies are called a "second edition" even though they might not contain any changes. After a publishing house agrees to print a given book, Soviet authors are paid 40% of their fee in advance and the remainder upon approval. If no copies of a book are sold, the author is paid regardless. Authors can receive more than their original contract fee if the book goes through additional "editions." For non-fiction books, a printing of 15,000 is regarded as an edition.

Each year, 15-20 translations of American fiction are published in the USSR; each major publishing house turns out three or four works within the limits of an "unofficial" quota. Occasionally, some are published in minority languages as well as Russian. The largest project for the publication of American books in the Soviet Union is the Library of American Literature. Originally, this was a joint project with the United States, but the U.S. ended its participation in 1980 as U.S.-Soviet contacts were curtailed in general. As a result of this 60-volume project, all American authors of any literary significance have been published in the USSR according to the Soviets.

A significant number of Soviet citizens apparently enjoy a wide range of American literature, including classics and popular novels. In recent years, William Faulkner and William Styron have become very popular in the Soviet Union as was Hemingway in the 1950s and 1960s. Theodore Dreiser and Jack London are popular, and Mark Twain is so familiar to Soviet children that many don't know he's American. An effort has been made to publish only high quality literature, but novels such as Airport and Jaws have been published recently.

Depictive Arts

Soviet painting has a long tradition of superb artistry. The twentieth century has not diminished the talent. People tend to forget that Kandinsky and Chagall are not French, but Russian. Of course, next to literature, this art medium has experienced the most severe ups and downs. There are periods when only the heroic factory worker and peasant woman may be seen; there are other periods when the most experimental art receives approval. On the one hand, completely unrealistic art is displayed in the museums; on the other hand, personal exhibitions in parks are broken up by the police. There should be no misunderstanding of this point which has received so much publicity in the West: These exhibitions are only partly attacked because of the extremely modernistic quality of the paintings shown. Primarily they are disrupted because the exhibitors have failed to get permits to exhibit. Like any totalitarian state, the USSR cannot tolerate any kind of organized occurrance which is outside its control.

In general, art is strongly supported. There is even strong emphasis on the restoration of old ikons in churches which are now state museums. Also folk painting is constantly encouraged. For example, there is an entire museum in Moscow which features only hand painted trays. There are other museums which display a favorite of Caucasian artists - metal chasing.

The following are at the present time the most well known younger painters: E. Moiseenko; Iu. Pimenov; A. Plastov; and S. Gerasimov. Among the more experimental, younger painters are: G. Korzhev; V. Ivanov; L. Kabachek; V.

Zagonek; A. Mylykov; V. Kabanov; I. Utkin; V. Titov; G. Moskovchenko; E. Vasil'ev; M. Ushats; V. Fomichev; E. Gurov (the last three are primarily cartoonists); L. Stil'; A. Iakovlev; and Z. Arshakuni. Lenin Prize winners in painting include Arkadii Plastov for his portraits of Kolkhoz members; Sergei Gerasimov for the landscape of the Land of Russia series; Evsei Moiseenko for the Years of War series; and Iurii Pimenov for the New Neighborhood series. In 1978, Sviatoslav Roerikh was designated an honorary member of the Academy of the Arts of the USSR.

Possibly the most talented contemporary Soviet painter is Ernst Neizvestnyi who was asked to leave Russia in 1975. He is best remembered for his running battle with Premier Khrushchev when the latter stated that Neizvestnyi's work could have been daubed "by the tail of an ass" and was fit "only for the walls of urinals." Ironically, when Khrushchev died Neizvestnyi was asked by the Khrushchev family to design the monument which is now standing over his grave.

Most sculpture in the Soviet Union are heavy, massive examples of overpowering conspicuousness. Size, heroic figures and realistic simplicity of line are stressed. Foremost sculptors in the USSR today include M. Anikushin; L. Kerbel; A. Kibalnikov; and G. Iokubonis. The most recent winners of Lenin prizes are Iurii Gradov for the Khatyn Memorial in Belorussia; Gunar Asaris for the memoral ensemble entitled "To the Memory of the Victims of Fascist Terror" in Salaspils, Latvia; and Evgenii Vuchetich for his Heroes of the Battle of Stalingrad in Volgograd.

Folk art is also strongly supported, especially since it is an excellent source of hard-currency income. The lacquer boxes produced in Palekh, Kholui, Fedoskino and Mstera are truly exquisite. Khokhloma wooden bowls and implements produced primarily in the Ukraine are both colorful and utilitarian. Inlaid straw pictures produced in Belorussia are quite decorative. Copper chasing in Armenia and Georgia are true works of art on a high level. The same is true of hand-painted ceramics and precious metal jewelry in Central Asia. Carpets produced in the same area are among the finest in the world.

READINGS

Barabash, Iurii. Aesthetics and Poetics. Moscow: Progress, 1977.

Brown, Deming. Russian Soviet Literature Since Stalin. Cambridge: Cambridge University Press, 1978.

Brown, Edward J. Major Soviet Writers. London: Oxford University Press, 1973.

Carlisle, Olga Andreyev. Voices in the Snow: Encounters With Russian Writers. New York: Random House, 1962.

Crouch, Martin & Porter, Robert, (eds.) Understanding Soviet Politics Through Literature. Winchester: Allen & Unwin, 1984.

Dodge, Norton and Hilton, Alison, (eds.) New Art From the Soviet Union. Washington: Acropolis Books, Ltd., 1977.

Dunham, Vera S. In Stalin's Time: Middleclass Values in Soviet Fiction. Cambridge: Cambridge University Press, 1976.

Friedberg, Maurice. A Decade of Euphoria. Bloomington: Indiana University Press, 1977.

Hayward, Max, ed. On Trial. New York: Harper and Row, 1966.

Hayward, Max and Crowley, Edward, (eds.) Soviet Literature in the Sixties. New York: Praeger, 1964.
James, C. V. Soviet Socialist Realism: Origins and Theory. New York: St. Martin's Press, 1973.
Johnson, P. Khrushchev and the Arts. Cambridge: MIT Press, 1965.
Juenger, Harri, (ed.) Literatures of the Soviet Peoples. New York: Frederick Ungar, 1970.
Khrapchenko, M. The Writer's Creative Individuality and the Development of Literature. Moscow: Progress, 1977.
Khrushchev, N. S. The Great Mission of Literature and Art. Moscow: Progress, 1964.
Lif, A., (ed.) Forbidden Laughter. Los Angeles: Almanach, 1979.
Lindstrom, Thais S. A Concise History of Russian Literature From 1900 to the Present. New York: New York University Press, 1978.
Mathewson, Rufus W. Jr. The Positive Hero in Russian Literature. Stanford: Stanford University Press, 1975.
Obolensky, Dimitri. Art Treasures in Russia. New York: McGraw-Hill, 1970.
Rybakov, Anatoli. Heavy Sand. Book-of-the-Month Club, 1981.
Shneidman, N. N. Soviet Literature in the 1970's: Artistic Diversity and Ideologial Conformity. Toronto: University of Toronto Press, 1979.
Sinyavsky, Andrei. For Freedom of Imagination. New York: Holt, Rinehart and Winston, 1971.
Slonim, Mark. Soviet Russian Literature: Writers and Problems 1917-1977. New York: 1977.
Solzhenitsyn, Aleksandr. The Mortal Danger: How Misconceptions About Russia Imperil America. New York: Harper & Row, 1980.
_____. Detente. New Brunswick: Transaction Books, 1976.
Stacy, Robert H. Russian Literary Criticism. Syracuse: Syracuse University Press, 1974.
Williams, Raymond. Marxism and Literature. Oxford University Press, 1977.

XXII. The Performing Arts

If one accepts the profound influence of literature on the Soviet citizen, and its potential danger, one would have to agree that drama and theatre are even more potentially dangerous. Of course, drama falls within the area of belles lettres and is subject to all interpretation and censorship of any other literary genre In addition, however, there are many more moods and intonations which may be superimposed on the drama when it is performed on the stage Obviously, the statement that "Gorbachev is a great leader!" may be voiced in many different ways, some of which may convey a meaning which is diametrically opposite to the written word. Censorship is also more difficult since the performance in the presence of an official observer may be straight, and in his absence quite different. Added to this is the fact that the theater-going public in the USSR is immense and that playwrights, actors and especially directors have a very large following.

During the Stalin-era the theatre-going audience was starved for decent performances which showed some semblance of character development and internal conflict. Instead, they were shown only steely-eyed "leather men" and black or white situations which existed only to support Stalins policies and interpretations. The only non-didactic performances were simple, even infantile, humorous sketches in which obvious targets such as the United States, tsarists and the church were vilified. Playwrights who attempted to produce anything with depth, were not published. Many did not even try to publish, but wrote "for the drawer."

During the "Thaw" of 1953-55, many plays suddenly appeared out of the drawer and were published in numerous minor publications, books and journals. A number of these plays were concerned with satire - a genre sorely neglected during preceeding years. Most plays, however, delved into a subject area which was previously out of bounds - the fallibility of even high Soviet officials and the injustices resulting from the misuse of authority and the desire to accumulate wealth. Among the best known examples of such plays were The Guests by Leonid Zorin and A Personal Affair by Aleksandr Shtein. This was also the time of the emergence of two giants of post-Stalinist drama, who are still writing today: Aleksei Arbuzov with his Years of Wandering and Victor Rozov with his Good Luck! Both plays make attempts at psychological development and are amply endowed with negative characters whose self-centered and ruthless-qualities were difficult to find in plays of the Stalin era

During the several years following the "Thaw," playwrights attempted to capitalize on the new "liberalism." In the spirit of Dr. Zhivago playwrights elaborated on the individuality of their characters and man's right to internal privacy. Nikolai Pogodin's A Petrarchan Sonnet is probably the best example of this period, closely followed by Samuil Aleshin's Alone. Possibly the most successful play of the period was Rozov's Alive Forever which was subsequently made into a film (The Cranes are Flying). Although on the surface it may appear to be cut from the same pre-thaw mold, and it really is a patriotic play about World War II, the character-development and the weaknesses present in several of the main characters, set it aside as an excellent example of the "new realism." Aleksandr Volodin's Five Evenings is interesting in that it is narrative without any ideological thrust. Arbuzov's Irkutsk Story seems to be a rather superficial romantic drama which takes place in a typical setting of cranes and excavators. Nevertheless it was highly successful. Later plays by Arbuzov, including The Lost Son, The Happy Days of an Unhappy Man and My Poor Marat (entitled The Promise in New York productions) were also extremely successful and eminently theatrical.

In the 1960's and early 1970's a number of dissident writers also tried their hand at plays which were, obviously, never staged in the Soviet Union. These included Andrei Amalrik who wrote six plays, mostly one-acters in the vein of absurdist theatre. Also included must be the three plays of Solzhenitsyn (Candle in the Wind; The Feast of Conquerors and, the best, The Love-Girl and the Innocent) which further develop the same themes contained in his novels. The most bitter satire and parody is evident in Andrei Remezov's Is There Life on Mars? which centers on Soviet anti-Semitism under the guise of minority affairs on Mars as viewed through a telescope from Earth.

Rozov continued writing plays during this period and produced one of his most successful, "Class Reunion," which exposes the socio-political and economic development of its characters over a twenty-year period and questions the true meaning of success in life. Volodin, whose Factory Girl was quite successful, wrote Never Part From Your Loved Ones, probably his best and most theatrical play, about the below-surface emotional relationship between a young couple. Another eminently romantic plot was in Valentin and Valentina by Mikhail Roshchin, one of the biggest Soviet box office hits, depicting the emotional stresses of a very young couple deeply in love. Roshchin's Echelon, his best play, was successfully staged in Houston (Alley Theatre) in 1977. The action takes place in a boxcar in which people of diverse backgrounds are being evacuated during World War II.

One of the most interesting playwrights of the period, Aleksandr Vampilov, died unexpectedly in 1972 Although he was quite prolific, two plays require special attention: Duck Hunting was successfully performed at the Arena Stage in Washington, D.C. in 1978, and is still constantly on the playbill in the USSR. It depicts the weakness, egoism and lack of direction of the young Russian and is pervaded with farcical and ironic elements. The other play, Last Summer in Chulimsk, is undoubtedly his best. It, also is constantly performed. It is a "slice-of-life" play in which several people from all walks of life are made to interact with frustrating, ennervating and destructive results.

Chingiz Aitmatov's and Kalai Mukhamedzhanov's Ascent of Mount Fuji is a most attractive and theatrical play which is alledgedly based on the true story of the persecution of a well-known poet (Bulat Okudzhava) by the Soviets It portrays individual and collective guilt and the egoistic drive for self-preservation. The play was performed by Arena Stage in 1975 and is being itermittently performed on the Soviet Stage.

Vasilii Aksenov wrote two full-length plays, Your Murderer and Always on Sale. Both are totally out of character with the plays presently written and produced in the USSR. They are grotesque, phantastic and symbolic, and often hard to understand. They attempt contact with western dramatic traditions, e.g. Ionesco and Brecht, much more so than other plays written before or since For this reason they have never been published, although Always on Sale was staged in Moscow for a very short time

The recent period saw the emergence of new playwrights with considerable talent, the foremost of whom is probably Edvard Radzinskii. His play Conversations with Socrates develops the inter-personal relationship between Socrates, his betrayers, his wife and his hypocritical followers. His play I, Mikhail Sergeevich Lunin is based on a real key figure in the Decembrist Uprising of 1825 and has obvious strings connected to the present day. It is also beautifully theatrical and profoundly, powerfully effective His most recent play was Theatre in the Time of Nero.

Liudmilla Petrushevskaia is the leading woman playwright in the USSR although, at this writing, she really has not yet gained a nation-wide reputation. Her plays Love, Come Into the Kitchen and Cinzano, are powerful indictments of the young intelligentsia and the superficiality of the self-seeking new Soviet middle class. She has great talent and a fine future if she can remain uncorrupted.

An older playwright, Rozov, must also again be mentioned here. His Nest of the Wood Grouse which was performed at the Kennedy Center, is probably his best play. He depicts the dishonesty, destructive competitiveness and moral perversion of the Soviet upper class No wonder Rozov was severely chastized for this play and is now no longer in favor.

In general, someone who appreciates western drama, or even East European dramas such as Polish, would find Soviet drama to be stagnant, listless and far behind normal evolution. It should be remembered, however, that there are significant exceptions and that the Soviet playwright has labored under much more severe restrictions than his western counterparts

At the present time there are 567 professional theaters in the USSR, including 372 drama and musical comedy theaters, 42 opera and ballet stages and 152 children's theaters. The annual theater audience is approaching 120 million. Nearly all Soviet theaters are repertory theaters with their own troop, their own permanent building and an average repertory of 15 plays including both classics and contemporary dramatic works. There are also a limited number of traveling repertory theaters which were formed to bring culture to the more remote rural areas. Normally these troops are made up of young, aspiring actors or of third-rate older performers who have been downgraded from permanent stages. All theaters receive a reasonable subsidy from the State

Similar to New York, Moscow is the theater-center of the Soviet Union. There are 29 major legitimate stages in Moscow, most of which are open at any given time The following is a listing of the most important of them:

a. The Malyj Theatre is generally considered to be a "museum" rather than a live stage Its director, Vladimir Andreev, formerly of the Ermolova Theatre, is old, untrained and unimaginative. The only lively elements are the guest performances by ensembles of theatres outside of Moscow.

b. The New Stage of MXAT has experienced considerable revitalization under its present director Oleg Efrejmov who is not afraid of innovative staging and the selection of plays by controversial playwrights.

c. The Ermolova Theatre has traditionally become known as an unimaginative house which relied mainly on Russian and foreign classics that were politically fully acceptable. This perception has changed this season because of the work of the new director, Valerii Fokin.

d The Malaja Bronnaja Theatre is totally ineffectual, primarily due to the incompetence of director Evgenii Lazarev, a former actor.

e The Taganka does not fare much better, but is simply banking on its former reputation which it no longer deserves.

f. The Vaxtangov has an excellent cast but has found a bad director in Evgenii Simonov. It has a much better reputation than it deserves.

g. The Majakovskij Theatre has adopted cheap effects and a low artistic level. Its director, Andrei Goncharov, is an old man who has little competence or imagination to offer.

h. The Komsomol Theatre is on the rise, primarily due to the talent and courage of its director Mark Zakharov.

i. The Gogol' Theatre is not faring well under a director, Boris Golubovskii, who will gladly accept any play offered him. There is some hope for the theatre with the help of an energetic, young director, Dolgochev.

j. The Theatre of Satire has an excellent cast and a good repertoire. However, its director, Valentin Pliucek, is mediocre at best and has little taste or courage.

k. The Mossovet Theatre has become one of the least interesting houses under the uninspired direction of Pavel Khomskii, who has recently had one failure after another.

l. The Sovremennik Theatre has a good future under its present director, Galina Volchok, the only woman permanently assigned that position in a major theatre. She is courageous, innovative, and not afraid to show the work of controversial playwrights.

m. The Puskin Theatre has done little innovative or exceptional under its mediocre director, Boris Morozov.

n. The Stanislavskii Theatre is one of the most interesting at the present due to its energetic director Aleksandr Tovstonogov.

Examples from
The 1987 Theatre Season in Moscow

The past two decades the Ermolova Theater, located in the heart of Moscow on Gorkii Street, a few steps from the Kremlin, has been considered a rather conservative house which never displayed any innovative motivation. This was changed virtually overnight. Today its tickets are among the most difficult to obtain. The reason for this change is the new managing director, Valerii Fokin.

Not that he is that outstanding an artist — rather, what he has been doing coincides with the political objectives of the new Soviet leadership. The two most successful plays of the season are a case in point.

The first play is Speak out! (Govori...). According to the announcements, the play was written by Aleksandr Buravskii, based on the themes of "Raionnye budni" and on segments of the biography of Valentin Ovechkin, its author. It is directed by Fokin himself and has a cast of over 30. The program, one tabloid-size sheet, is quite eye-catching. On one side it has the normal listing of the cast and other pertinent information. The other side is a copy of the edict by the Party concerning land apportionment, dated October 28, 1917.

As the curtain opens, the audience reaction was immediate. On a pedestal, center stage, is a bust of Josef Stalin. (Incidentally, according to one member of the cast, the bust, which was made of papier mache, had to be transported by metro through Moscow. Those involved still recollect the stares of disbelief by the other passengers.) The scene was set right after the Revolution. There are no villains but simply overzealous Party officials whose actions in the agricultural communities of the country often have detrimental effects. Moreover, the people most affected suffer in silence. They refuse to question Party decisions no matter how much they must suffer. This continues on through the decades until the present time. Officiousness coupled with disregard of the effects of actions is just as prevalent today as before. The most humorous scene of the play which evoked a great deal of laughter from the audience, is the depiction of a district Party meeting. The chairman simply mumbles a catechism of stock phrases. No one really listens — some read newspapers, others sleep, some have personal conversations. At the end of his speech the Party head asks for a vote. Of course, all raise their hands in unanimity He calls for comments from the membership. Of course, no one speaks up.

The end of the play is an appeal to all good communists to voice their opinions openly and freely. That is, to disagree with Party proposals whenever they feel that they are erroneous. This, of course, is not heretical or even revisionist — it is simply an illustration of Gorbachev's insistence on "glasnost."

The second play at the Ermolova is much more subtle and effective The Last Visitor (Poslednii posetitel) was written by Vladlen Dozortsev and directed by Mikhail Tsitriniak in conjunction with Valerii Fokin. It has only a cast of five There are no scene changes. The entire action takes place on a set depicting the office of the First Deputy Minister of Health. As the curtain opens, we see the minister and his assistant, a physician, getting ready to go home. A clerk enters and announces that there are two persons who are still waiting outside for an audience. The minister agrees to see them. It is a man and a woman -- she is the wife of the central subject of the play, while he is simply an interlocutor whose specific function and background are never defined in the play. It seems that the woman's husband had become ill, had been taken away by ambulance, and that she had lost all trace of him within the health care system. She had turned to a journalist for help and had also obtained documents which indicated her husbands need for surgery, and also the possibility of gross negligence by the system. As the play progresses, the verbal fencing between the male visitor and the assistant heightens. There is a clear impression that things are not as they should be. Finally, the visitors agree to leave behind all the documentation in return for the assurance by the minister of the patient's well being, that he will receive the surgery which he requires, and that he will be reunited with his wife very soon. After the visitors leave, the minister and his assistant discuss the matter and make a few telephone calls. The result is one which the chief of staff, quite obviously, had been aware of all along. The man in question had died two weeks earlier as a result of the wrong medical care and other malfeasance. There had been a gigantic cover-up which would be perpetuated by the minister and his assistant in their future actions on this case.

This is a much more dangerous play than the first one, since it undermines the trust of the viewer in an agency which has control over his physical well-being Nevertheless, it fits in excellently with Gorbachev's anti-corruption campaign and was therefore permitted to be shown.

Three examples of the new Soviet approach to Jewish themes on the Moscow stage should also be included here:

On several previous occasions, the Jewish Musical Cameo Theater (JMCT), the principal music group in Birobidzhan, has come to Moscow to perform before a prodominantly Jewish audience The 1987 season was no exception. What was definitely different was that the posters advertising the events were pasted on billboards in several conspicuous places right in the center of Moscow. Also, tickets, which previously could be obtained only at the box office, were easily available at numerous theatre kiosks throughout the city. In addition, quite a number of non-Jews were in attendance at these performances which alas, were of mediocre quality at best. There were evenings of traditional Jewish folk music, and also a gala performance of an operetta called Anatevka which was primarily based on the Broadway musical Fiddler on the Roof. Its success was primarily due to the fact that for the first time, Soviet Central Television aired this performance in 1986 during prime time under the title Tevye the Milkman. It was estimated that approximately 100 million Soviets watched it. There seems to be a plan afoot to use the JMCT as proof to the outside world that the Jews do enjoy full rights in the USSR. One example of this is a four-page spread on the JMCT, with photographs, in the September, 1986 issue of the official Soviet publication Soviet Life.

The next example, the performance of Five Stories by Isaak Babel (Piat Rasskazov I. Babelia) was quite different. It is one of the major plays of the 1987 season being performed on the main stage of the Taganka Theater which is know as one of the most innovative houses in Moscow, particularly under the strong leadership of Iurii Liubimov who is now an expatriate. Isaak Babel, one of the finest prose writers of the early Soviet period who was later eliminated by Stalin, was partially resurrected after Stalin's death. He has traditionally been considered the outstanding representative of the Odessa school of Jewish writers. Although the Soviets admit to his existence, it is truly impossible to buy his works which are printed in only very small editions. It was therefore a rare threat to attend a performance in which theatrical versions of four of his short stories were presented The audience was predominantly non-Jewish, but thoroughly enjoyed the play, the small group of musicians who played traditional Jewish music in a lively rhythm, and even the constant references to "our people" in the script. The play was not particularly good. There was virtually no improvisation since all the lines were taken directly from Babel's stories. Also, the four stories chosen, were politically the most harmless ("Konkin," "Evening," "The Story of My Dovecot," and

"Awakening"). Nevertheless, the official resurrection of Babel and his Jewish themes was a "first" and was therefore considered a precedent by the audience. The director is Efim Kucher, a young man who didn't even rate having his name mentioned in the printed program.

Our third and final example is by far the most significant. It is the repertory performance of No. 40 Sholem Aleikhem Street (Ulitsa Sholom Aleikhema, dom 40), written by Arkadii Stavitskii. The performance is at one of the major Moscow houses, the Stanislavsky Theater. The overall responsibility for production is that of the principal director A. G. Tovstonogov who himself has won a number of major awards, and who is also the son of G. Tovstonogov, certainly the most respected director in the Soviet Union today. He was ably assisted by a younger director - A. Rafikov. Although the Stanislavsky Theater is a comparatively large house, there were literally thousands of people on the street begging for tickets It seemed as if the major portion of the Jewish population of Moscow was there. The theme of the play was a fascinating one, since it was totally unexpected and unprecedented. As soon as the premise became clear, there were gasps of disbelief from the audience that the censors permitted it to be performed.

The action takes place in a Jewish section of Odessa, in the home of what would here be called an upper-middle-class Jewish family. The members of this family consist of an elderly, typically Jewish woman (even her Russian had a strong Jewish inflection), the main role of the play, superbly portrayed by R. Bykova; her husband, an old man who is still working in the local government and who loves his everyday existence and doesn't want it to change; an older son, a professional who is quite successful, whose daughter is attractive, but a punker who has gotten into bad company; a younger son who is a talented surgeon but who cannot get the advancement he deserves -- it is implied that his being a Jew holds him back unfairly. The two sons decide that they can no longer cope with Soviet society and decide to emigrate to the United States via Israel.

This causes extreme disruption within the family. Although the mother loves her home, she decides to leave with her children. Her granddaughter doesn't want to leave, partly because she rebels against all authority, but particularly because she is ambivalent about a young man who is right before his doctoral examination in the sciences, and who is in love with her. The grandfather is totally shocked by the plan and absolutely refuses to tear himself away from the home. He makes references to how terrible it used to be for the Jews (obviously under Stalin) compared to how things are now, and how they all fought together against the nazis. Nevertheless he realizes that, in the final outcome, he will have to accompany his family. Near the end of the play he commits suicide. His wife stays behind as her moral commitment to him. The rest of the family departs. The young scientist continues professing his love for the young girl although he realizes, as does his father, that his career is over because of this "anti-Soviet" attachment. The entire family is destroyed.

The play is filled with innuendos and unvoiced commentary on the position of the Jews in the USSR. For example, the centerpiece of the apartment is a large breakfront which has been in the family for generations. The mother, who is extremely attached to it, realizes that she will have to leave it behind. She therefore offers it as a gift to several of her non-Jewish neighbors. They all refuse although it is a handsome piece of furniture, virtually unobtainable on the Soviet market. Their refusal, although never stated in so many words, is based on their conviction that the possession of property bestowed upon them by enemies of the state (as all emigrants are), would have negative repercussions upon their lives.

Another interesting relationship in the play is the one which the family has with the janitor, a man in his late eighties, who used to be a nobleman and an officer in the White Army during the Civil War. He subtly but clearly finds a greater meeting of the minds with the Jews than with the new "Soviet Man."

Of course the play cannot be more outspoken because it would not have passed the censorship otherwise Nevertheless, despite some minor faults, it is a courageous, artistically superb drama and, in the eyes of most Moscow theatre-goers, a milestone in the constant fight between playwright/director and the Party.

The houses which primarily produce musical programs include:

a. The Bolshoi Theatre, for opera and ballet.
b. The Palace of Congresses, for opera and ballet.
c. The Stanislavskii and Nemirovich-Danchenko Musical Theatre, for opera and ballet
d. The Chamber Music Theatre
e. Chaikovskii Hall

Children's and puppet theatres include:

a. The Central Children's Theatre.
b. The Young Playgoer's Theatre
c. The Children's Musical Theatre
d. The Obraztsov Puppet Theatre
e. The Puppet Theatre

All the theaters listed above are located in the city of Moscow. In all fairness, two theatres in Leningrad must be added to this list.

a. The Pushkin Theatre: This is the former Aleksandrinskii Theatre It had declined during the late Tsarist and early Soviet period but was called back to life by a series of plays directed by Georgii Tovstonogov. It is now one of the principal stages of the USSR

b. The Gorky Theatre: Again, Tovstonogov played a definite part making it an important stage through his revivals of Three Sisters and The Inspector General which were said to be superior to Moscow staging.

As is well known, the circuses in the USSR are of superior quality especially in the choreography of the acts and in artistic excellence The same may be said of its ice skating reviews

Soviet Ballet, especially of the Kirov Theatre in Leningrad and the Bolshoi in Moscow, is of the finest possible quality. The techniques are flawless. One may see a performance of Swan Lake one year, return the next year, and not a single motion has been altered. There is absolutely no innovative spirit in this art form which accounts for the many defections of ballet artists to the west.

Shostakovich and Khachaturian are dead Among the younger Generation of composers, the following may be listed: M. Blanter; I. Dunaevskii; N. Bogoslavskii; Kara Karaev; A. Aleksandrov; the Pokrass Brothers; R. Shchedrin; V. Soloviev-Sedoi; A. Ostrovskii; B. Mokrusov; A. Novikov; E. Kolmanovskii; T. Khrennikov; and A. Pakhmutova.

There are 133 philharmonic societies and 652 musical groups in the country. Each year they present more than a half million concerts attended by more than 250 million persons.

Moscow and Leningrad also have frequent guest performances by other national groups. This includes Gypsy musicians, Georgian dancers, Armenian singers and Kazakh actors Russians, especially, enjoy these programs and also vaudeville presentations. Of course, the youth would rather go to a rock concert or listen to rock records which bring a high price on the black market. There are numerous concerts by foreign artists, e.g. Elton John, which are sold out as soon as they are announced.

By far, however, the most frequently visited form of entertaiment are films. The Soviets turn out many films of extremely low calibre - civil war films depicting evil Tsarists; World War II films about nasty German spies; and more contemporary films about rapacious western capitalists. Every once in a while, however, there are superb films produced The three great, original talents who did so much for silent films and laid the groundwork for the film industry of the West, Eisenstein, Pudovkin and Dovzhenko, all had their roots in pre-revolutionary times. Although they lived for a considerable time after the revolution (Eisenstein died in 1948 and Dovzhenko in 1956), they were virtually put out to pasture during the Stalin period. Nevertheless their influence was profound on the next Soviet generation of filmmakers which included Sergei Iutkevich, Iosif Geifits and Mark Donskoi, all of whom are now approaching old age.

"Soviet Film Under Gorbachev"

A few current statistics would help to bring Soviet cinematographic activity into better focus. The Soviet film industry is headed and managed by the USSR State Committee for Cinema, better known as GOSKINO. Its governing board is appointed by the USSR Council of Ministers to which it is accountable. GOSKINO supervises the management of film studios, motion picture theaters, other cinematic enterprises, and film distribution and exhibition Since it is responsible for the selection of scripts and all facets of production and distribution down to the number of copies to be made of each finished product, it acts as the primary censorship authority and is closely supervised by the Party.

At the present time there are thirty-nine major, permanent film studios in the USSR. Each of the fifteen Union Republics houses at least one such studio in its capital. Of course, the more important and densely populated republics have more than one studio -- for example, the RSFSR has five and the Ukraine three. These thirty-nine studios presently produce approximately 150 full-length feature films annually, of which thirty-five are created in the MOSFILM Studios in Moscow. Additionally, about one hundred films for television and a total of 1,450 short films, documentaries, popular science films and cartoons are also released every year. The daily Soviet attendance at motion picture theatres is approximately 12 million, which clearly supports Lenin's declaration that "film is the most important art " The average cost of admission, depending on the length of the film, is either forty or eighty kopeks. There are 153,000 motion picture theatres in the Soviet Union of which 16,500 are in urban and 126,500 in rural areas. One hundred thousand of these have wide-screen capability. There are an additional 71,300 premises not open to the general public (for example, institutional, organizational and educational entities), which show films on a regular basis

The average cost of a normal length ("one-series") film is 600,000 rubles; the "two-series" film costs a million. Films, except for those whose release has been stopped or restricted by the authorities, are expected to earn a profit. Earnings above the cost, and these are often very substantial, go into the State coffers except for the sums that are allocated to pay for equipment, operational costs and expansion of studio facilities. In addition, two and one-half percent of the gross receipts are divided among the director, writer and composer who worked on the film, depending on its genre For example, the composer would get a larger share for a musical. A drama by an important writer who also did the screenplay would assure him of a sizable portion. Often the director himself has written the screenplay and receives the "lion's share" of the funds. This sharing plan has caused some of the top directors, composers and writers to become millionaires.

The salary for actors depends on their politics, popular appeal, experience and professional training. The base pay for extras is six rubles a day. The actors above this level are classified into several pay categories. The maximum salary for a top actor is 3,500 rubles for a one-series film. This low figure is misleading for several reasons. The average Soviet film is made in a much shorter time than its American counterpart. In addition, if the film receives any of the Soviet or foreign cash awards, the monies are distributed among the actors and staff. Top actors, artistic staff and technical personnel receive end-of-year bonuses which often exceed their annual salaries. Members of the film industry in top positions enjoy substantial privileges: Foreign travel, special housing, access to special stores, automobiles, summer homes, etc.

Of course film, as all other arts in the Soviet Union, must follow whatever political direction that is propagated at any given time. The present is no different and should be understood in the light of the objectives and style of Mikhail Gorbachev. It is no longer acceptable to paint the governing authorities only in rosy colors. Nor is it enough to produce propagandistic works which tell ludicrous stories which are of little interest to and are believed by no one. Too many are based on the traditional eternal triangle of girl loves boy, boy loves tractor, girl eventually loves tractor too. The average Soviet urban citizen in the late 1980s is much too sophisticated for this. The audience insists on increased preoccupation with the private life of the individual and his personal hopes, aspirations, and internal and interpersonal conflicts Contrary to official doctrine, the more courageous writers and directors want to point out that the life of the individual is the prime element of importance which, in turn, fashions the life of the collective, and not the doctrinaire reverse. This is the period of rejuvenation for some of the outstanding older directors including Danelia, Ioseliani, Konchalovskii, Chkheidze, Shengelaia, Abuladze and others; and the emergence of highly talented younger directors including Gubenko, Nakhapetov, Nikonenko, Tsilinskii, Liubshin, Menshov, Kozakov, Mikolaichuk, Grammatikov, Burliaev and Tokarev.

One must understand why Gorbachev is permitting these highly sensitive subjects to be portrayed. He is fighting corruption. He is fighting the Stalinists and other ultra-conservatives. He is trying to prove to the West that limited freedom of speech can exist in the USSR. His primary intent, however, is to woo the intellectual and artistic community -- the people of his own social class.

During the Party Congress in March, 1986, virtually nothing was said about the arts. Filmmakers and theatre directors dispaired For six months there was a lull in innovative production. Then, a long list of events occurred which gave them new hope:

a. Highly controversial plays were permitted to be performed on the stage.

b. The reactionary Minister of Culture, Demichev, was removed from his position. A Council for the Arts was created with Raisa Gorbacheva as one of its members, which clearly inflated its importance.

c. A number of previously restricted films were released for general consumption, for example, "Agony" which was distributed in the West as "Rasputin," and the anti-Stalinist "Repentance "

d. Several of the most important representatives of the performing arts such as the dean of Soviet stage directors Tovstonogov, and the head of the Filmmakers Union Klimov, spoke out against restrictive censorship methods. More significantly, their comments were printed in national publications.

e. Major figures of the Soviet cinema and their products were brought back from oblivion or semi-obscurity -- some posthumously. This included an outstanding film director, Paradzhanov, who was released from prison and has started making films again; and the brilliant writer-director-actor Vasilii Shukshin who had died a decade earlier.

f. The kind words that are being spoken in the USSR about defectors such as Soviet theatre director Iurii Liubimov and the brilliant film director Andrei Tarkovskii who died in Paris in 1987.

g. The increased volume of artistically innovative non-Russian films. As in all the arts, the further away one is from Moscow, the more daring one may be. This is certainly true of the Baltic Republics but is most applicable to Georgia. Fortunately, even MOSFILM and other RSFSR studios have had to recognize this high quality of talent and have availed themselves of the services of some of the best Georgian directors for many of their most successful films, among them Abuladze, Chkheidze, Danelia, Gaidai, Kalatozov, Khutsiev, Kobakhidze, Shengelaia, Ioseliani and others. Important Lithuanian directors include Krumin, Vabalas, Zalakevicius and Zhebriunas.

Now let us turn to a discussion of several films which have been distributed since 1984. In general, among the latest examples of Soviet films, with few exceptions, there are few worthwhile products. Gorbachev's most recent edicts have not yet had time to affect the industry's products. There is another rash of World War II films, since this is a relatively safe subject. The most interesting of this genre, released in January 1985, entitled "Marshall Zhukov -- Biographical

Pages", was directed and written by M. Babak. It is a semi-documentary of the now fully rehabilitated, controversial World War II general. This period also produced many comedies which were the biggest box-office hits. There were also a number of espionage thrillers starring the KGB, in an attempt to humanize it in the eyes of the public — a feat never previously attempted The best example is a serialized film for television which was avidly watched by everyone, entitled "TASS is Authorized to Report."

One of the most astonishing films "The Blonde Around the Corner," directed by Vladimir Bortko, was released in 1984. It is about the underground world of black market, under-the-counter favors, influence peddling, and all other forms of economic and social corruption. Natasha, the blonde, works in a government food supermarket. The audience receives a view of the back room which is filled with all desirable delicacies while the open shelves in front are nearly empty. The scope widens with promises of automobiles, trips abroad, summer homes and other virtually unattainable luxuries. Natasha's answer to all requests is "No problem!" Of course, there is a happy ending when Natasha is shown the error of her ways by her upright boyfriend and his simple, patriotic, hard-working parents. She drops her sinful ways to take her place in the building of communism in Siberia -- this, incidentally, caused quite a bit of cynical laughter among Soviet audiences. The film was originally condoned by Gorbachev's mentor, Andropov, as part of the anti-corruption campaign which is continuing now.

Another recent film, "The Legend of Princess Olga," was directed by the Ilienko brothers at the Dovzhenko studios in Kiev. It is an extremely expensive, three-hour-long production, an historical pageant patterned after the Russian Primary Chronicle. Its significance lies in its obvious Ukrainian nationalism.

"A Thorny Path to the Stars" of 1985 is the Soviet answer to "Star Wars." It was directed by Rikhard Viktorov and contains many special effects never before used in Soviet films. Contrary to normal procedures, the star was not a trained actress but was discovered in the sweater section of the GUM department store in Moscow where she worked as a salesgirl. The film bears a clear anti-war message.

Evgenii Evtushenko directed his first film, "The Kintergarten," (released in 1985), an autobiographical study of his wartime evacuation to Siberia as a child. It created a sensation because it contains two nude scenes and the highly reverential treatment of a rabbi. There are also some surrealistic scenes, for example, Russian soldiers marching with rifles and carrying goldfish bowls to a slow-motion cadence. There is an unusually sympathetic portrayal of a nazi officer played by Klaus Maria Brandauer. The film received only a three-line announcement in the major Soviet film periodical.

"Wartime Romance" completed by Petr Todorovskii in late 1984, is particularly attractive because it is totally devoid of propaganda. In fact, the initial scenes at the front lines during World War II do not portray heroes, but a young woman who is being kept by a major as his mistress. Most of the film takes place in Moscow after the war and portrays the infatuation of a meek, married schoolteacher for this uncouth, immoral mistress. The film has all the successful ingredients — tears, nostalgia, melancholy and a good amount of gentle humor It was one of the Academy Award nominees for best foreign film of 1984.

Quite different is "Begin at the Beginning" directed by Aleksandr Stefanovich and released in 1986. It features Vladimir Vysotskii's songs and stars Andrei Makarevich, the leader of the top Soviet rock group "Time Machine." In the film, officials and critics accuse Makarevich of leading Soviet youth into "hooliganism" and implore him to follow the example of his more cooperative, conformist contemporaries who have earned official acceptance. He rejects this path, allies himself with underground poets, and even defends the memory of Vysotskii in a fistfight.

"Repentance" directed by Tengiz Abuladze was first screened in November, 1986 for select audiences in Moscow and Tbilisi where it was made. The film clearly attempts to face the horrors perpetrated under the Stalin regime although Stalin himself never appears in it. The principal character, however, is clearly recognizable as Lavrentii Beria, Stalin's secret police chief. Although, in the final scene, everything turns out to have been just a dream, the message is clear: the actions of the past cannot be buried but must be discussed and, when appropriate, condemned. The film is to be distributed to 150 selected urban theatres in February, 1987.

READINGS

Hecht, Leo, (ed.) NEWSNOTES on Soviet and East European Theatre and Drama. All issues. NEH subsidized. George Mason University, Fairfax, VA 22030.

Krebs, Stanley D. Soviet Composers and the Development of Soviet Music. New York: W. W. Norton, 1970.

Leyda, Jay. Kino: A History of the Russian and Soviet Film. London: Allen and Unwin, 1960.

Marshall, Herbert. The Pictorial History of the Russian Theatre. New York: Crown Books, 1977.

Ruehle, Juergen. Theater und Revolution. Munich: DTV, 1963.

Segel, Harold B. Twentieth Century Russian Drama. New York: Columbia University Press, 1979.

Velekhova, Nina. Moscow Theatres. Moscow: Planeta, 1979.

Zis, Avner. Foundations of Marxist Aesthetics. Moscow: Progress, 1977.

XXIII. Religion

When a Soviet philosopher is asked for the reasons why the Soviet Union is so strongly opposed to religion on a philosophical basis, he will be full of answers and explanations which may be read in every Soviet primer. Religion is reactionary by definition; it is ancient superstition which has been converted into a dogmatic system; it is based on irrationality and refuses to allow itself to be asked sensible questions on the basis that man is too ignorant to understand the answers. Religion cloaks itself in piety but has been responsible for more bloodshed than any other force on earth. Even in times of relative quiet, religion lulls mankind into a sense of false security and offers a cloak of protection in return for blind faith. In order to be able to continue its soporific function it allies itself with the most reactionary forms of government.

It is not the intent of this chapter to discuss the relative merits of these arguments. Suffice it to say, that they reflect good Marxist-Leninist doctrine. The main point is, however, that be they true or not, they are not the real main reason why religion is so strongly combatted. The honest reason is that religion competes with the State and a totaliterian state cannot bear such competition which would be contradictory to the central concept of "control." There cannot be any entity outside the jurisdiction of the Party and, religion, if practiced correctly, would be such an entity. Therefore, it must be combatted and, if possible, eradicated at all cost. The Soviet Law Concerning Religious Associations which was originally published in April, 1929 and completely revised in June, 1975, attempts to accomplish this by making it extremely difficult for any Soviet citizen to express his religious faith.

The key to understanding the problems religion faces in the USSR is contained in Article 52 of the Constitution which states that the State must be separated from the Church and the Church from the school. It further assures two freedoms: Freedom of religious worship and freedom of anti-religious propaganda. These two freedoms are not equal There is no freedom of pro-religious propaganda. Religion is not supported by the State, but anti-religion is heavily supported. Not only is there freedom of anti-religious activity, but it is the political obligation of every good communist to combat religious influence. In addition, especially in urban areas, younger citizens become laughing stocks or social outcasts if they profess to be devoutly religious. More importantly, it is very difficult for an individual to obtain professional or social advancement if it is known that he is religious. Not only does the State not support the Church materially, but does everything in its power to reduce its material possessions. More and more churches are being closed to services and being changed into museums at the whim of the State More and more works of religious art are removed from the churches and transported to urban places of exhibition. Even more insidiously, some major churches have been converted into Museums of Atheism; the beautiful Cathedral of Kazan' in Leningrad is an excellent but sad example of such a fate Another example, a small eighteenth century church along the Moskva River, in the shadow of the Kremlin, has been converted into a motorcycle club. Far from being democratic, the treatment of the churches in the USSR is purely suppressive.

The Constitution also states that "Incitement of hostilities or hatred on religious grounds is forbidden." The unsuspecting reader may interpret this to be for the protection of the devout, and, of course, a few token instances are thus enforced. In the vast majority of cases, however, the reverse application is employed. It is the religious person who more often than not incites hostility by his opposition to a system of beliefs and mores which is accepted by the socialist majority of his society. It is also considered an incitement to hatred if the religious person attempts to teach his values to the very young to be used to hurt society as a whole. On the other hand, Western observers should not make the mistake based on observing overflowing crowds in churches on major holidays like Easter, that there is a resurgence of religious feeling in the USSR. One should remember that, if most of the churches are closed for services, the remainder will naturally overflow. On days other than holidays, one will see virtually exclusively old women at church services. This is especially the case in major urban areas. Religion in the USSR has always been strongest in the rural setting.

The following are the major churches and denominations operating in the Soviet Union today:

a. The Russian Orthodox Church: This is by far the largest church in the nation. The Patriarch and head of the Holy Synod is Pimen who has an administrative office in Moscow and his religious seat in the beautiful Saint Sergius complex in Zagorsk. The patriarchate is considered by many to be a figurehead position dependent upon the whims of the State, and with no power to make any decisions outside of very narrow religious boundaries. This is why this religion is tolerated more than others. The church is divided into a number of dioceses both in the USSR and in foreign lands (e.g., in France, USA and Austria). Only five seminaries are still open, the largest one being in Zagorsk The number of students is severely restricted. Although most devout orthodox Soviets accept things as they are, there have been tenacious rumors that in several geographic areas priests have been openly protesting against governmental infringements upon church rights There have been quite a number of arrests and a considerable number of banishments from priestly assignments. Nevertheless the number of petitions to various governmental and Party agencies by the disaffected church-going public has increased dramatically in recent years. This is not proof that the church is strengthening its ranks, but only that it has become more vocal.

b. The Old Believers: This is a group which separated from the official Russian Orthodox Church during the great schizm in the seventeeth century, and formed its own church. It still has a surprisingly large number of adherents in the USSR and abroad, with significant pockets in the Moscow vicinity and the northern regions of the RSFSR, the Baltic Republics, the Ukraine and Belorussia.

c. The Georgian Orthodox Church: Theoretically this church is a separate denomination with its own Patriarch, David V, whose seat is in Tbilisi, the capital of Georgia In reality, it is administratively completely subordinated to the Patriarch of the Russian Orthodox Church, and severely persecuted by the latter. In fact, it retains only a small number of churches and a handful of clergy. In addition, it no longer has its own seminary and is dependent on other denominations for its young clergy.

Chart 37

PRINCIPAL RELIGIOUS GROUPS IN THE SOVIET UNION

	Religion	Where Majority of Membership Found
1.	Russian Orthodox	Russia, Eastern Ukraine, Byelorussia.
2.	Moslems	Central Asia: Kazakh, Uzbek Tadzhik, Turkmen, and Kirghiz SSR's. Caucasus: Azerbaidzhan SSR. Crimea.
3.	Roman Catholic	Western Ukraine, Lithuania.
4.	Catholic of the Eastern Rite (Uniate)	Western Ukraine.
5.	Protestant	Latvia, Estonia, larger cities.
6.	Jewish	Birobidzhan, Byelorussia, Ukraine, larger cities.
7.	Armenian Christian Georgian Christian	Armenia, Georgian SSR's.
8.	Buddhist	Buryat.

9. Others:

   a. Old Believers (Russian Orthodox Sect).

   b. Denominations identified with small national groups (mostly local modifications of Christian or Moslem beliefs).

   c. Pagans.

d. <u>The Armenian Gregorian Church</u>: This is a separate church headed by Patriarch Vazgen I, whose seat is in Echmiadzin (a major monastery located in the outskirts of Erevan, the capital of Armenia) He is an important figure since he is the spiritual leader of not only Soviet Armenians, but also of a considerable number of Armenians living on foreign soil.

e. <u>The Roman Catholic and Uniate Churches</u>: When the USSR incorporated a great deal of Polish land after World War II, they incorporated an area which was predominantly Roman Catholic and Uniate, an Eastern Rite which submits to papal authority. Most of the Catholics and Uniates in the Soviet Union live in the Ukraine, Belorussia, and Lithuania which was historically united with Poland for centuries. There is no central hierarchy for the Roman Catholic or Uniate Church in the USSR. Everything is conducted on a local level. There is strong evidence that the Soviet State has had a great deal of success in forcing a decline in the organization of these churches. There has been a significant decrease in the number of churches, priests and seminaries, in some areas by as much as 80%.

f <u>Islam</u>: There are approximately 40 million Moslems in the Soviet Union, mostly Sunnites. As are most Moslems, the ones in the USSR are relatively devout. Because the USSR, in its international policy, is attempting to show the Moslem world its best face, the Moslems within the country have not been persecuted as have the other religions. Nevertheless, this large population of Moslems must cause the authorities some degree of worry, since there is a great deal of community of culture and social thought among this large segment of the population and because Moslem fundamentalism, e.g. Iran, seems to be on the increase Therefore, although no steps are being taken against the religion, the Soviet powers are engaging in a concerted effort to make the various segments of Moslem population conscious of ethnic and cultural differences rather than similarities. Fragmented and segmented Moslem pockets of population are much less dangerous than a united Moslem populace. One step in this direction was the creation of four independent religious centers:

1 The Moslem Board for the European part of the USSR and Siberia, in Ufa which is the capital of the Bashkir Autonomous Republic.

2. The Moslem Board for Transcaucasia, located in the capital of Azerbaidzhan, Baku.

3. The Moslem Board for Central Asia and Kazakhstan in Tashkent, the capital of the Uzbek SSR.

4. The Moslem Board for the North Caucasus in Buinaksk, Dagestan ASSR.

g. <u>The Evangelical Lutheran Church</u>: Nearly all the members of this church are in Latvia and Estonia. It is estimated that there are at least 800,000 adherents in these Republics. Both Republics are being saturated with Russian immigration, while many young Balts are being offered lucrative careers in Russia. This programmed thinning of the population is starting to hurt church membership

h. The Baptist Church: There are conflicting reports as to membership figures, ranging from 1/2 million to 3 million. This denomination has traditionally been severely persecuted because of the devoutness of its members and the collaboration with Baptists outside the county.

i. Buddhism: It is practiced in the Kalmyk, Buriat and Tuva Autonomous Republics. Since the Soviets do not really consider Buddhism a fully-fledged religion, and since it is practiced only in very remote areas, the authorities have paid relatively little attention to it

j. Smaller demoninations: There are also a limited number of Mennonites, Seventh Day Adventists, Molokans, Reformists, Methodists and additional splinter groups.

k. Judaism: This religion has been left to the last, since the Soviet consider it to be not a religion but a nationality. It is possible to be both a Catholic and a Ukrainian; or a Baptist and a Russian; or an Orthodox and a Tartar. It is, however, impossible for a Jew to have any nationality listed on his internal passport other than Jewish. This is due to the fact that Birobidzhan has been designated as the Jewish Autonomous Region with all the rights and privileges of any other ethnic AO. Although only slightly more than 20% of the entire population of Birobidzhan is Jewish, it is the home region of the Jews and all the Jews must carry its nationality Since no one in the USSR can have two nationalities, the Jews can never be Russians or Ukrainians or anything other than Jews. This has been an effective means whereby Jews have been eliminated from local politics and from access to national-level posts of authority through an unwritten quota system There are approximately 2 million Jews in the USSR. Approximately one-third of them are attempting to obtain exit visas. Considering that an abnormally high percentage of Soviet intellectuals, engineers and scientists are Jewish, this would constitute a great "brain drain" for the country. In addition, from a purely theoretical point of view, the USSR argues thus about all attempted emigration: Here the society has spent many years and a great deal of money educating and training persons to take their intended positions for the boon of society. Now that their education has been completed, they wish to leave, i.e., deprive society of the service which is due it, and wish to work for another society which is an enemy of socialism. This line of thought is coupled with the important ingredient of a long Soviet history of violent anti-semitism and the realization that Jews constitute the largest segment of the make-up of dissident elements

READINGS

Benningsen, A and Quelquejay, C. Islam in the Soviet Union. New York: Praeger, 1967.

Brizgys, Bishop Vincent. Religious Conditions in Lithuania under Soviet Russian Occupation. Chicago: Lithuanian Catholic Press, 1968.

Conquest, Robert (ed.) Religion in the USSR. London: Bodley Head, 1968.

Galitskaia, I.A. Mysli o religii. Moscow: Gos. izd. polit. lit., 1962.

Goldberg, B.A. The Jewish Problem in the Soviet Union. New York: Crown, 1961.

Hayward, Max and Fletcher, William C. Religion and the Soviet State. New York: Praeger, 1969.

Israel, Gerard. The Jews in Russia. New York: St. Martins Press, 1975.
Kolarz, Walter. Religion in the Soviet Union. New York: St. Martins Press, 962.
Rabinovich, Solomon. Jews in the Soviet Union. Moscow: Novosti Press, undated.
Ro'i, Yaakov, (ed.) The USSR and the Muslim World. Winchester: Allen & Unwin, 1984.
Rubin, Ronald I., (ed.) The Unredeemed: Anti-Semitism in the Soviet Union. Chicago: Quadrangle Books, 1968.
Soviet Jews: Fact and Fiction. 2nd ed. Moscow: Novosti Press, 1972.
Struve, Nikita. Christians in Contemporary Russia. New York: Scribner, 1967.
Ware, Timothy. The Orthodox Church. London: Penguin, 1964.
Wheeler, Geoffrey. Racial Problems in Soviet Muslim Asia. 2nd. ed. London: Oxford University Press, 1962.

XXIV. Philosophy, Morality, Freedom

Before a discussion of Soviet philosophy is possible, a number of concepts and definitions will have to be introduced These are the basic Marxian concepts which were later to be interpreted by Plekhanov, Lenin and other most frequently invoked Russian communist mentors. They are discussed here in the most simple, basic terms:

a. Idealism: The philosophical definition has nothing to do with the lay terms of idealistic behavior. Rather, this is the philosophical concept that it is ideas which run the universe, not material things. In fact, material things are only a reflection of ideas and depend on them for their existence. This concept was expounded by idealist philosophers such as Hegel, Kant, Schelling, Fichte, Schopenhauer and others. Certainly the Marxists reject this philosophy completely, and fully support the opposite concept of materialism.

b. Materialism: Again, the philosophical concept is totally different from the lay definition of materialism and materialistic. This term signifies a direction in philosophy which insists that material things lay the basis for everything else in the universe, including ideas. In other words, first you have material things, then you derive all ideas from them. Material things are the foundation for all human endeavor.

c. Dialectics: This is an ancient concept of the interaction between opposite forces. The Yin-Yang, for example, is symbolized by a circle with an uneven line through its center dividing it into a black and a white half. Each of the two segments, however, also contains a small globule of the opposite; i.e., there is a small sphere of black in the white field, and a small sphere of white in the black field. Everything in the world is divided into opposing forces: black and white; day and night; good and evil; powerful and weak; male and female, etc., ad infinitum. Each force does, however, contain a seed of the opposite force which shows that there is a possibility for change Instead of "being," everything is "becoming."

In Platonic-Socratic philosophy the same idea also arises, specifically in definitions. One person is called upon to define a concept His definition, or statement, or proposal is called the thesis. Another person is called upon to define the same concept, and has a totally opposite definition or point of view. This is called the antithesis. The two are then called upon to discuss their differences and to come up with a single definition acceptable to both sides. This is called the synthesis.

The German idealist philosopher Hegel adopted this Plantonic dialectic and applied it to his philosophical pronouncements. In his view, the world has developed through a series of conflicting ideas. Of course, the Marxists did not agree with his idealism, but definitely accepted Hegel's view that there has been a definite upward movement, i e., that what has been synthesized, is on a higher plane of development than the thesis and antithesis which formed it. The Marxists were definitely favorably inclined towards the optimistic feelings thus expressed. In fact, Hegel is traditionally one of the Soviet Union's favorite western philosophers, and he is frequently erroneously celebrated as the father of dialectics.

d. Dialectic Materialism: If we accept the premise that everything is based on material things; and if we also believe that there is a confrontation and conflict between opposing factors, we will logically arrive at dialectic materialism. This philosophy states that certain material conditions exist; they, in turn, are contradicted by proponents of another material condition; out of this opposition comes a third material conditions, i.e., the synthesis. This synthesis is on a higher plane, that is, some progress in the right direction is already visible. Nevertheless, this synthesis is only a temporary solution. Eventually it will itself become a thesis and will be opposed by an antithesis to form another synthesis which, in turn, will then become a thesis, and so forth. The process is never ending. It is not an evolutionary, but a revolutionary process since we are not talking about something new evolving from something old, but a condition of eternal combat between strongly opposed concepts. The revolution never ends, and after each step a higher plateau has been reached.

The very heart of dialectic materialism is the conviction that the conflict between two sides of a "materialistic," or, in more modern language, "economic" confrontation is the class struggle. The confrontation is always between two classes of opposite economic function. This was true in the beginning of time, between the patriarch and the family; between segments of a clan; between slave holders and slaves; between the feudal lords and serfs; between monarchs and subordinate princes; between the Church and the State; and between many other opposing concepts finally arriving at the ultimate confrontation between the capitalists and the proletariat. Since everything is in motion all the time, there cannot be a static society. There will continue to be change for the better, even after a communist world has been created, and classes no longer exist

In a wider sense, dialectic materialism also forms the basis for all change, not only political and economic After all, everything is a derivitive of economics Certainly the form of government and the state of international relations depend on economics; that is easy to see. But everything else, also, is a direct result of the economic base. All art and music, for example, is either financed by a ruling class, or is a product of those who oppose this ruling class. This is, of course, just as true for palace architecture, or ostentatious bank buildings, or monuments to national leaders and heads of corporations. Religion is also traditionally based on economics. In the early days, the Church was an economic stabilizing force in empires. It is therefore not at all strange that in some nations the Church evolved as the strongest economic force and the largest single landlord. Even in more modern times, the Church is frequently a big business venture For example, certain states supported missionary activities in those areas of the world which were either rich in undeveloped raw materials, or were potential markets Even ethics and morality are constantly changing in accordance with the economic situation prevalent at a given time. In nearly all countries, for example, immorality has increased greatly in proportion to an uncontrolled increase in the standard of living.

Another cornerstone in the philosophy of the Soviet Union is the strong belief in determinism. This means, that the world must function in accordance with economic laws which are inviolate These are the laws of nature in accordance with which the world will move no matter what anyone attempts to do. If a strong force opposes it, it may temporarily delay the inevitable outcome Sooner or later, however, the outcome will be the same, and those who opposed it will be

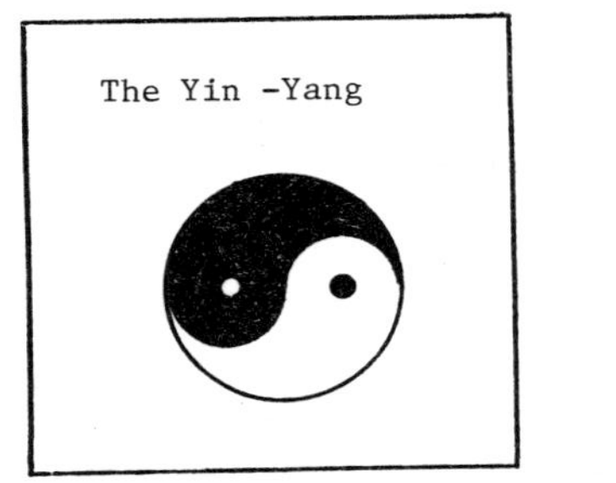

A Diagram of Marxian Dialectics

SYNTHESIS: Communism

THESIS: Reactionary capitalists ⇄ ANTITHESIS: Class-conscious proletariat

SYNTHESIS: Industrial capitalism

THESIS: Reactionary feudal nobility ⇄ ANTITHESIS: Commercial bourgeoisie of rising European towns.

SYNTHESIS: Feudalism

THESIS: Slave-owning elite of classical Rome and Greece ⇄ ANTITHESIS: Invading Germanic tribes of fourth through ninth centuries

Chart 38

destroyed. Anyone who accepts this deterministic philosophy must also accept the fact that freedom can only be highly limited. If everything in the future is scientifically founded and follows the strict rules of economic revolution, then it would logically follow that there could be no freedom, since such freedom would have to do combat with the fact of an inevitable end result. Therefore, the only freedom which any true communist society may admit, is the freedom to recognize the inevitable and to work towards its realization. The freedom to work against the perfection of society cannot be allowed since it temporarily harms society, although the final outcome will be the same There can be no real freedom to defy the laws of nature and the natural upward development of mankind. One cannot believe in the freedom to exploit the masses for the benefit of a few, or to yell "fire" in a crowded theatre. If one is free to believe in and accept the economic laws which govern his existence, one must be able to understand these laws. Therefore, an absolute ingredient of the philosophy of freedom in a communist society must be the education of the masses.

Once the people understand what is good for them, they will no longer be attracted by the momentary pleasures which the "false freedoms" of capitalist societies could afford them. They will realize that useless luxury, pornography, abstract art, the ability to attack openly what is good for them and the ability to support what is bad for them, is not real freedom, but enslavement of the mind It is the Party whose leadership is staffed by persons who have spent their lives studying Marxian philosophy, who will guide the way. They are not to be looked upon as interpreters of Marx, but rather as scientists who are totally altruistic and who can clearly state what the inalienable laws, which they did not themselves devise, are. These are also the leaders who may free communist society from the most harmful so-called freedom of them all, i.e., the freedom to become the slave of a religious doctrine. Religion is a tool which has been devised as a form of economic shackles, and is also highly unscientific The Soviets may, however, be accused of having substituted one religion for another. They have created a Father (Marx), a Son (Lenin) and High Priests (the Central Committee), complete with a holy corpse, relics, temples of communist worship, ikons (the cult of Lenin) and all other paraphernalia normally associated with a primitive religion.

Morality from the Soviet point of view is also diametrically opposed to western concepts. Is it moral to create standards of morality which support the economic status quo to the detriment of the proletariat? It is moral to allow money-making pornographic movie houses which cater to sado-masochistic appetites, but at the same time to condemn people who steal a piece of fruit because they are hungry and cannot afford it? Is it moral to create an entire body of laws, from anti-discrimination to honesty in politics, and then not to pay heed to them if they infringe upon the rights of the leading economic class? Is it moral for wealthy murderers and drug dealers to get suspended sentences while poor people may spend years in jail for lesser transgressions?

Similar questions may be asked as concerns international relations. Is it moral to condemn one nation of crimes against humanity while tacitly supporting other nations whose antisocial activities have been a matter of record for ages? Can there be such a thing as selective morality which condones the transgressions of friends while condemning the misbehavior of international competitors?

There is another side of international ethics which must be seen from the Soviet view simply to understand how they think. Let us say, that they enter into a treaty with the West in 1988. They signed this treaty because it is of benefit to the nation and to society. But let us say that in 1990 the international and economic situation changes, and adherence to this treaty would cause grave damage to the Soviet society. Would it be moral to continue adhering to the principles of this treaty despite the harm that it would do to the Soviet State? In the view of the Soviets, this would not only be hypocrisy, but the height of immorality. Treaties, are created for the benefit of both sides. When one side knows that it is no longer morally feasible to adhere to the provisions of a treaty, it cannot be forced to adhere to them despite the jaded paragraphs in musty tomes on international law.

The most common accusation against the Soviets by the West is the immorality in the treatment of the Soviet citizen by the State. We talk about atrocities, labor camps, suppression, persecution and many other facets which seem to be highly unjust to us Let us not dwell on our own concept of these Soviet acts; they are all very well known to us and justly condemned by us. Let us rather, at this point, try to understand the Soviet rationale which commits these acts and still considers them to be not at all in conflict with the Soviet version of morality.

In the West we have persistently adhered to the adage that it is better that a hundred guilty not be punished rather than to have one innocent unjustly condemned. This view is thoroughly discredited by the Soviet philosophy of morality. The overriding question is not the guilt or innocence of a particular individual, but the effects of certain actions on the totality of society. The individual is only a cell in the social organism which must, according to the laws of nature, practice self-preservation. Whenever the individual is in conflict with society, society must win even if the individual has to be destroyed. Therefore, it is better to condemn a hundred innocent people rather than to let one guilty person go, if this one guilty person can cause a great deal of harm to the organism. One rotten apple will spoil an entire barrel of healthy apples. When a group of persons is rounded up and it is known that one of them is a danger to society, but this one has not been clearly identified, it will be necessary to neutralize the entire group. When a surgeon removes a cancer, he does not very carefully try to follow the outline of the cancerous growth with his scalpel. He deliberately cuts a good portion of healthy tissue and removes it with the cancer in order to make certain that not a single cancerous cell remains. The State must remove all cancers from its healthy body, even if it has to lose healthy tissue. In the long run, this is the only way it can sustain itself. In support of this doctrine the Soviets point with pride to their crime rate when compared with ours.

One thing that any western intellectual will learn very quickly, is that it is extremely difficult to argue with a Soviet intellectual on a philosophical question, and to convince him. The most that the westerner may hope for, is a draw. A great strength of Soviet philosophy is the fact that it has an answer for everything. There are no dubious areas like in western philosophies, or areas which are taboo, like in religion. The Soviets feel very comfortable with their philosophical system and consider it much more logical and much more scientific than any western alternative. It is also extremely optimistic, sometimes even romantically so. For this reason the Soviets have been so successful in swaying so many underdeveloped nations who have been exposed to western economic philosophy for centuries and have developed a strong aversion to it.

READINGS

Ballestrem, Karl G. Russian Philosophical Terminology. Fribourg: "Sovietica," University of Fribourg, 1964.

Basmanov, Mikhail Where are Trotskyites Leading the Youth? Moscow: Novosti Press, 1973.

Blakeley, Thomas J. Soviet Philosophy. Dordrecht: Reidel, 1964.

Davydova, N. S. Na puti k kommunismu. Moscow: Izd. polit. lit, 1968.

De George, Richard T. Soviet Ethics and Morality. Ann Arbor: The University of Michigan Press, 1969.

Dialektika stroitel'stva kommunisma. Moscow: Mysl', 1968.

Gilison, Jerome M. The Soviet Image of Utopia. Baltimore: Johns Hopkins Univ., 1975

Ilitskaia, Lenina. ABC of Dialectical and Historical Materialism. Moscow: Progress, 1978.

Khomenko, E. A. and Iasiukov, M. I. Kurs Marsksistko-Leninskoi filosofii. Moscow: Voennoe izd., 1968.

Laszlo, Ervin, (ed) Philosophy in the Soviet Union. New York: Praeger, 1967.

McNeal, Robert H. The Bolshevik Tradition. 2nd ed. Englewood: Prentice-Hall, 1975

Mills, C. Wright The Marxists. New York: Dell, 1962.

Moser, Charles A. Russia: The Spirit of Nationalism. New York: St. John's University, 1972

Parkin, Frank. Class Inequality and Political Order. London: Granada Books, 1970

Sheptulin, A. P. Marxist-Leninist Philosophy. Moscow: Progress, 1978

Vostrikov, A. V. et als. Marksistko-Leninskaia filosofiia-dialekticheskii materialism. Moscow: Izd. "Mysl'" 1968.

Wetter, Gustav A. Soviet Ideology Today. New York: Praeger, 1962

What is Communism: (Questions and Answers). Moscow: Novosti Press, 1976

XXV. Women

Women are guaranteed absolute equality under the law. They may not be discriminated against in any occupational activity except for those which require a great deal of manual strength and might be detrimental to the health and well being of a woman. Yet, women are the workhorses of the nation. Despite the edict outlawing heavy physical work for the weaker sex, one may see many women working on road construction, pouring tar, doing roof repair work, carrying heavy loads, etc. On the personal plots on Kolkhozes and Sovkhozes, it is not unusual to see a woman hitched to a plow.

There are also a number of professions that are traditionally female and others which are nearly exclusively male. Normally, most of the occupations relegated to women are the lowest paying ones. It is women who constitute the vast army of sweepers and moppers and who receive an absolutely minimum wage. It is nearly exclusively women who have sales jobs in stores or are street vendors. Of course the subdivisions of health services such as nurses, laboratory technicians and dental assistants, are typically female jobs However, the same is true for doctors - nearly 70% of them are women. One must remember that they are normally graduates of Institutes, not of Universities, and therefore have less prestige. This profession is also not very well paid if the doctor is a staff member of a polyclinic, as most women doctors are. The upper reaches of medicine, i.e., the respected top-notch surgeon or cardiologist or cancer expert, is well paid and highly respected, but this is the category into which the 30% of male doctors fit

The field of education is similar. Virtually all graduates of pedagogical institutes are women. Virtually all school teachers on the primary and secondary levels are female. At the universities, the predominant number of "instructors" and "senior instructors" are women. The vast majority of junior professors (dotsent) are male, and in the upper reaches, the full professors, a woman is extremely rare.

Despite all this, one must admit that the Soviets have made tremendous progress in equal rights for women. Considering that the woman in Russia before the Revolution was a second class citizen, uneducated, illiterate, with virtually no hope for professional advancement, the present day Soviet woman has made great strides. Until recently, for example, there were virtually no women in jurisprudence. At present, more than half of the lawyers are women. A short time ago, it would have been virtually impossible for a woman to make a career in engineering or technology; now there are many women in this field. There are a considerable number of women in the managerial field in jobs with great authority and responsibility.

Women are also starting to occupy important positions on the local Soviet government level, and significant ceremonial functions on the top level. There are even Union Republics with female Presidents. Albeit that these are positions which carry little authority, yet they contribute tremendous prestige to women in general. On the other hand, despite the fact that there are more women than men in the country, and the fact that women have a large share of the delegates in the Supreme Soviet, only some of the minor ministerial posts go to women The power positions and the strategic posts in the Council of Ministers are all occupied by men. The same is true for the Party. Only about one fourth of the members are female. Although women do occupy some minor Party posts on the local level, and although there are several token women in the Central Committee, there was not a single woman in either the Politburo or in the Secretariat until the recent appointment of A.P. Biriukova. The same statement may be made for the press. Very few political journalists, editors and foreign corespondents are women.

We have already discussed the importance and significance of literature and art. Here again, we see a predominance of male writers (of course there are significant exceptions), male painters and sculptors, male architects and male stage directors. The Union of Writers and the Union of Artists have always been governed by virtually all-male councils.

In some respects, however, the Soviet woman has even more freedom than her western counterpart. We have already discussed the fact that all workers receive a vacation. More often than not, the wife may take a vacation to a different place and at a different time from her husband, just to get away from her family. Even more unusually, the wife may be offered a better job a thousand miles away, and may accept it although it would mean years of separation from her husband. Of course, the choice would be up to her. The wife may also decide that she no longer wants to have sexual relations with her husband. This is her perfect right and no grounds for divorce. It is purely up to her to decide whether she wants to bear children or not. She may interrupt any pregnancy during the first twelve weeks and be aborted at one of the many women's clinics at only a minute, nominal charge This right is enforced despite the fact that the State is extremely interested in a higher birth rate.

In spite of these freedoms the Soviet woman experiences numerous frustrations. She cannot afford to buy attractive clothes partly because of unavailability and partly because of extremely high cost. She cannot readily buy any cosmetics; most are imported from Poland and Czechoslovakia and quite expensive She has a tendency to age rather rapidly as soon as she reaches middle age. One thing is quite noticeable to the foreigner when he first comes to the Slavic part of the USSR. The women are quite attractive and have good figures while they are in their late teens and in their twenties. As soon as they reach the age of thirty they have a tendency towards obesity which accellerates the older they get. It has come to a point where, for the first time in history, the State has started to publish posters pointing out the inherent dangers in being overweight There are several reasons for female obesity, some of which may afford additional insight into the mentality of a Soviet woman:

a. In most parts of the Soviet Union, traditionally, fat on women was not considered unattractive. In fact, corpulence was always associated with good health

b. People eat out of frustration when they feel unhappy or are under pressure. There are many opportunities in the western USSR to overeat; and it is mostly women who avail themselves of this opportunity.

c. Women are more involved with food, i.e., its purchase and preparation.

Chart 39

Women in the USSR

Occupation	*Percentages of Total Population in Respective Pursuits*
Industry	50%
Construction	30%
Agriculture and Timber	43%
Communications and Transport	30%
Public Sales and Food	76%
Community Services	53%
Scientific Research	50%
Health Services	86%
Culture and Education	73%
Supreme Soviets of the Republics	35%
Soviets of Regions, Districts & Localities	48%
Judges of People's Courts	32%
Secondary or Higher Education	59%
Engineers	33%
Agriculturalists and Vetinarians	38%
Economists	65%
Medical Workers (incl. Dentistry)	94%
Teachers and Librarians	86%
Doctorate in Science	14%
Professors and Academy Members	9%

d. They have gone through many famines. Unconsciously there is a desire to take advantage of this relatively affluent period and to store up fat for possibly austere times in the future

As was pointed out before, women's rights have made tremendous strides in the past two decades. Even the Soviets admit, however, that there are still inequities in this field Most of the problem is shrugged away with statements pointing out that a woman loses much time towards professional advancement due to a very liberal Soviet pre-natal and post-natal leave-of-absence policy. When there are several such lengthy leaves, the woman may lose a total of several years of valuable work experience and therefore miss promotion. Additionally, a woman is much more preoccupied with her children and problems at home than the man is, and therefore would not be able to concentrate fully on her profession Besides, when the man finishes work, he may rest. The woman has to do quite a bit of daily shopping (there are few large, well-functioning refrigerators), has to prepare food, clean house, sew clothes, look after the children, and work full-time besides. Obviously, with so many various duties to fulfill, her occupational work cannot possibly be as efficient as that of a man. There are many more excuses, including the conviction by most Soviet men that women are neither as logical nor as intelligent as men. One of the main real reasons, however, is the fact that the Slav has traditionally had a patriarchial society and not sufficient time has passed to overcome this heritage.

As one important member of a public organization stated, the main reason for establishing a Women's Committee was to bring about total equality for women. Obviously this has not yet been achieved, since the Women's Committee still exists.

READINGS

Biriukova, A. P. Zabota o trudiashcheisia zhenshchine v SSSR. Moscow: Profizdat, 1975

Dodge, Norman. Women in the Soviet Economy. Baltimore: Johns Hopkins Press, 1966.

Hansson, Carola and Liden, Karin. Moscow Women. New York: Pantheon, 1983.

Holland, Barbara (ed.) Soviet Sisterhood. Bloomington: Indiana University Press, 1985

Konenko, Yelena Soviet Women: Their Role as Homemakers and Citizens. Moscow: Novosti Press, 1976.

Mamonova, Tatyana. Women and Russia. Boston: Beacon Press, 1984.

McAuley, Alastair. Women's Work and Wages in the Soviet Union. Winchester: Allen & Unwin, 1981

St. George, George Our Soviet Sister. Washington: Robert B. Luce, Inc., 1973.

Vavilina, V. Vysokaia sud'ba. Moscow: Profizdat, 1975.

Zhenshchina v sotsialisticheskom obshchestve. Moscow: Sekretariat S.E.V., 1975.

XXVI. Marriage, Family and Divorce

An integral part in any discussion of marriage is the relationship between men and women and the moral posture towards sex. Although there is a great deal of prudishness in the Soviet Union, e.g., it is impossible to ask a member of the opposite sex for the location of the bathroom; magazines such as Playboy are anathema; there are quite a number of incongruities. For example, it is not at all unusual for a man to be assigned a berth in a cramped railroad compartment with three women. There is virtually no prostitution except for the larger cities where the customers are generally foreigners and the women are generally working as informants for the KGB. By the same token, there is a great deal of pre-marital sex. Even under Stalin it was considered important for a woman to be a virgin until marriage. This is certainly no longer the case. It is quite common for a young Soviet woman to see a doctor for the surgical removal of her hymen long before she has any intention to be married. Young people engage in sexual relations regularly before marriage, but usually not promiscuously, i.e., normally with the same partners for extended periods of time. Although somewhat primitive contraceptive measures are available, most Soviets fail to use them. The common means of interrupting a pregnancy is abortion, to which no stigma is attached. There are also quite a number of illegitimate births. The children of unwed mothers enjoy all the rights of any other children. The law permits the mother to enter any patronymic name she chooses as the father of the child on its birth certificate Upon reaching the age of 18, the young person may then change his name to any he desires. The principle of illigitimacy does not exist in the Soviet Union.

To a large extent the prevalence of pre-marital relations is a testimony to the increased standard of living. Until relatively recently, it was extremely difficult for a man and woman to find a place sufficiently private to engage in sexual activities. It should be remembered that there are no motels, and that most unmarried Soviets live with their parents who are still conservative. The fact that such activities have accellerated proves that the housing situation is improving. In addition, this is one way in which some extra money may be made illegally: a family may take a weekend away from the city, let us say at the home of a relative. In the meantime they may rent their apartment to a young, unmarried couple which would like to set up housekeeping for a weekend, for a relatively high rental charge.

There are more than two million marriages registered in the Soviet Union every year. This figure constitutes approximately 87 marriages for every 10,000 persons of marriagable age, and is virtually identical with the figure in the United States. Of course, marriage percentages differ with the geographic locations. For example, the highest marriage rates are on the new frontiers in Siberia and Central Asia, since most of those pioneers are young people. The age of those getting married has also changed Most of the people are considerably older than the teen-age applicants of two decades ago. It has become vogue to wait for marriage until one is professionally established and until one has the assurance that the place of residence will not change in the near future. Just as an example, more than 21% of all brides in urban areas and 17% of the brides in rural areas are more than 33 years old. This would have been unthinkable before. Also, the age difference between the bride and groom has shrunk Two-thirds of all marriages take place between people whose age difference is less than three years.

All marriages have to be recorded at the local Citizens Records and Licensing Bureau (ZAGS). The act of registering with ZAGS constitutes an official marriage and no further ceremony is required. In recent years couples have preferred a more solemnly ceremonious occasion. For this purpose, Palaces of Weddings have been founded near the ZAGS offices The bride dresses up in a beautiful wedding dress and white veil; the groom wears a black suit. A ceremony is conducted with non-religious vows, e.g., promises to love one another and to become good and loyal citizens in the spirit of the Communist Party. The newlyweds then pay tribute by laying a bouquet of flowers on the grave of the Unknown Soldier. In Moscow, they will view the remains of Lenin. Afterwards, there will be a large and extremely expensive celebration where the vodka will flow like water.

After a couple marries, they may live with one of the in-laws until they are assigned separate quarters. This may take a rather long period of time and does put a great strain upon the marriage right from the beginning. Both the husband and wife normally work, which makes it difficult to plan for children until a sufficient income and sufficient savings have been effected. Although the woman still has not attained all the rights which will make her equal to man, there is no doubt that she has taken great strides towards being liberated. She therefore enjoys not being only a housewife, but a productive member of the working class She is loathe to give up her freedom for having to raise children, since the permitted absence from work, adding pre- and post-natal release, is nearly a year for every child This is one reason why the birthrate, especially in the industrial, urban areas of the European part of the USSR, has dropped so radically. This is also a good reason why women who do have children are ready to give up a good part of their privacy and let an old relative move into the apartment, so that they are released from a good part of housekeeping and taking care of the children. Nevertheless, children do play a tremendous part in Soviet society All material goods are lavished upon them; they are placed upon pedestals and catered to in every way. Nevertheless, deep within, many urban mothers do feel that their children have robbed them of a definite amount of opportunity to compete professionally. Russian marriages and Russian families have always been considered quite close, despite the overwhelming sociological problems of alcoholism. In recent times, however, marriages have taken on a much looser character.

The divorce rate in the USSR has been steadily climbing for the past two decades, so that now it has become the highest in the world. Fully one-third of all Soviet marriages end in divorce Since this is an overall figure for the entire nation, it is easy to understand why in some large cities one marriage out of two will fail. In a recently conducted survey, a number of reasons for this extremely high rate were listed:

a. The economic independence of working wives has weakened the traditionally strong family ties.

b. For two decades after World War II there were many more women than men in the country. By 1980, men and women in the marriagable age group were nearly equal in number. Women are now less afraid of not being able to find another husband and agree to divorces more readily.

c. The older generation of traditional family-oriented, pre-revolutionary conservatives, has died out. In fact, older people are no longer as respected as they used to be Their peace-making efforts to reunite husband and wife therefore normally fail.

d. The level of education and the ranks of the intelligentsia have risen perceptibly. This group believes that incompatible marriages should be dissolved for the benefit of both partners.

e. Society is no longer as intolerant of divorces as during the Stalin period. There are no social stigmata attached to a divorced person.

f. The rate of alcoholism for both men and women has climbed, despite government efforts to curb it. Many divorces result from it.

g. Couples are waiting to have children. Childless marriages can be dissolved much more easily.

h. There has been a great increase in marriage across cultural and ethnic lines. Statistics show that such marriages have a high potential for failure.

i. There are many marriages of financial convenience, e.g. to obtain residency permits, which are dissolved as soon as possible.

The two major deterrents to divorce were listed as:

a. The desire to stay together despite incompatibility for the sake of the children.

b. The desire of both partners to continue having optimum privacy by retaining their separate apartment which they would lose upon divorce

If there are no children, divorce is extremely simple. Both partners go to ZAGS and register the divorce without a hearing before a judge, and with the payment of a minimal fee. They have to give no reason for their decision. When there are children, there must be a hearing and reasons must be presented. In a recent poll where a Soviet professor of sociology surveyed the reactions of 1,000 couples petitioning for the divorce, the following reasons were cited by women:

a. 29.2%, drunkedness by the husband.
b. 26.6%, wife-beating and extremely rude behavior.
c. 15%, infidelity.
d. 12.4%, loss of love for the husband.
e. 9%, psychological incompatibility.
f. 3%, husband in prison.
g. 1.4%, love for another man.
h. 1%, inadequate sex life.

The men were polled separately and cited the following reasons for the dissolution of the marriage:

a. 30.5%, psychological imcompatibility
b. 24.5%, loss of love for their wives.
c. 15.5%, wife's infidelity.
d. 12.3%, love for another woman.
e. 7%, shrewish behavior of wife.
f. 2.5%, mother-in-law problems.
g. 2.5%, inability of the wife to bear children.
h. 2.2%, inadequate sex life.
i. 1.7%, jealousy of wife.

A number of western sociologists insist that there are other reasons which are more valid, specifically the absence of religion to cement the home. Also, since divorces were so difficult to obtain before and are so easy to get now, the floodgates have been opened and people are not taking a chance that they may close again. Another important reason is the fact that wives do not have to worry about bearing the financial costs of bringing up their children after the divorce. The husband still carries pecuniary responsibility and the State makes certain that he lives up to it. In addition, the State will be only too glad to contribute financially towards the costs of rearing children.

READINGS

Fundamentals of the Legislation of the USSR and the Union Republics on Marriage and the Family. Moscow: Novosti, 1975.

Gazaryan, Spartak. Children in the USSR. Moscow: Novosti, Press, 1973.

Inkeles, Alex and Geiger, Kent (eds.) Soviet Society. London: Constable, 1961.

Kassof, Allen. Prospects for Soviet Society. New York: Praeger, 1968.

Kohler, Foy D. Understanding the Russians: A Citizen's Primer. New York: Harper and Row, 1970.

Schecter, Leona and Jerrold. An American Family in Moscow. Boston: Little, Brown, 1975.

Smith, Hedrick. The Russians. New York: Quadrangle, 1976.

Stern, Mikhail. Sex in the USSR. New York: Times Books, 1980.

XXVII. Dissidence

Dissidence in the Soviet Union receives wide-spread press coverage in the West. Alas, most of the stories reported by the media are little more than wishful thinking. Any idea that the overt dissident incorporates within himself the true feelings of a large segment of the population is certainly untrue. There also seems to be the conception in the West that Soviet dissidents receive publicity in the USSR. Nothing could be further from the truth. Soviet media are interested in propagating only the positive factors of society. It may be an oversimplification, but let us accept for the moment that there are three types of dissidents and that the State reacts to them in the following different ways:

a. Virtually every human being in every society finds things wrong with some aspect of his society and gives vent to his spleen by complaining. This is certainly true in the Soviet Union. There are complaints about the lack of consumer items, about the inadequacy of housing, about the slow service given by civil servants, about the unfairness of plant officials, labor union leaders or Party and government functionaries. Of course the State realizes that it would be foolish to shut off this escape valve. It therefore encourages criticism and self-criticism but attempts to organize it and channel it in the right direction. Virtually every local newspaper has a "Letters from the Readers" column where people actually do contribute complaints which are printed (Pravda receives 600,000 letters anually, answers all and publishes 6,000). Certainly the editorial staff is very careful to publish only those complaints which seem reasonable, which do not attack the system and for which a remedy will be implemented to show the public that it does have a voice in running things. Frequently single individuals in responsible positions will be attacked, but only in those cases where there is good reason to believe that the individual is ripe for demotion. Occasionally, the Party will mount an attack and cloak it as a contribution by an interested reader, just to lay the foundation for a purge. The State considers such dissent to be healthy, since it is carefully controlled.

b. The second type of dissent is the one which has received the most wide-spread publicity in the West. This group of dissenters is interested in a total revision of the system of government and the socio-political leadership in the USSR. Whenever we think of this group, names such as Sakharov, Ginzburg, Bukovskii, Sharanskii and Solzhenitsyn come to mind. There are a number of important items of information we must remember when we read western press reports on this movement. First of all, it is an absolute fact that this is not a well-organized movement with common interests. In fact, elements within this grouping oppose each other quite strongly on an ideological basis. Sakharov, who would like to see the elimination of all severe restraints, has frequently accused Solzhenitsyn of desiring to substitute the autocracy of the traditional Russian Orthodox Church for the present autocratic regime. Similarly, one segment of overt dissidents which is not at all publicized in the West, are extreme radicals who feel that the Soviet State has become much too liberal and has strayed from the path of true socialism by entering into an accomodating relationship with the West; many members of this grouping may be considered neo-Stalinists. There are even several ultra-nationalists who resent any intercourse with foreign countries and Pan-Slavists who would like to revive this idyllic nineteenth-century unfeasible doctrine.

The ideological difference takes on added significance when one realizes that the number of overt dissidents is extremely small. One illustration is the fact that when a vote was taken whether to expel Solzhenitsyn from the Writers Union, only eight out of a total voting membership of 6,792 members voted against it. A great weakness of the dissident group is also the fact that it argues on the terms of the Party, i.e., it invokes Lenin, the Soviet Constitution and Party policy and falls into the communist dialectic jargon which insures their defeat from the outset. It is also true that there are quite a number of illegal Samizdat publications circulating in the country, most of them either hand-written or typed. Certainly some of the articles attack various facets of Soviet society. Nevertheless, contrary to Western belief, most of the items in Samizdat are rather apolitical. They are poetry, fiction and articles which do not fall into the present concept of Socialist Realism and could therefore not be published anywhere else.

Despite the fact that this grouping of overt dissidents is rather small and ineffectual, the System cannot tolerate them and is forced to persecute them. First of all, the State sees to it that an absolute minimum of publicity is given to this group. They receive virtually no coverage by the media, therefore the vast majority of the population doesn't even know of their existence. Solzhenitsyn is known for his One Day in the Life of Ivan Denisovich but not for any of his great later novels or his Gulag Archipelago. The system sees no reason why it should publicize its enemies. It deals with this opposition by various methods. Some, like Solzhenitsyn, may be expelled to the West and therefore branded as treasonous defectors. Others may lose their jobs and be barred from living in major population centers (virtually all dissidents in this group are from large cities). Still others, especially those who engage in anti-Soviet activities or overt propaganda, may be sentenced to prison for up to ten years or may be exiled to remote areas. Those dissidents who persist in attacking the system no matter what the personal consequences may be, are obviously mad and are confined to mental institutions. This eliminates the necessity for a public trial and requires no publicity whatsoever.

c. The third form of dissidence is by far the most important and by far the most dangerous for a conservative Soviet leadership. This is the dissidence which is extremely wide-spread among the intelligentsia. In simple terms, it can be defined as follows: The desire to bring about a liberalization and more freedoms within the parameters of the present system. The writer wants to be able to discuss subjects previously taboo; the scientist wants a greater exchange of scientific data with the West; the intellectual wants more access to written materials produced in the West; all would like a liberal policy of travel to the West and the elimination of the travel restrictions and internal passports within their own country; the scientist wants permission to conduct his own research on subjects which interest him rather than only on projects devised by the State. The traditional system is built on the idea that everything must be painted in black and white with no grey areas. The dissenters in this category feel that grey areas are extremely important and are the very areas in which progress in all fields may be made. Rigidity is not conducive to healthy development and optimum efficiency. Gorbachev understands this quite well.

The importance to the West as to the potential success of this group is far reaching. If conservative leadership persists, Soviet-Western relations will be ill-defined and will continue to fluctuate between "detente" and an impregnable "iron curtain." Internally, the USSR will continue to function at less than optimum efficiency. If the dissenting intelligentsia is victorious, the relationship with the West will be greatly improved. At the same time, knowledgeable, well educated, efficient leaders in the image of Gorbachev will replace others. This would greatly strengthen the Soviet Union as a world power and would make its socio-political philosophy much more attractive to non-aligned nations. To a large extent the situation is quite similar to the cultural revolution in China, where the traditional Maoists were pitted against the technocrats.

d. The most vociferous and numerically the largest group has been the Jews. First of all, it would be wrong to create a separate category for Jewish dissidents; there are Jewish representatives in each of the three categories of dissenters listed above. The Jews enjoy a special position both in the international press and in the Soviet Union, since it is the only group most members of which want to leave the country. Their voice is most clearly heard since they represent an inordinately large percentage of the intelligentsia. By the same token, the State may always answer that this segment of the population which has been so well educated and supported by society, now wants to deprive society of what is due it. The Jews also have a destination, a place where they will be accepted, be it Israel or any western country with a significant Jewish population Other ethnic minorities are also severely suppressed; most of them are not heard from because they consist primarily of culturally deprived and uneducated people. The fate of the Tartars, for example, is quite severe. There are very few Tartar intellectuals, however; nor is there a place to which the Tartars could logically emigrate

There are divergent views as to whether the notoriety endowed upon Soviet dissenters in the West is contributing to the effectiveness of dissention in the USSR. Some state that the embarrassment caused to the Soviet Union by pointing out internal transgressions against human rights puts dissent into the limelight and makes it difficult for the USSR to apply severe suppressive measures without exposure. Others believe that by calling a great deal of attention to dissention, the West is impressing upon the Soviet State the political importance of these dissenters, thereby forcing the State not to overlook any embryonic dissention, and making it increasingly difficult for moderates to work towards evolutionary changes The dissenters themselves feel that notoriety in the West is extremely helpful to their cause. Considering the recent release of many dissidents by Gorbachev and the return from exile of Sakharov, they may be right. Also interesting is the recent invitation to well-known expatriates to return to the USSR.

READINGS

Alexeyeva, Ludmilla. Talking Back to the Kremlin: Soviet Dissent. Wesleyan University Press, 1985.

Blake, Patricia and Hayward, Max (eds.) Dissonant Voices in Soviet Literature. London: Allen and Unwin, 1965.

Bonavia, David. Fat Sasha & the Urban Guerilla: Protest and Conformism in the Soviet Union. New York: Atheneum, 1973.

Bosley, K., Sapiets, J. and Pospielovsky, D. (eds.) Russia's Other Poets. London: Longmans, 1968.

Bromke, Adam and Rakowska-Harmstone, Teresa (eds.) The Communist States in Disarray 1965-1971. Minneapolis: University of Minnesota Press, 1972.

Bukowski, Wladimir Opposition. Munich: Carl Hanser Verlag, 1971.

Churchward, L. The Soviet Intelligentsia. London: Routledge, 1973.

Gaucher, Roland. Opposition in the USSR. New York: Funk and Wagnalls, 1969.

Kontinent. All copies of this journal of literary, social, political and religious commentary. Garden City, N.Y.: Anchor Press/Doubleday.

Labedz, Leopold (eds.) Solzhenitsyn: A Documentary Record. New York: Harper and Row, 1971.

Medvedev, Roy. Samizdat Register 2. New York: W. W. Norton, 1981.

Medvedev, Z. Ten Years After Ivan Denisovich. New York: Random house, 1974.

Parchomenko, Walter. Soviet Images of Dissidents and Nonconformists. London: Greenwood, 1986.

Reddaway, Peter (ed.) Uncensored Russia: Protest and Dissent in the Soviet Union. The Unofficial Journal Chronicle of Current Events. New York: American Heritage Press, 1972.

Rothberg, Abraham. The Heirs of Stalin: Dissidence and the Soviet Regime, 1953-1970. Ithaca: Cornell University Press, 1972.

Sakharov, Andrei. Progress, Coexistence and Intellectual Freedom. New York: W. W Norton, 1968.

______. Sakharov Speaks. New York: Knopf, 1974.

Solzhenitsyn, Alexander. Letters to the Soviet Leaders. New York: Harper and Row, 1974

Tokes, Rudolf L. Dissent in the U.S.S.R. Baltimore: Johns Hopkins, 1975.

XXVIII. Strengths, Weaknesses and Prospects

There are a number of strengths which are easily identifiable in every totalitarian state. Obviously, the State does not have to adhere to due process and may impose its decisions without question. Since the State has only the good of the nation in mind, any opposition, by definition, must intend to hurt the nation and is therefore an act of treason easily dealt with. The State does not have to justify its decisions or to ask for popular approval. To a great extent, the individual in the Soviet Union, who has for centuries been told what to do and not to question the source of power, is not too unhappy about his status All decisions are made for him; he thereby avoids the agony of choice. His life is orderly and totally predictable.

On the economic plane, planning is completely centralized. The economy of the country is geared to what is actually needed, rather to what could make more money. In case of emergency, the entire economy can quickly be geared to overcome the problem. As far as the individual is concerned, he knows that he will never be unemployed and that he will make a sufficient amount of money to be able to afford a reasonably comfortable life despite intermittent periods of shortages. The only exception to this are Kolkhoz residents whose number is rapidly shrinking. In general, the Soviet worker has security, well realizes it, and appreciates it. Of course, he knows that he may be earning a great deal less than other segments of the population. He sees beautiful limousines, sumptuous summer homes, western imported clothes, jewelry, etc. But he has the realization that he, or his children, will be able to attain the same level if they have the drive and the intelligence. He knows that his family is not caught in as rigid a caste system as it was before the Revolution.

Although the average citizen will never be wealthy, he does have a number of rights which will insure his making ends meet. He has absolutely free medical and dental care for himself and his family. He knows that his children will receive a free education through all levels of schooling, and that they will be able to progress as far as their abilities will take them. He also knows that he will get virtually free vacations and will be able to take part in cultural activities without cost.

The Soviet citizen is sheltered from evil impulses. His media expose him only to what is uplifting and progressive. He is taught not to look back, but to look forward, and to accept the fact that things are getting better all the time The Soviet does accept this and is grateful for it. He gets only the good news and the moral catalysts in everything he reads. He is constantly instilled with the healthy feeling of "manifest destiny" which we had in the United States at the turn of the century and which we have partly lost. If all this exposure brainwashes him to believe that the USSR is the greatest nation with the greatest potential, that things will constantly get better, that socialist morality is preferable to capitalist immorality. If he is instilled with the idea that there is only one reasonable philosophy and that all others are detrimental, this unifies the nation spiritually.

One great strength which is all too easily overlooked is the Soviet commitment to culture There is no anti-intellectual trend as in some western countries, but rather the opposite. Intellect is something to be highly respected and to be aspired to. This is traditional not only in the Russian but in some of the other major nationalities of the USSR. The Soviet reads voraciously, attends theatre performances whenever he can, visits his many museums and attends concerts All these activities are attainable in the Soviet Union because they cost so little and are encouraged by the state. True that some of the material is of a propaganda nature, but certainly not as much as one would think. The favorites are still the old nineteenth century masters who were certainly not socialists However, it does instill in the present day Soviet a feeling of pride and patriotism to see to what level culture has evolved in his own land. The tradition of culture has not abated. The western observer must realize that a people which has been able to produce such giants as Tolstoy, Dostoevsky, Mendeleev, Pavlov, Solzhenitsyn, Sakharov and hundreds of others of similar stature, cannot be underestimated no matter in which aberrational direction the national energy may now be expended. The potential, nevertheless, is there

The other side of the coin, the weaknesses, are, alas, just as convincing. The economic unity of the country has many pitfalls. The red tape is immense, and frequently gross errors are made which can be covered up by the leadership since there is no accountability. All this encourages inefficiency and cheating. No leader is willing to accept responsibility for fear of failing and being purged for it. Since the real leadership is not derived by popular election, this leadership may be removed without a popular vote This "passing of the buck" is the normal procedure not only in the economics of the country, but in all major political and cultural activities. It will take Gorbachev a long time, if ever, to change this.

A few more words must be said about the economic efficiency of the system. Although it is true that the economy may be targeted to overcome a crisis, it may also be targeted to support a political decision. Frequently this means that production may be shifted from needed consumer items to the production of tactical materials whose utility may become obsolete soon thereafter. In other words, it is not really the needs of the nation which are important, but the political interpretation of these needs by the members of the Politburo Whenever power is placed in the hands of a few, without recourse by the many, this power will invariably tend to corrupt and to be misused if there is no effective system of checks and balances.

It is true that the individual worker has a great degree of security as far as employment is concerned. This security is only valid if he is extremely careful not to overstep his role as an ordinary worker. He is forced to apprise himself of the Party line so that he does not support an unpopular cause; he has to be careful about the friends he keeps; he has to take care that a jealous co-worker cannot accuse him of economic sabotage; he has to pacify the Party functionaries and the trade union leaders; he knows that he cannot strike or walk off his job if he is unhappy with his working conditions; he sees inefficiency all around him and can do nothing to change it; he lives in a world of organized chaos, and knows it. He is constantly vulnerable and constantly on the defensive, despite "glasnost."

Despite the high standards of morality which are constantly propagated, corruption is evident everywhere. The system, which eliminates private enterprise and a great deal of personal initiative, seems to ask for illegal behavior from the lowest workman to the highest economic director. Such corruption is partly condoned since its elimination would halt the entire economic system; partly it is not clearly recognized because of the complex, inefficient system which makes it an obvious victim for embezzlement, misappropriation and mismanagement

The State has stressed the subordination of the individual to the social organism. This is an objective which cannot be achieved. Individualism will always be a major driving force On the economic plane, this simply means that the person with more drive and more intelligence will attempt to gain more material advantage than his neighbor. If he cannot accomplish this legally, he will try to do it illegally. On the philosophical plane he will try to obtain a basis for comparison. He will not be satisfied with knowing and fully accepting only his own philosophy, but will want to know something about other schools of thought.

There also seems to be every indication that a number of social problems in the Soviet Union are quite severe and that others are on the increase. Alcoholism, despite governmental programs to curb it, even the tremendous increase in the price of vodka, has not abated. There seems to be quite an increase in the number of criminals some of whom have organized into gangs, judging from several Soviet films released in recent years. The fact that a relatively small drug problem does exist, especially in the Leningrad area, seems to be implied by the fact that several dime detective novels have appeared recently, which center around police activities to apprehend drug smugglers and pushers. There are allegedly 40,000 drug users in the USSR. Divorce rates are astronomically high; by the same token the birth rate in the western USSR has fallen to a dangerous low. There is a clear desire by the little man to accumulate as much money as possible, which has forced the leadership to adopt philosophically controversial measures (for example, the State Lottery advertises that "you, too, can win 100,000 rubles"). Long hair, bluejeans and sneakers are becoming the uniform of youth. Uplifting, heroic music is giving way to western rock. Other nationalities are "thinning down" the "superior Russian bloodline" and are threatening its numerical superiority

Of course, of particular importance in the evaluation of future prospects of the USSR and all nations who deal with it, is the stability of its leadership. Gorbachev, no doubt, has good intentions. Were all his proposals accepted by the more conservative elements in the Party, the world balance of power would shift perceptibly in favor of the Soviets -- particularly in the economic sphere. It is also significant that the new leader is comparatively young and should have some 20 years of power before him. Yet, we must not be misled by him. He will continue to try to expand Soviet power, to thwart the United States in the race for raw materials and markets, to use any means at his disposal, fair or dirty, to achieve his national objectives. On the other hand, he may find it difficult to consolidate his power completely, and thus would be unable to initiate the majority of his planned reforms. If that is the case, little change will result, the Soviet Union will continue on its road of economic inefficiency, and the West will gain a considerable upper hand We cannot forecast what will happen. No one in the USSR knows for sure. Gorbachev may very well stay on as leader for many years without meeting his objectives. He may, in the opinion of some observers, be replaced by more conservative elements. Or, he may push through his reforms successfully. Only time will tell.

As far as US relations with the USSR are concerned, we must remember that the Russians, for centuries, have had good reason to distrust the West. Every schoolchild is reminded that there were US troops on Soviet soil fighting on the side of the Tsarists against the communists during the Civil War. The present-day Soviet believes that, just as communism is militant, so is capitalism, and that the Soviet State must be ever watchful to prevent western economic and military imperialism from making inroads in Eastern Europe or anywhere else in the world where it could potentially threaten the well-being of the USSR. Every child is made to believe that the US wants the destruction of the Soviet State both politically and economically.

It is, of course, true that the Soviet educational system teaches a great number of facts about the United States at all levels. The Soviet is, generally speaking, quite knowledgeable about us Unfortunately he is given only the negative side of our culture, which creates an extremely distorted picture. This distortion is aided by a barrage of destructively self-critical reports from our own media, on the premise that the communist world would be impressed by the freedom which we have to attack our own system. The Soviet citizen sees us putting our worst foot forward and does not realize that we are hiding our good points. Although he is basically sceptical, he then naturally believes a good deal of the propaganda about us which he is being fed, and which contains just enough truth to be logically accepted.

Similar arguments are even more pertinent from our own perspective. We are taught very little about the USSR in our schools. We are, as a nation, eminently ignorant about the Soviet Union. Even our highest representatives in our national government all to often commit errors in judgement which would be unthinkable if they had even a rudimentary knowledge of the USSR and the character of the Soviet people. The obvious answer lies in education, in giving our people as much valid information about the USSR as is available, even if some of it is flattering to their system. It is the author's hope that this book has, to a small measure, contributed to this objective. It is also fervently hoped that some day a similar book about the United States may be published in the Soviet Union

READINGS

Amalrik, Andrei. Will the USSR Survive Until 1984? New York: Harper and Row, 1970

Bialer, Seweryn The Soviet Paradoc: External Expansion, Internal Decline. New York: Knopf, 1985.

Brown, Archie and Kaser, Michael (eds.) Soviet Policy for the 1980s. Bloomington: Indiana University Press, 1984.

Brown, J. F. The New Eastern Europe: the Krushchev Era and After. New York: Praeger, 1966.

Crowe, Barry. Concise Dictionary of Soviet Terminology, Institutions and Abbreviations. New York: Pergamon Press, 1969.

Florinsky, Michael T. Encyclopedia of Russia and the Soviet Union. New York: McGraw-Hill, 1961.

Gerhart, Genevra. The Russian's World: Life and Language. New York: Harcourt Brace Jovanovich, 1974.

Hollander, Paul. Soviet and American Society: A Comparison. New York: Oxford University Press, 1973.

Law, David A. Russian Civilization. New York: MSS Corp., 1975.

Mihajlov, M. Russian Themes. New York: Farrar, Straus and Giroux, 1968.

Sailsbury, Harrison E. (ed.) The Soviet Union: The Fifty Years. New York; Signet, 1968.
Schapiro, L. and Boiter, A. (eds.) The USSR and the Future. New York: Praeger, 1963.
Schopflin, George (ed.) The Soviet Union and Eastern Europe: A Handbook. New York: Praeger, 1970.
Werth, Alexander Russia: The Post-War Years. New York: Taplinger Publ., 1971.

APPENDIX 1

Transliteration

Transliteration from Russian into English in the United States has always been problematic. Unfortunately there are three major transliteration systems in full use:

a. U.S. Board on Geographic Names System: As the name implies, this system is used on all maps. In addition, most U.S. Government agencies use it in their publications. The Chicago Manual of Style recommends it.

b. The Library of Congress System: This system is used by the Library of Congress and by most other libraries. The majority of humanities and social science journals also use it, however the diareses and ligatures are frequently ommitted

c The International Linguistic System: This is the system which Slavic scholars all over the world use to communicate with each other. A number of scholarly publications require it. The Slavic and East European Journal, the Russian Language and the PMLA Bibliography insist upon it. This system is quite cumbersome since the diacritical marks (hacheks) have to be put in by hand if a Czech typewriter is not available.

Unfortunately there are numerous self-devised systems besides, which are used by newspapers and magazines or by individual writers who tend to be confused by the three other systems. It should also be pointed out that there is a serious problem in trying to look a word up in a card file or index, since, for example, a Russian word starting with the letter ю may be found under "yu," or "iu," or "ju," depending upon which system is being used. In this book the Library of Congress system, without diacritical marks, is used throughout, except in the bibliographies where the transliteration of the original publication is used

The following transliteration chart lists all three major systems. It also attempts to indicate, as closely as possible, what the English sounds of the letters are. It is only the underlined portion of the English word which is pertinent.

TRANSLITERATION SYSTEMS

RUSSIAN	U.S. BOARD ON GEOGRAPHIC NAMES	LIBRARY OF CONGRESS	INTERNATIONAL LINGUISTIC SYSTEM	SOUND IN ENGLISH
А а	a	a	a	art
Б б	b	b	b	boy
В в	v	v	v	vote
Г г	g	g	g	go
Д д	d	d	d	dog
Е е	e, ye*	e	e	end, yes
Ё ё	ë, yë**	ë	e	York
Ж ж	zh	zh	ž	je (Fr.)
З з	z	z	z	zone
И и	i	i	i	antique
Й й	y	ĭ	i	toy
К к	k	k	k	king
Л л	l	l	l	love
М м	m	m	m	map
Н н	n	n	n	nap
О о	o	o	o	sort
П п	p	p	p	pot
Р р	r	r	r	Pedro (Span.)
С с	s	s	s	sun
Т т	t	t	t	top
У у	u	u	u	dubious
Ф ф	f	f	f	fan
Х х	kh	kh	x	ach, ich (Germ.)
Ц ц	ts	t͡s	c	tsetse fly

Ч	ч	ch	ch	č	chair
Ш	ш	sh	sh	š	shoot
Щ	щ	shch	shch	šč	fresh cheese
Ъ	ъ	"	"	"	hardens preceding consonant
Ы	ы	y	y	y	bill
Ь	ь	'	'	'	softens preceding consonant
Э	э	e	e	e	era
Ю	ю	yo	i͡u	ju	you
Я	я	ya	i͡a	ja	yard

*Transliterated as ye after vowels, at the beginning of a word or syllable, and after " or '. In all other situations it is transliterated as e.

**Transliterated as yë after vowels, at the beginning of a word or syllable, and after " or '. In all other situations it is transliterated as ë.

The arched line over two connecting letters which is used in the Library of Congress Transliteration system is sometimes ommitted.

Chart 40

APPENDIX 2

Terminology

Whenever we, in the West, read a newspaper which contains the text of a recent speech by a Soviet dignitary, or the wording of a Soviet communique, we hit upon terms which are highly familiar to us, but which are used in a way which seems to distort the original meaning. The following are a number of the more common terms which are interpreted in accordance with the Soviet definition:

Agitation: This word is normally coupled with propaganda. It denotes the duty of every communist to educate the public so that it may understand and more fully appreciate the system. Agit-prop is conducted in all occupational endeavors, in all organizations and at all levels. It may be very basic or highly sophisticated. Persons engaged in this activity are called activists.

Amateur: One is not actually paid for a specific activity outside his normal profession, but who may receive bonuses and privileges which far exceed his normal income.

Anarchism: The doctrine which proposes the immediate elimination of all government and centers of authority, i.e., before society is ready for it. The communist idea of the "withering away of the State" is a process which will take many years and which will develop naturally after all preliminary revolutionary processes have been accomplished

Blat: One of the most commonly used words in the Soviet Union today. It denotes the attempt or ability to obtain any service, privilege or material benefit outside of normal channels It may range from a simple favor, to the exertion of political influence, to outright bribery.

Bourgeoisie: The so-called middle class which has been created by the capitalists as a buffer between them and the proletariat. The bourgeois looks down on the worker and up to the capitalist. Because of their numbers, they constitute the backbone of the capitalist system. They are conservative, uninformed, complacent and self-satisfied with their own petty economic position and the hypocritical exploitation of the factory worker and peasant.

Capitalism: The economic doctrine whereby the means of production and distribution are in the hands of a few, for personal profit. Capitalists are not themselves involved in the production process and exploit those who are The products of nature belong to a privileged class.

Chauvinism: The doctrine which places the benefits to one's own nation above the benefits to mankind. This doctrine causes wars and economic injustice. Of course, if a nation has only the good of mankind in mind when it attempts to aggrandize itself, it cannot be called chauvinistic.

Cosmopolitanism: The conscious desire to become an over-sophisticated, urban "world citizen" with no allegiances to either national or politico-economic doctrine. The major transgressors are traditionally Jews.

Creative Marxism: The CPSU is the Party of Creative Marxism. Obviously Marx could not foresee all the changes which were to occur a century later and therefore could prescribe no laws and regulations to fit every possible future condition. Although Marxian laws of economics are profound, monumental and immutable, it may, on occasion, be necessary to be creative in those areas on which Marx remains mute. This is the function of the Party, not the individual who might be accused of revisionism were he to attempt such an act

Cult of Personality: The attempt of any functionary of the Party or Government, on any level, to disavow that he is only "the first among peers," and to consider himself as an extraordinary individual with special powers, who cannot be replaced. Stalin and Khrushchev were both guilty of this crime. The answer is collective leadership in which no single individual reigns supreme.

Democratic Centralism: It is the duty of every good communist to voice his opinions whenever anything is going through the process of being decided. This included the formulation of a new law or an election. However, once a decision has been made, either by the majority or by those empowered to make decisions, it is binding on everyone. There is no such concept as a "loyal opposition."

Deviationism: The attempt to stray from the firm precepts of Marxism-Leninism. To some extent this is more insidious than Revisionism, since the latter is an open attempt at change.

Dictatorship of the Proletariat: This is the natural extension of Democracy. The people as a whole govern themselves with an iron hand and have the last word in matters which affect their existence. If there is a conflict between the will of the people and the law, the people must win. Justice is meted out not from law books, but out of the conscience of the people.

Dogmatism: The refusal to recognize that the Soviet system is based upon "creative Marxism" i.e., on the fact that, although the basic concepts of socialism are inviolate, their application has to be adapted to the changing times. Such people hamper progress and refuse to accept the fact of a continuous revolutionary process. (The line between anti-dogmatism and deviationism is a fine one and, on occasion, a very dangerous one.)

Economic Sabotage: A stock phrase which is used to indict anyone who hampers the orderly production or distribution process. This may range from the actual destruction of a piece of machinery, to repeated absences from work due to alcoholism.

Fellow Traveler: An opportunist who does not really believe in the communist system but plays along with it in order to survive. He is not to be trusted since he is uncommitted and may adopt another allegiance if he considers it to be his personal benefit. There can be no neutrality. This is why novels such as Dr. Zhivago cannot be permitted

Glasnost: Openness, open speech. A policy initiated by Gorbachev in late 1986 in which all citizens are invited to speak openly about problems and faults within the system and the government and Party administration This freedom does not include any attack upon or disagreement with the basic tenets of socialism or the Party leadership principles, but simply with inequities as to their application. The policy of glasnost is also applied to foreign relations and foreign press releases as to major setbacks or accidents in the Soviet Union which have previously been hushed up.

Hero: Any Soviet citizen, engaged in any pursuit, who has contributed significantly to the furtherance of communism and the elevation of society. He is normally decorated, given bonuses, and placed on a pedestal as an example for all the people to emulate

Hooliganism: Named after a turn-of-the-century American comic strip, "Happy Hooligan." It designates rowdy behavior in public and petty destructiveness caused by intoxication. Most frequently it is applied to the misbehavior of young people. Although it is not caused by political motives or economic unrest, it is frequently interpreted thus by the western media.

Imperialism: The attempt by capitalist forces to extend their spheres of influence over yet uncommitted and underdeveloped territories. Such imperialism may be political, (war, insurrection, subversion of present regimes), or economic, (capturing export markets, using large corporations to gain control over raw materials.) Of course, when the USSR does this it is not imperialism but the intent to awaken in those backward and uncommitted areas the recognition of the value of a socialist system under the spiritual and politico-economic guidance of the USSR

Intelligentsia: In the widest sense, everyone who has attended an institution of higher learning. In the narrower sense, the best intellectuals who are primarily to be found in the fields of research, education, literature and art.

Liberalism: The inability to have firmly founded convictions, thereby laying oneself open to harmful influences; permitting such harmful influences to take root and to be spread among the people, despite the fact that they are clearly recognizeable as harmful.

Monopoly: The attempt to exert complete control over a production or distribution process, or over a source of raw materials, in order that the possibility of competition be eliminated and in order that the maximum surplus value may be enforced.

Nomenklatura: A listing of several thousand positions at the top levels of Party, government, and public organizations throughout the Soviet Union. This is the leadership of the nation which can either be supportive of, or a thorn in the side of the General Secretary, CPSU. These are the most firmly entrenched functionaries who are loathe to give up any of their perquisites or power. For this reason, they are the most opposed to political change or to social liberalization as proposed by Gorbachev.

Objectivity: The concept that all questions should be considered objectively, i.e., with an open mind, without pre-conceived ideas. This concept completely disregards all the socio-economic lessons which mankind has learned over the centuries and is considered a highly negative trait.

Parallel Structure: For each level of government or major mass organization, there is a level of the Party which supervises it. Frequently members of the Party wear two hats, i.e., the hat of the controller and the hat of the controlled.

Parasitism: The refusal of an individual to become involved in the production or distribution process or to contribute to society in any manner. At the same time, a parasite takes advantage of all the benefits bestowed upon society by the working class.

Perestroika: Reconstruction. This term is primarily but not exclusively applied to economics. It concerns itself with changes within the means of production and distribution in order to make the USSR more competitive with capitalist nations. Examples are changes in the application of planning principles, private enterprise and the sharing of authority in major industries.

Proletariat: All the people who contribute to the benefit of society by becoming engaged in production, distribution, education, intellectual life or Party/Government functions.

Provocation: Any question directed by a foreign non-communist concerning the achievements of communism, the answer to which may be embarrassing to the system. For example: Why are the best quality products grown on private plots? Why is it so difficult for a Soviet citizen to get permission to travel abroad? Why is there such severe censorship?

Religion: The apparatus designed to feed the irrational and detract from the scientific by conjuring up mystical and mysterious entities which cannot be logically explained; the no longer necessary tool to create an opiate which will pacify the primitive and detract their minds from social inequities. A parasitic, money-making enterprise.

Revengism: Despite the fact that they were soundly beaten by the glorious Soviet Army in World War II (with a very little outside assistance), certain people still have not learned their lessons and are trying to stir up old sentiments which will rekindle the flames of war. This charge is primarily levied against West Germany which is supported by the United States. It is also partially true for Japan which decided to capitulate only after the USSR had declared war on it.

Revisionism: The desire and intent to revise the teachings of Marx and Lenin and thereby stray from the true path of socialism and communism as defined by the Party leadership.

Self-Criticism: This criticism is always destructive. In any endeavor which has shown poor results or serious flaws, scapegoats must be found. The result is a ritual with much breast-beating and pronouncements of mea culpa, after which the culprits promise to mend their ways. This is a special form of catharsis.

Socialism: The production and distribution process of goods belongs to all those who are involved in the process, but not to those who have not contributed.

The products of nature belong to all the people who want to use them not for profit, but to benefit mankind.

Speculator: One who buys items on the market legally and tries to sell them at a profit illegally. This could be small items such as theater tickets, or bulk items such as the produce of several personal plots.

Subjectivism: The healthy manner of looking at all socio-economic questions with clear pre-conceptions based on Marxist-Leninist doctrine. This creates invulnerability to the tricky, pseudo-attractive arguments of capitalism.

Subotnik: A Soviet worker who is fully employed but who voluntarily contributes a number of his Saturdays, without pay, to work on an important construction project, e.g., excavation of a canal, harvesting, road building, which is of strategic importance to the State. This activity is more symbolic than productive.

Surplus Value: The cornerstone of the capitalist system. The additional price placed upon a manufactured item above and beyond the cost of the raw materials and the production process, which is to profit a class which has had no direct hand in the process and exploits the worker

Third-World Nations: Those nations which are favorably inclined towards the USSR and socialism, but are not yet fully in the Soviet camp. Wholly uncommitted nations which are just as friendly towards the West as towards the Soviet Union are normally treated as members of the capitalist camp, although this fact does not curb the attempts of the USSR to proselyte.

Trotzkyism: The doctrine that there should be simultaneous world-wide revolution, including in all the capitalist nations. This would cause a global bloodbath needlessly. This doctrine also suggests that each nation may plot its own socialist course dependent upon its own local situations and preferences, and that no one nation such as the Soviet Union may presume to dictate policy to other communist nations. On an ideological plane, this doctrine is considered to be the most dangerous to the USSR by the Party leaders.

APPENDIX 3

THE CONSTITUTION OF THE UNION OF SOVIET SOCIALIST REPUBLICS

I
PRINCIPLES OF THE SOCIAL STRUCTURE AND POLICY OF THE USSR

Chapter 1
THE POLITICAL SYSTEM

Article 1. The Union of Soviet Socialist Republics is the socialist state of the entire people and expresses the will and interests of the workers, peasants, and intelligentsia, the working people of all nations and nationalities of the country.

Article 2. All the power in the USSR belongs to the people.

The people exercise their state power through the Soviets of People's Deputies which constitute the political foundation of the USSR.

All other bodies of the state are under the control of, and accountable to, the Soviets of People's Deputies.

Article 3. The Soviet State is organized and functions according to the principle of democratic centralism, that is, the fact that all bodies of state authority from the lowest to the highest are elected, that they are accountable to the people, and that lower bodies are obligated to abide by the decisions of higher ones. Democratic centralism combines central leadership with local initiative and creative activity, and with the responsibility of each state body and official for the work entrusted to them.

Article 4. The Soviet State and all its bodies function on the basis of socialist law, insure the maintenance of law and order, and protect the interests of society and the rights and freedoms of the citizens.

State organizations and public organizations and officials shall observe the Constitution of the USSR and Soviet laws.

Article 5. Major matters of state shall be subject to nationwide discussion and shall be put to a popular vote (referendum).

Article 6. The Communist Party of the Soviet Union is the leading and guiding force of Soviet society and the nucleus of its political system and of all state and public organizations. The CPSU exists for the people and serves the people.

The Communist Party, armed with Marxism-Leninism, determines the general perspectives of the development of society and the course of domestic and foreign policy of the USSR, directs the great constructive work of the Soviet people, and bestows a planned, systematic and theoretically substantive character upon their struggle for the victory of communism.

All party organizations shall function within the framework of the Constitution of the USSR.

Article 7. Trade Unions, the All-Union Leninist Young Communist League, cooperatives and other public organizations, participate in managing state and public affairs and in deciding political, economic, social and cultural matters in accordance with the aims enunciated in their statutes.

Article 8. Work-Collectives participate in discussing and deciding state and public affairs, in planning production and social development, in training and assigning personnel; and in discussing and deciding matters pertaining to the management of enterprises and institutions, the improvement of working and living conditions, and the use of funds allocated both for developing production and for social and cultural purposes and financial incentives.

Work-Collectives promote socialist competition, the propagation of progressive methods of work, and the strengthening of production discipline. They educate their members in the spirit of communist morality and to strive intensify their political consciousness and raise their cultural level, skills and qualifications.

Article 9. The extension of socialist democracy is the principal objective in the development of the political system of Soviet society. This entails increasingly broader participation of citizens in managing the affairs of society and state, continuous improvement in the mechanism of state, increasing activities of public organizations, strengthening the system of People's Control, consolidating the legal foundations for the functions of state and public life, greater openness and publicity, and constant responsiveness to public opinion.

Chapter 2
THE ECONOMIC SYSTEM

Article 10. The basis for the economic system of the USSR is socialist ownership of the means of production in the form of state property (belonging to all the people), and collective-farm and cooperative property.

Socialist ownership also includes the property of trade unions and other public organizations, which they require to carry out their purposes under their statutes.

The state protects socialist property and provides and conditions for its growth.

No one has the right to use socialist property for personal gain or other selfish purposes.

Article 11. State property, that is, the common property of the Soviet people, is the principal form of socialist property.

The land, its minerals, waters and forests are the exclusive property of the state. The state owns the basic means of production in industry, construction and agriculture; the means of transportation and communication; the banks; the property of state-run trade organizations and public utilities and other state-run enterprises; most urban housing; and other property necessary for the purposes of the state.

Article 12. The property of collective farms and other cooperative organizations, and of their joint enterprises, is comprised of the means of production and other assets which they need for the purposes prescribed in their statutes

The land held by the collective farms is secured to them, in perpetuity, for their free use

The state promotes the development of collective farm and cooperative property and its gradual convergence into state property.

Collective farms, like other users of the land, are obligated to make effective and frugal use of the land and to increase its fertility

Article 13. Earned income forms the basis for the personal property of Soviet citizens. Personal property of citizens in the USSR may include articles for everyday use, personal consumption and convenience; tools and other objects on a small landholding; a house; and earned savings. The personal property of citizens and the right to inherit it are protected by the state.

Citizens may be granted the use of plots of land in the manner prescribed by law, for augmentative cultivation (including the keeping of livestock and poultry), for fruit and vegetable growing, or for construction of an individual dwelling. Citizens are required to make reasonable use of the land allocated to them. The state and collective farms provide assistance to citizens in working their small landholdings.

Property owned or used by citizens may not be used as a method of obtaining unearned income, or be employed to the detriment to the interests of society.

Article 14. The labor of the Soviet people, free from exploitation, is the source of growth of social wealth and of popular and individual well being.

The state exercises control over the apportionment of labor and consumption in accordance with the principle of socialism: "From each according to his ability, to each according to his work." It fixes the tax rate on taxable income.

A person's status in society is determined by socially useful work and its results. Through a combination of material and moral incentives, and the encouragement of innovation and creative work attitude, the state helps to transform labor into the primary vital need of every Soviet citizen.

Article 15. The primary objective of social production under socialism is the fullest possible satisfaction of the people's growing material, cultural and intellectual needs.

By relying on the creative initiative of the working people, socialist competition and scientific and technological progress; and by improving the forms and methods of economic management, the state insures the growth of labor productivity, the increase of production efficiency and work quality, and the dynamic, planned, proportionate development of the economy.

Article 16. The economy of the USSR is an integrated economic complex which comprises all elements of social production, distribution and exchange on its territory

The economy is managed on the basis of state planning for economic and social development, with due consideration given to the sectoral and territorial principles; and by combining centralized direction with managerial independence and initiative of individual and amalgamated enterprises and other organizations. Active use is made of management accounting, profit and cost factors, and other economic levers and incentives.

Article 17. In the USSR, individual labor in the handicrafts, farming, the providing of public services, and other activities based exclusively on the personal work of individuals and members of their families, is permitted by law. The state regulates such work to insure that it serves the interests of society

Article 18. In the interest of future generations, necessary steps are taken in the USSR to protect and to make rational use of the land and its mineral and water resources, and of the plant and animal kingdoms; and to preserve the purity of air and water, to insure the replenishment of natural resources, and to improve the human environment.

Chapter 3
SOCIAL DEVELOPMENT AND CULTURE

Article 19. The unbreakable alliance between the workers, peasants and intelligentsia constitutes the social basis of the USSR.

The state assists in the enhancement of the social homogeneity of society, that is, the elimination of class differences and of the essential distinctions between urban and rural and between intellectual and physical labor, thereby drawing together all nations and nationalities of the USSR.

Article 20. In accordance with the communist ideology that "The free development of the individual is the condition for the free development of society," the state pursues the aim of giving citizens an increasing number of genuine opportunities to apply their creative energy, ability and talent, and to develop their personalities in all ways possible.

Article 21. The state is concerned with improving working conditions, safety and labor protection and the scientific organization of work, and with the reduction and eventual elimination of all heavy physical labor through comprehensive mechanization and mechanization of the production processes in all branches of the economy.

Article 22. A program is being consistently implemented in the USSR to convert agricultural labor into a variant of industrial labor, to extend the network of educational, cultural and medical institutions, and of trade, public catering, service and public utility facilities in rural localities, and to transform hamlets and villages into well-planned and well-supplied settlements.

Article 23. The state is pursuing a continuing policy of raising the pay level and real income of the people by means of an increase of productivity.

In order to satisfy the needs of the Soviet people more fully, social expenditure funds have been created The state, with broad participation by public organizations and work collectives, insures the growth and just distribution of these funds.

Article 24. State systems of health protection, social security, trade, public catering, communal services and amenities, and public utilities, are in operation and are being augmented in the USSR.

The state encourages cooperatives and other public organizations to provide all types of services for the populace. It also encourages the development of mass physical culture and sports.

Article 25 In the USSR there is a uniform system of public education which is being constantly improved, which provides general education and vocational training for the citizenry, and which serves the communist education and the intellectual and physical development of youth and trains them for work and social activity.

Article 26. In accordance with the needs of society the state provides for the planned development of science and the training of scientific personnel, and organizes the introduction of the results of research into the economy and into other spheres of life

Article 27. The state is concerned with the protection, augmentation and the making of extensive use of the cultural wealth of society for the moral and esthetic education of the Soviet people and for the raising of their cultural level.

The development of professional, amateur and folk arts is encouraged in every manner in the USSR.

Chapter 4
FOREIGN POLICY

Article 28. The USSR resolutely pursues the Leninist policy of peace and supports the strengthening of the security of nations and broad international cooperation.

The foreign policy of the USSR is aimed at insuring international conditions favorable for the building of communism in the USSR, safeguarding the state interests of the Soviet Union, consolidating the positions of world socialism, supporting the struggle of peoples for national liberation and social progress, preventing wars of aggression, achieving total universal disarmament, and consistently implementing the principle of peaceful coexistence of states with different social systems

War propaganda is outlawed in the USSR.

Article 29. The relations of the USSR with other states are based on the observance of the following principles: sovereign equality; mutual renunciation of the use or threat of force; inviolability of frontiers; territorial integrity of states; peaceful settlements of disputes; non-intervention in internal affairs; respect for human rights and fundamental freedoms; equal rights for peoples and their right to decide their own destiny; cooperation among states; and fulfillment, in good faith, of obligations arising from the generally recognized principles and rules of international law, and from the international treaties signed by the USSR.

Article 30. As a part of the world system of socialism and the socialist community, the USSR promotes and strengthens friendship, cooperation, and comradely mutual assistance with other socialist countries on the basis of the principle of socialist internationalism, and takes an active part in socialist economic integration and the socialist international division of labor

Chapter 5
DEFENSE OF THE SOCIALIST MOTHERLAND

Article 31. Defense of the socialist motherland is the concern of the entire people, and is one of the most important functions of the state

In order to defend the gains of socialism, the peaceful labor of the Soviet people, and the sovereignty and territorial integrity of the state, the USSR maintains armed forces and has instituted universal military service.

The duty of the Armed Forces of the USSR to the people is to provide reliable defense of the socialist motherland and to be in constant combat readiness, guaranteeing that any aggressor may be instantly repulsed

Article 32. The state insures the security and the defensive capability of the country and supplies the Armed Forces of the USSR with all that is necessary for that purpose.

The duty of state bodies, public organizations, officials and citizens in regard to safeguarding the security of the country and strengthening its defense capability are defined in the laws of the USSR.

II.
THE STATE
AND
THE INDIVIDUAL

Chapter 6
CITIZENSHIP OF THE USSR.
EQUAL RIGHTS OF CITIZENS.

Article 33. Uniform federal citizenship has been established in the USSR. Every citizen of a Union Republic is a citizen of the USSR.

The bases and procedures for acquiring or forfeiting Soviet citizenship are defined by the Law of Citizenship of the USSR.

When they are abroad, citizens of the USSR enjoy the protection and assistance of the Soviet state.

Article 34 Citizens of the USSR are equal before the law, without distinctions based on origin, social or property status, race or nationality, sex, education, language, religious attitudes, nature and type of occupation, domicile, or other factors of status.

The equal rights of citizens of the USSR are guaranteed in all fields of economic, political, social and cultural life.

Article 35 Women and men have equal rights in the USSR.

The exercise of these rights is insured by affording women equal access with men to education and vocational and professional training, equal opportunities in employment, compensation and promotion, and in social, political and cultural activities, and through special labor and health protection measures for women; by providing conditions which enable mothers to work; by legal protection and material and moral support for mothers and children, including paid leaves and other benefits for pregnant women and mothers; and by the gradual reduction of working hours for mothers with small children.

Article 36. Citizens of the USSR of different races and nationalities have equal rights

The exercise of these rights is insured by a policy of total development and cohesive bonds of all the nations and nationalities of the USSR; by educating the citizenry in the spirit of Soviet patriotism and socialist internationalism; and by making possible the use of native languages and other languages of other peoples of the USSR.

Any direct or indirect limitation of the rights of citizens or the creation of direct or indirect privileges on the grounds of race or nationality, or any advocacy of racial or national exclusiveness, hostility or contempt, are punishable by law.

Article 37. Citizens of other countries or stateless persons in the USSR are guaranteed the rights and freedoms provided by law, including the right to apply to a court and other state bodies for the protection of their personal, property, family, and other rights.

Citizens of other countries and stateless persons, when in the USSR, must respect the Constitution of the USSR and observe Soviet laws.

Article 38. The USSR grants the right of asylum to foreigners who are persecuted for defending the interests of the working people and the cause of peace, or for participating in revolutionary or national-liberation movements, or for progressive social, political, scientific or other creative activity.

Chapter 7
THE BASIC RIGHTS, FREEDOMS AND OBLIGATIONS OF CITIZENS OF THE USSR

Article 39. Citizens of the USSR fully enjoy the social, economic, political and personal rights and freedoms proclaimed and guaranteed by the Constitution of the USSR and by Soviet law. The socialist system insures the expansion of the rights and freedoms of citizens and the continued improvement of their standards of living, as programs to develop social, economic and cultural life are fulfilled.

Enjoyment by citizens of their rights and freedoms must not be to the detriment of the interests of society or the state, or infringe upon the rights of other citizens.

Article 40. Citizens of the USSR have the right to work (that is, to guaranteed employment and pay in accordance with the quantity and quality of their work, and not below the state-established minimum), including the right to choose their trade or profession, type of job or employment in accordance with their desires, abilities, training and education, with necessary attention to the needs of society.

This right is assured by the socialist economic system, the steady growth of productive forces, free vocational and professional training, improvement of skills, training in new trades and professions, and the development of systems of vocational guidance and job placement.

Article 41. Citizens of the USSR have a right to rest and leisure.

This right is assured by establishing a working week not to exceed 41 hours for workers and other employees, a shorter working day in a number of trades and industries, and shorter hours for night work; by providing paid annual vacations, weekly days of rest, enlargement of the network of cultural, educational and health improvement institutions and a mass-scale development of sports, physical culture, camping and tourism; by providing neighborhood recreational fascilities and other opportunities for judicious use of free time

The length of working and leisure time for collective farmers is determined by their collective farms.

Article 42. Citizens of the USSR have the right to health protection

This right is assured by free, qualified medical care provided by state health institutions; by extending the network of therapeutic and health improvement institutions; by developing and improving safety and hygiene in industry; by conducting widespread prophylactic measures; by measures to improve the environment; by special care for the health of the new generation, including the prohibition of child labor but excluding the work done by children as part of the school curriculum; and by developing research to prevent or reduce the incidence of disease and to assure citizens of a long and active life.

Article 43. Citizens of the USSR have the right to support in old age, in illness, and in the event of complete or partial disability or death of the breadwinner

This right is guaranteed by the social insurance of workers and other employees and of collective farmers; by allowances for temporary disability; by provision, either by the state of the collective farms, of retirement pensions, disability pensions, and pensions for the death of the breadwinner; by providing employment for the partially disabled; by care for the elderly and the disabled; and by other forms of social security

Article 44. Citizens of the USSR have the right to housing.

This right is assured by the development and upkeep of state and socially owned housing; by assistance for cooperative and individual housing construction; by fair distribution, under public control, of the housing that becomes available through fulfillment of the program of constructing well-equipped dwellings, and by low rents and low charges for utilities. Citizens of the USSR shall take good care of the housing allocated to them.

Article 45. Citizens of the USSR have the right to education.

This right is assured by the free provision of all forms of education, by the institution of universal, compulsory secondary education, and by the broad development of vocational, specialized secondary, and higher education in which instruction is oriented to practical activity and production; by the development of off-campus correspondence and evening courses; by the provision of state scholarships, grants and privileges for students; by the free distribution of textbooks; by the opportunity to attend schools where instruction is in the native tongue; and by providing facilities for self-education.

Article 46. Citizens of the USSR have the right to enjoy cultural benefits.

This right is assured by broad access to the cultural treasures of their own land and of the world which are preserved in state and other public collections; by the development and equitable distribution of cultural and educational institutions throughout the country; by developing radio and television broadcasting and the publishing of books, newspapers and periodicals and by expanding free library services; and by increasing cultural exchanges with other countries.

Article 47. Citizens of the USSR, in accordance with the aims of building communism, are guaranteed the freedom of scientific, technical and artistic work. This freedom is assured by widening scientific research, encouraging invention and innovation, and developing literature and the arts. The state provides the necessary material conditions for this, and supports voluntary societies and unions of workers in the arts, organizes the introduction of inventions and innovations in production, and in other spheres of activity.

The rights of authors, inventors and innovators are protected by the state.

Article 48. Citizens of the USSR have the right to take part in the management and administration of state and public affairs and in the discussion and adoption of laws and measures of national and local significance.

This right is assured by the opportunity to vote and to be elected to Soviets of People's Deputies and to other elected state bodies, to take part in nationwide discussions and referendums, in People's Control Commissions, in the work of state bodies, public organizations, and local community groups, and in meetings at places of work and residence.

Article 49. Every citizen of the USSR has the right to submit proposals to state bodies and public organizations for improving their activities, and to criticize shortcomings in their work.

Officials are obligated, within established time limits, to examine the proposals and requests of citizens, to reply to them, and to take appropriate action.

Persecution for criticism is prohibited Persons guilty of such persecution shall be liable.

Article 50. In accordance with the interests of the people and in order to strengthen and develop the socialist system, citizens of the USSR are guaranteed the freedoms of speech, press, assembly, meetings, street processions and demonstrations.

Exercise of these political freedoms is assured by putting public buildings, streets and squares at the disposal of the working people and their organizations, by broadening the dissemination of information, and by the opportunity to use the press, television and the radio.

Article 51. In accordance with the aims of building communism, citizens of the USSR have the right to associate in public organizations which promote their political activity and initiative and the satisfaction of their various interests

Public organizations are guaranteed the conditions necessary for the successful performance of the functions defined in their rules.

Article 52. Citizens of the USSR are guaranteed freedom of conscience, that is, the right to profess or not to profess any religion, and to conduct religious worship or atheistic propaganda. Incitement of hostilities or hatred on religious grounds is forbidden.

In the USSR the church is separated from the state, and the school from the church.

Article 53. The family enjoys the protection of the state

Marriage is based on the free consent of the woman and the man; the spouses are completely equal in their family relations.

The state helps the family by providing and developing a wide-spread system of child care institutions, by organizing and improving communal services and public catering, by paying grants upon the birth of children, by providing children's allowances and benefits for large families, and by other forms of family allowances and assistance

Article 54. Citizens of the USSR are guaranteed the inviolability of the person. No one may be arrested except by a court decision or by a warrant from a procurator.

Article 55. Citizens of the USSR are guaranteed the inviolability of their home. No one may, without lawful grounds, enter a home against the will of those residing in it.

Article 56. The privacy of citizens, and of their correspondence, telephone conversations and telegraphic communications is protected by law

Article 57. Respect for the individual and the protections of the rights and freedoms of citizens is the duty of all state bodies, public organizations and officials

Citizens of the USSR have the right to protection by the courts against infrigements upon their honor and reputation, life and health, and personal freedom and property

Article 58. Citizens of the USSR have the right to lodge complaints against the actions of officials, state bodies and public bodies. Complaints shall be examined in accordance with the procedures and within the time limits established by law

Actions by officials which conflict with the law or exceed their authority and infringe upon the rights of citizens may be appealed in court in the manner prescribed by law.

Citizens of the USSR have the right to compensation for damage resulting from unlawful actions by state organizations and public organizations, or by officials in the performance of their duties.

Article 59. The exercise of rights and freedoms by citizens is inseparable from the performance of their duties and obligations

Citizens of the USSR are obligated to observe the Constitution of the USSR and Soviet laws, to comply with the standards of socialist conduct, and to uphold the honor and dignity of Soviet citizenship.

Article 60. It is the duty of, and a question of honor for, every able-bodied citizen of the USSR to work conscientiously in his chosen socially useful occupation, and to observe labor discipline strictly. Evasion of socially useful work is incompatible with the principles of socialist society

Article 61. Citizens of the USSR are obligated to preserve and protect socialist property. It is the duty of a citizen of the USSR to resist misappropriation and squandering of state and socially owner property, and to make frugal use of the people's wealth.

Persons encroaching in any way on socialist property shall be punished in accordance with the law

Article 62 Citizens of the USSR are obligated to safeguard the interests of the Soviet State and to enhance its power and prestige.

Defense of the Socialist Motherland is the sacred duty of every citizen of the USSR.

Betrayal of the Motherland is the gravest of crimes against the people.

Article 63. Military service in the ranks of the Armed Forces of the USSR is the honorable duty of every Soviet citizen.

Article 64. It is the duty of every citizen of the USSR to respect the national dignity of other citizens, and to strength friendship between the nations and nationalities of the multinational Soviet State.

Article 65. A citizen of the USSR is obligated to respect the rights and lawful interests of other persons, to be uncompromisingly opposed to antisocial behavior, and to help maintain public order.

Article 66. Citizens of the USSR are obligated to concern themselves with the upbringing of children, to train them for socially useful work, and to raise them as worthy members of socialist society Children are obligated to care for their parents and to help them

Article 67. Citizens of the USSR are obligated to protect nature and to preserve its wealth.

Article 68. Concern for the preservation of historical monuments and other cultural values is the duty and obligation of citizens of the USSR

Article 69. It is the internationalist duty of citizens of the USSR to promote friendship and cooperation with peoples of other lands and to help maintain and strengthen world peace

III
THE NATIONAL-STATE STRUCTURE OF THE USSR

Chapter 8
THE USSR - A FEDERAL STATE

Article 70. The Union of Soviet Socialist Republics is and integral, federal, multinational state formed on the principle of socialist federalism as a result of the free self-determination of nations, and the voluntary association of equal Soviet Socialist Republics.

The USSR embodies the state unity of the Soviet people and draws all its nations and nationalities together for the purpose of building communism jointly.

Article 71. The Union of Soviet Socialist Republics unites:

the Russian Soviet Federated Socialist Republic
the Ukrainian Soviet Socialist Republic
the Belorussian Soviet Socialist Republic

the Uzbek Soviet Socialist Republic
the Kazakh Soviet Socialist Republic
the Georgian Soviet Socialist Republic
the Azerbaidzhan Soviet Socialist Republic
the Lithuanian Soviet Socialist Republic
the Moldavian Soviet Socialist Republic
the Latvian Soviet Socialist Republic
the Kirgiz Soviet Socialist Republic
the Tadzhik Soviet Socialist Republic
the Armenian Soviet Socialist Republic
the Turkman Soviet Socialist Republic
the Estonian Soviet Socialist Republic.

Article 72. Each Union Republic shall retain the right freely to secede from the USSR.

Article 73. The jurisdiction of the Union of Soviet Socialist Republics, as represented by its highest bodies of state authority and administration shall encompass:

1. the admission of new republics into the USSR; endorsement of the formation of new autonomous republics and autonomous regions within Union Republics;

2. determination of the state boundaries of the USSR and the approval of changes in the boundaries between Union Republics;

3. establishment of general principles for the organization and functions of republic and local bodies of state authority and administration;

4. the assurance of uniformity of legislative norms throughout the USSR, and the establishment of the fundamentals of legislation for the Union of Soviet Socialist Republics and Union Republics;

5. pursuance of a uniform economic and social policy; direction of the country's economy; determination of the main avenues for scientific and technological progress and of general measures for the efficient exploitation and conservation of natural resources; drafting and approval of state plans for the economic and social development of the USSR, and endorsement of reports on their fulfillment

6. drafting and approval of the Consolidated Budget of the USSR, and endorsement of the report on its execution; management of a single monetary and credit system; determination of the taxes and revenues forming the Budget of the USSR; and formulating price and wage policy;

7. direction of the sectors of the economy and of enterprises and amalgamations under Union jurisdiction, and the general supervision of industries under Union-Republic jurisdiction;

8. issues of war and peace, defense of the sovereignty of the USSR and the safeguarding of its frontiers and territory, and the organization of defense; direction of the Armed Forces of the USSR;

9. state security;

10. representation of the USSR in international relations; the relations of the USSR with other states and with international organizations; establishment of general procedures for, and corrdination of, the relations of the Union Republics with other states and with international organizations; foreign trade and other forms of external economic activity on the basis of state monopoly;

11. control over observance of the Constitution of the USSR and assurance of the conformity of the Constitutions of the Union Republics to the Constitution

of the USSR.

12. and disposal over other matters of All-Union importance.

Article 74. The law of the USSR shall have the same force in all Union Republics. In the event of a conflict between a Union Republic law and an All-Union law, the law of the USSR shall prevail.

Article 75. The Territory of the Union of Soviet Socialist Republics is a single entity composed of the territories of the Union Republics

The sovereignty of the USSR extends throughout its territory.

Chapter 9
THE SOVIET SOCIALIST "UNION REPUBLIC"

Article 76. A union Republic is a sovereign Soviet socialist state that has united with other Soviet Republics into the Union of Soviet Socialist Republics.

Outside the spheres listed in Article 73 of the Constitution of the USSR, a Union Republic exercizes independent authority on its territory.

A Union Republic shall have its own Constitution conforming to the Constitution of the USSR, with the specific features of the Republic being taken into consideration.

Article 77. Union Republics participate in the decision making in the Supreme Soviet of the USSR, the Presidium of the Supreme Soviet of the USSR, the Government of the USSR, and other bodies of the Union of Soviet Socialist Republics in matters that come within the jurisdiction of the Union of Soviet Socialist Republics.

A Union Republic shall assure comprehensive economic and social development on its territory, facilitate the exercise of the powers of the USSR on its territory, and implement the decisions of the highest bodies of state authority and administration of the USSR.

In matters that come within its jurisdiction, a Union Republic shall coordinate and control the activities of enterprises, institutions and organizations subordinate to the Union.

Article 78. The territory of a Union Republic may not be altered without its consent. The boundaries between Union Republics may be altered by mutual agreement of the Republics concerned, subject to ratification by the Union of Soviet Socialist Republics

Article 79. A Union Republic shall determine its division into territories, regions, areas and districts, and shall decide other matters relating to its administrative and territorial structure

Article 80. A Union Republic has the right to enter into relations with other states, to conclude treaties with them, to exchange diplomatic and consular representatives, and to take part in the activities of international organizations.

Article 81. The Sovereign rights of Union Republics shall be safeguarded by the USSR.

Chapter 10
THE AUTONOMOUS SOVIET SOCIALIST REPUBLIC

Article 82. An Autonomous Republic is a constituent part of a Union Republic.

In spheres not within the jurisdiction of the Union of Soviet Socialist Republics and the Union Republic, an Autonomous Republic shall deal independently with matters within its jurisdiction.

An Autonomous Republic shall have its own Constitution conforming to the Constitutions of the USSR and the Union Republic, with specific features of the Autonomous Republic being taken into consideration

Article 83. An Autonomous Republic takes part in decision making in matters that come within the jurisdiction of the USSR and the Union Republic, through the highest bodies of state authority and administration of the USSR and of the Union Republic respectively.

An Autonomous Republic shall assure comprehensive economic and social development on its territory, facilitate the exercise of the authority of the USSR and the Union Republic on its territory, and implement decisions of the highest bodies of state authority and administration of the USSR and the Union Republic.

In matters within its jurisdiction, an Autonomous Republic shall coordinate and control the activities of enterprises, institutions and organizations subordinate to the Union or the Union Republic

Article 84. The territory of an Autonomous Republic may not be altered without its consent.

Article 85. The Russian Soviet Federated Socialist Republic includes the Bashkir, Buriat, Dagestan, Kabardin-Balkar, Kalmyk, Karelian, Komi, Mari, Mordovian, North Ossetian, Tartar, Tuva, Udmurt, Chechen-Ingush, Chuvash, and Yakut Autonomous Soviet Socialist Republics.

The Uzbek Soviet Socialist Republic contains the Kara-Kalpak Autonomous Soviet Socialist Republic.

The Georgian Soviet Socialist Republic contains the Abkhasian and Adzharian Autonomous Soviet Socialist Republics.

The Azerbaidzhan Soviet Socialist Republic contains the Nakhichevan Autonomous Soviet Socialist Republic.

Chapter 11
THE AUTONOMOUS REGION AND AUTONOMOUS AREA

Article 86. An Autonomous Region is a constituent part of a Union Republic or Territory The Law of an Autonomous Region, upon being submitted by the Soviet of People's Deputies of the pertinent Autonomous Region, shall be adopted by the Supreme Soviet of the Union Republic

Article 87. The Russian Soviet Federated Socialist Republic contains the Adygei, Gorno-Altai, Jewish, Karachai-Circassian, and Khakass Autonomous Regions.

The Georgian Soviet Socialist Republic contains the South Ossetian Autonomous Region.

The Azerbaidzhan Soviet Socialist Republic contains the Nagorno-Karabackh Autonomous Region.

The Tadzhik Soviet Socialist Republic contains the Gorno-Badakhshan Autonomous Region.

Article 88. An Autonomous Area is a constituent part of a Territory or Region. The Law of an Autonomous Area shall be ratified by the Supreme Soviet of the pertinent Union Republic

IV
SOVIETS OF PEOPLE'S DEPUTIES AND THE PROCEDURES FOR THEIR ELECTION

Chapter 12
THE SYSTEM AND WORK-PRINCIPLES OF SOVIETS OF PEOPLE'S DEPUTIES

Article 89. The Soviets of People's Deputies, that is, the Supreme Soviet of the USSR, the Supreme Soviets of Union Republics, the Supreme Soviets of Autonomous Republics, the Soviets of People's Deputies of Territories and Regions, the Soviet's of People's Deputies of Autonomous Regions and Autonomous Areas, and the Soviet's of People's Deputies of districts, cities, city districts, settlements and villages, shall constitute a single system of bodies of state authority.

Article 90. The term of the Supreme Soviet of the USSR, the Supreme Soviets of the Union Republics, and the Supreme Soviets of Autonomous Republics shall be five years.

The term for local Soviets of People's Deputies shall be two and a half years.

Elections to Soviets of People's Deputies shall not be later than two months before the expiration of the term of the pertinent Soviet.

Article 91. The most important questions within the jurisdiction of the respective Soviets of People's Deputies shall be considered and concluded at their sessions

Soviets of People's Deputies shall elect standing committees and form executive-administrative and other bodies accountable to them.

Article 92. Soviets of People's Deputies shall form people's control bodies combining state control with control by the working people at enterprises, collective farms, institutions and organizations.

People's control bodies shall check on the fulfillment of state plans and assignments, fight against breaches of state discipline, local prejudices, narrow-minded departmental attitudes, mismanagement, extravagance and waste, red tape and bureaucracy, and shall help improve the operation of the state mechanism.

Article 93. Soviets of People's Deputies shall direct all sectors of state, economic, social and cultural development either directly or through bodies created by them, make decisions and insure their implementation and verify their adoption.

Article 94. Soviets of People's Deputies shall function publicly on the basis of collective, open, constructive discussion and decision-making; on the basis of systematic reports submitted to them and the people by their executive-administrative and other bodies; and on the basis of involving citizens in their work on a broad scale

Soviets of People's Deputies and the bodies constituted by them shall systematically inform the public about their work and about the decisions arrived at by them.

Chapter 13
THE ELECTORAL SYSTEM

Article 95. Deputies to all Soviets shall be elected on the basis of universal, equal, and direct voting by secret ballot.

Article 96. Elections shall be universal: all citizens of the USSR who have reached the age of 18 shall have the right to vote and to be elected, with the exception of persons who have been legally declared insane.

To be eligible for election to the Supreme Soviet of the USSR a citizen of the USSR must have reached the age of 21

Article 97. Elections shall be equal: each citizen shall have one vote; all voters shall exercise their franchise on an equal basis.

Article 98. Elections shall be direct: deputies to all Soviets of People's Deputies shall be elected by citizens by direct vote.

Article 99. Voting at elections shall be secret: restrictions on the exercise of the voting process is forbidden.

Article 100. The following shall have the right to nominate candidates: branches and organizations of the Communist Party of the Soviet Union, trade unions, the All-Union Leninist Young Communist League, cooperatives and other public organizations, work collectives, and meetings of servicemen in their military units.

Citizens of the USSR and public organizations are guaranteed the right to free and complete discussion of the political and personal qualities and competence of candidates, and the right to campaign for them at meetings, in the press, on television and the radio.

The expenses involved in holding elections to Soviets of People's Deputies shall be met by the state.

Article 101. Deputies to Soviets of People's Deputies shall be elected by their constituencies

A citizen of the USSR, as a rule, may not be elected to more than two Soviets of People's Deputies.

Elections to the Soviets shall be conducted by electoral committees consisting of representatives of public organizations and work collectives, and of meetings of servicemen in military units

The procedures for holding elections to Soviets of People's Deputies shall be defined by the laws of the USSR and of Union and Autonomous Republics

Article 102. Electors give mandates to their deputies.

The pertinent Soviet of People's Deputies shall examine electors' mandates, take them into consideration in the drafting of economic and social development plans and in drawing up the budget, shall arrange for the implementation of the mandates, and shall inform citizens about their realization

Chapter 14
PEOPLE'S DEPUTIES

Article 103. Deputies are the plenipotentiary representatives of the people in the Soviets of People's Deputies.

In the Soviets, Deputies deal with matters concerning state, economic, social and cultural development, organize the implementation of the decisions of the Soviets, and exercise control over the work of state bodies, enterprises, institutions and organizations.

Deputies shall be guided in their activities by the interests of the state, shall take the needs of their constituency into account, and shall work to implement the mandates of their electors.

Article 104. Deputies shall exercise their powers without discontinuing their regular employment or duties

During sessions of the Soviet, and in order to exercise their powers as deputies in other areas as stipulated by law. Deputies shall be released from their regular employment and duties with retention of their average salaries at their permanent place of work.

Article 105. A Deputy has the right to address inquiries to the appropriate state bodies and officials, who are obliged to reply to them at sessions of the Soviet.

Deputies have the right to approach all state or public bodies, enterprises, institutions and organizations on matters arising from their work as deputies and to participate in the consideration of the questions raised by them. Heads of state or public bodies, enterprises, institutions and organizations concerned, are obliged to receive Deputies without delay and to consider their proposals within the time limits established by law.

Article 106. Deputies will be assured conditions necessary for unhampered and effective exercise of their rights and duties.

The immunity of deputies and other guarantees of their activities as Deputies, are delineated in the Law on the Status of Deputies and other legislative acts of the USSR and of Union and Autonomous Republics.

Article 107. Deputies shall report on their own work and on the work of their Soviet to their constituency and to the work collectives and public organizations which nominated them

Deputies who have not been found worthy of the confidence of their constituents may be recalled at any time by a decision of a majority of the electors in accordance with the precedures established by law.

V.
HIGHER BODIES OF STATE AUTHORITY AND OF ADMINISTRATION OF THE USSR

Chapter 15
THE SUPREME SOVIET OF THE USSR

Article 108. The Supreme Soviet of the USSR is the highest body of state authority of the USSR.

The Supreme Soviet of the USSR is empowered to deal with all matters within the jurisdiction of the Union of Soviet Socialist Republics as defined by this Constitution.

The adoption and amendment of the Constitution of the USSR; admission of new Republics into the USSR; endorsement of the formation of new Autonomous Republics and Autonomous Regions; approval of state plans for economic and social development, of the budget of the USSR, and of reports on their execution; and the institution of bodies of the USSR accountable to it, are the exclusive prerogative of the Supreme Soviet of the USSR.

Laws of the USSR shall be enacted by the Supreme Soviet of the USSR or by a nation-wide vote (referendum) held by a decision of the Supreme Soviet of the USSR.

Article 109. The Supreme Soviet of the USSR shall consist of two chambers: the Soviet of the Union and the Soviet of Nationalities.

The two chambers of the Supreme Soviet of the USSR shall have equal rights.

Article 110. The Soviet of the Union and the Soviet of Nationalities shall have an equal number of deputies.

The Soviet of the Union shall be elected by constituencies of equal population

The Soviet of Nationalities shall be elected on the basis of the following representation: 32 deputies from each Union Republic; 11 deputies from each Autonomous Republic; five deputies from each Autonomous Region; and one deputy from each Autonomous Area.

The Soviet of the Union and the Soviet of Nationalities shall decide on the validity of the deputies' credentials upon their presentation by the credential committees elected by them; and, in cases where the election law has been violated, shall nullify the election of the deputies affected

Article 111. Each chamber of the Supreme Soviet of the USSR shall elect a Chairman and four Vice-Chairmen

The Chairmen of the Soviet of the Union and of the Soviet of Nationalities shall preside over the sessions of their respective chambers and conduct their affairs.

Joint sessions of the chambers of the Supreme Soviet of the USSR shall be presided over alternately by the Chairman of the Soviet of the Union and the Chairman of the Soviet of Nationalities.

Article 112. Sessions of the Supreme Soviet of the USSR shall be convened twice a year.

Special sessions shall be convened by the Presidium of the Supreme Soviet at its discretion, or upon the proposal of a Union Republic, or upon the proposal of at least one-third of the deputies of one of the chambers.

A session of the Supreme Soviet of the USSR shall consist of separate or joint sessions of the chambers, and of meetings of the standing committees of the chambers, or of committees of the Supreme Soviet of the USSR convened between the sessions of the chambers. A session may be opened or closed at either a separate or a joint session of the chambers.

Article 113. The right to initiate legislation in the Supreme Soviet of the USSR is vested in the Soviet of the Union and the Soviet of Nationalities, the Presidium of the Supreme Soviet of the USSR, the Council of Ministers of the USSR, the Union Republics through their highest bodies of state authority, committees of the Supreme Soviet of the USSR and standing committees of its chambers, Deputies of the Supreme Soviet of the USSR, the Supreme Court of the USSR, and the Procurator General of the USSR.

The right to initiate legislation is also vested in public organizations through their national-level bodies.

Article 114. Bills and other matters submitted to the Supreme Soviet of the USSR shall be debated by its chambers at separate or joint sessions. When necessary, a bill or other matter may be referred to one or more committees for preliminary or additional consideration.

A law of the USSR shall be considered adopted when it has been passed by each chamber of the Supreme Soviet of the USSR by a majority of the total number of its deputies. Decisions and other acts of the Supreme Soviet of the USSR are adopted by a majority of the total number of Deputies of the Supreme Soviet of the USSR.

Bills and other extremely important matters of state may be submitted for nation-wide discussion by a decision of the Supreme Soviet of the USSR or its

Presidium, arrived at on their own initiative or upon the proposal of a Union Republic.

Article 115. In the event of a disagreement between the Soviet of the Union and the Soviet of Nationalities, the issue shall be referred for settlement to an arbitration committee formed by the chambers on a parity basis, after which it shall be considered for the second time by a joint session of the Soviet of the Union and the Soviet of Nationalities. If again no agreement is reached, the matter shall be postponed for debate at the next session of the Supreme Soviet of the USSR or submitted by the Supreme Soviet to a nation-wide referendum.

Article 116. Laws of the USSR and decisions and other acts of the Supreme Soviet of the USSR shall be published in the languages of the Union Republics above the signatures of the Chairman and Secretary of the Presidium of the Supreme Soviet of the USSR.

Article 117. A deputy of the Supreme Soviet of the USSR is empowered to address inquiries to the Council of Ministers of the USSR, and to Ministers and the heads of other bodies formed by the Supreme Soviet of the USSR. The Council of Ministers of the USSR, or the official to whom the inquiry is addressed, is obligated to submit a verbal or written reply within three days, at the given session of the Supreme Soviet of the USSR.

Article 118. A Deputy of the Supreme Soviet of the USSR many not be prosecuted, arrested, or incur a court-imposed penalty without the sanction of the Supreme Soviet of the USSR or, between its sessions, of the Presidium of the Supreme Soviet of the USSR.

Article 119. The Supreme Soviet of the USSR, at a joint session of its chambers, shall elect a Presidium of the Supreme Soviet of the USSR, which shall be a standing body of the Supreme Soviet of the USSR, accountable to it for all its actions, and which shall exercise the functions of the highest body of state authority of the USSR between sessions of the Supreme Soviet of the USSR, within the limits prescribed by the Constitution.

Article 120. The Presidium of the Supreme Soviet of the USSR shall be elected from among the Deputies and shall consist of a Chairman, First Vice-Chairman, 15 Vice-Chairman (one from each Union Republic), a Secretary, and 21 members.

Article 121. The Presidium of the Supreme Soviet of the USSR shall:

1. designate the date of elections of the Supreme Soviet of the USSR;

2. convene sessions of the Supreme Soviet of the USSR;

3 coordinate the work of the standing committees of the chambers of the Supreme Soviet of the USSR;

4. assure observance of the Constitution of the USSR and the conformity of the constitutions and laws of Union Republics to the Constitution and laws of the USSR;

5. interpret the laws of the USSR;

6. ratify and abrogate international treaties of the USSR;

7. revoke decisions and ordinances of the Council of Ministers of the USSR and of the Councils of Ministers of the Union Republics should they fail to conform to the law;

8. institute military and diplomatic ranks and other titles of a special nature; and confer the highest military and diplomatic ranks and other special titles;

9. initiate orders and medals of the USSR and honorary titles of the USSR; award orders and medals of the USSR; and confer honorary titles of the USSR;

10. grant citizenship of the USSR, and rule on matters of renunciation and deprivation of citizenship of the USSR, and of granting asylum;

11. issue All-Union acts of amnesty and exercise the right of pardon;

12. appoint and recall diplomatic representatives of the USSR to other countries and to international organizations;

13. receive credentials and letters of recall of the diplomatic representatives of foreign states accredited to it;

14. form the Council of Defense of the USSR and confirm its composition; appoint and dismiss the high command of the Armed Forces of the USSR;

15. proclaim martial law in particular localities and throughout the country in the interest of the defense of the USSR;

16. order general or partial mobilization;

17. between sessions of the Supreme Soviet of the USSR, proclaim a state of war in the event of an armed attack on the USSR or when it is necessary to meet international treaty obligations relating to mutual defense against aggression;

18. and exercise other powers vested in it by the Constitution and laws of the USSR

Article 122. The Presidium of the Supreme Soviet of the USSR, between sessions of the Supreme Soviet of the USSR and subject to being submitted for its confirmation at the subsequent session, shall:

1. amend existing legislative acts of the USSR when necessary;
2. approve changes in the boundaries between Union Republics;
3. form and abolish ministries and state commissions of the USSR upon the recommendation of the Council of Ministers of the USSR;
4. relieve individual members of the Council of Ministers of the USSR of their responsibilities and appoint persons to the Council of Ministers on the recommendation of the Chairman of the Council of Ministers of the USSR.

Article 123. The Presidium of the Supreme Soviet of the USSR promulgates decrees and adopts decisions.

Article 124. Upon expiration of the term of the Supreme Soviet of the USSR, the Presidium of the Supreme Soviet of the USSR shall retain its powers until the newly elected Supreme Soviet of the USSR has elected a new Presidium

The newly elected Supreme Soviet of the USSR shall be convened by the outgoing Presidium of the Supreme Soviet of the USSR within two months of the election.

Article 125. The Soviet of the Union and the Soviet of Nationalities shall elect standing committees from among the deputies to make a preliminary review of matters coming within the jurisdiction of the Supreme Soviet of the USSR, to promote execution of the laws of the USSR and other acts of the Supreme Soviet of the USSR and its Presidium, and to inspect the work of state bodies and organizations. The chambers of the Supreme Soviet of the USSR may also establish joint committees on a parity basis.

When it considers it necessary, the Supreme Soviet of the USSR may set up commissions of inquiry and audit, and committee on any other matter

All state and public bodies, organizations and officials are obligated to respond to the requests of these commissions of the Supreme Soviet of the USSR and of its chambers, and to submit the required materials and documents to them.

Recommendations of the commissions shall be subjected to consideration by state and public bodies, institutions and organizations. The commission shall be informed of the results of such consideration or of the action taken, within the prescribed time limit.

Article 126. The Supreme Soviet of the USSR controls the activities of all state bodies accountable to it.

The Supreme Soviet of the USSR shall form a People's Control Commission of the USSR to supervise the system of people's control.

The organization and procedures of people's control elements are defined by the Law of People's Control of the USSR

Article 127. The procedures of the Supreme Soviet of the USSR and of its bodies shall be defined in the Rules and Regulations of the Supreme Soviet of the USSR and other laws of the USSR enacted on the basis of the Constitution of the USSR.

Chapter 16
THE COUNCIL OF MINISTERS OF THE USSR

Article 128. The Council of Ministers of the USSR, that is, the Government of the USSR, is the highest executive and administrative body of state authority in the USSR.

Article 129. The Council of Ministers of the USSR shall be constituted by the Supreme Soviet of the USSR at a joint session of the Soviet of the Union and the Soviet of Nationalities, and shall consist of the Chairman of the Council of Ministers of the USSR, First-Vice-Chairmen and Vice-Chairmen, Ministers of the USSR, and Chairmen of State Commissions of the USSR.

The Chairmen of the Councils of Ministers of the Union Republic shall be _ex officio_ members of the Council of Ministers of the USSR.

The Supreme Soviet of the USSR, on the recommendation of the Chairman of the Council of Ministers of the USSR, may insert into the Government of the USSR the heads of other bodies and organizations of the USSR.

The Council of Ministers of the USSR shall submit its resignation to the newly elected Supreme Soviet of the USSR at it opening session.

Article 130. The Council of Ministers of the USSR shall be accountable and answerable to the Supreme Soviet of the USSR and, between sessions of the Supreme Soviet of the USSR, to the Presidium of the Supreme Soviet of the USSR.

The Council of Ministers of the USSR shall report regularly on its activities to the Supreme Soviet of the USSR.

Article 131. The Council of Ministers of the USSR is empowered to deal with all matters of state administration within the jurisdiction of the Union of Soviet Socialist Republics as long as, according to the Constitution, they do not come under the competence of the Supreme Soviet of the USSR or the Presidium of the Supreme Soviet of the USSR.

Within its sphere of authority, the Council of Ministers of the USSR shall:

1. assure guidance to the economic, social and cultural development; draw up and implement measures to promote the well-being and cultural development of the people, to develop science and engineering, to insure rational exploitation and conservation of natural resources, to consolidate the monetary and credit systems, to pursue uniform price, wage and social security policies, and to organize state insurance and a uniform system of accounting and statistics; and to organize the management of industrial, construction, and agricultural enterprises and amalgamations, transport and communications facilities, banks, and other organizations and institutions of national subordination;

2. draft current and long-range state plans for the economic and social development of the USSR and the Budget of the USSR, and submit them to the Supreme Soviet of the USSR; take measures towards the execution of the state plans and Budget; and report to the Supreme Soviet of the USSR on the implementation of the plans and Budget;

3. implement measures to defend the interests of the state, protect socialist property and maintain public order, and guarantee and protect the rights and freedoms of citizens;

4. take measures to insure state security;

5. exercise general guidance of the development of the Armed Forces of the USSR, and determine the annual number of citizens to be inducted for active military service;

6. provide general guidance concerning relations with other states, foreign trade, and economic, scientific, technical and cultural cooperation between the USSR and other countries; take measures to assure the observance of the USSR's international treaties; and ratify or abrogate intergovernmental international agreements;

7. and, when necessary, form committee, central boards and other departments subordinated to the Council of Ministers of the USSR to deal with matter of economic, social and cultural development, and defense.

Article 132. A Presidium of the Council of Ministers of the USSR consisting of the Chairman, the First Vice-Chairmen, and Vice-Chairmen of the Council of Ministers of the USSR, shall function as a standing body of the Council of Ministers of the USSR to deal with matters concerning guidance of the economy, and with other matters of state administration.

Article 133. The Council of Ministers of the USSR, on the basis of and in pursuance of the laws of the USSR and other decisions of the Supreme Soviet of the USSR and its Presidium, shall issue decisions and ordinances and make certain of their execution. The decisions and ordinances of the Council of Ministers of the USSR shall be binding throughout the USSR.

Article 134. The Council of Ministers of the USSR has the right, in matters within the jurisdiction of the Union of Soviet Socialist Republics, to suspend the excecution of decisions and ordinances of the Councils of Ministers of Union Republics, and to rescind acts of ministries and state committees of the USSR and of other bodies subordinated to it.

Article 135. The Council of Ministers of the USSR shall coordinate and direct the work of All-Union and Union Republic ministries, state commissions of the USSR, and other subordinate bodies.

All-Union ministries and state commissions of the USSR shall direct the work of the branches of administration entrusted to them, or shall exercise inter-branch administration throughout the territory of the USSR either directly or through bodies established by them.

Union-Republic ministries and state commissions of the USSR direct the work of the branches of administration entrusted to them, or exercise inter-branch administration, as a rule, through the corresponding ministries and state commissions and other bodies of the Union Republics, and directly administer individual enterprises and amalgamations of Union subordination. The procedures for transferring enterprises and amalgamations from Republic or local subordination to national subordination shall be defined by the Presidium of the Supreme Soviet of the USSR.

Ministries and State Commissions of the USSR shall be responsible for the condition and development of the areas of administration entrusted to them.

Within their competence they issue orders and other acts on the basis of, and in execution of, the laws of the USSR and other decisions of the Supreme Soviet of the USSR and its Presidium, and of decisions and ordinances of the Council of Ministers of the USSR, and organize and verify their implementation

Article 136. The competence of the Council of Ministers of the USSR and its Presidium, the procedures for their work, relationships between the Council of Ministers and other state bodies, and the listing of All-Union and Union-Republic Ministries and State Commissions of the USSR are defined in the Law on the Council of Ministers of the USSR, on the basis of the Constitution.

VI
FUNDAMENTAL PRINCIPLES OF THE STRUCTURE OF THE BODIES OF STATE AUTHORITY AND ADMINISTRATION OF UNION REPUBLICS

Chapter 17
HIGHER BODIES OF STATE AUTHORITY AND ADMINISTRATION OF A UNION REPUBLIC

Article 137. The highest body of state authority of a Union Republic shall be the Supreme Soviet of the Republic

The Supreme Soviet of a Union Republic is empowered to deal with all questions within the jurisdiction of the Republic under the Constitutions of the USSR and the Republic.

Adoption and amendment of the Constitution of a Union Republic; endorsement of state plans for economic and social development, of the budget of a Republic, and of reports on their fulfillment; and the formation of bodies accountable to the Supreme Soviet of the Union Republic are the exclusive prerogative of the Supreme Soviet of the Republic.

Laws of a Union Republic shall be enacted by the Supreme Soviet of the Union Republic or by a referendum held by decision of the Supreme Soviet of the Republic.

Article 138. The Supreme Soviet of a Union Republic shall elect a Presidium which is a standing body of that Supreme Soviet and accountable to it for all its activities. The composition and powers of the Presidium of the Supreme Soviet of a Union Republic shall defined in the Constitution of the Union Republic.

Article 139. The Supreme Soviet of a Union Republic shall form a Council of Ministers of the Union Republic, that is, the government of that Republic, which shall be the highest executive and administrative body of state authority in the Republic.

The Council of Ministers of a Union Republic shall be responsible and accountable to the Supreme Soviet of that Republic or, between sessions of the Supreme Soviet, to its Presidium.

Article 140. The Council of Ministers of a Union Republic issues decisions and ordinances on the basis of, and in pursuance of, the legislative acts of the USSR and of the Union Republic, and of decisions and ordinances of the Council of Ministers of the USSR, and shall organize and verify their execution.

Article 141. The Council of Ministers of a Union Republic has the right to suspend the execution of decisions and ordinances of the Councils of Ministers of Autonomous Republics, to rescind the decisions and orders of the Executive Committees of Soviets of People's Deputies of Territories, Regions and cities (i.e., cities under the jurisdiction of the Republic), and of Autonomous Regions, and in Union Republics not divided into regions, of the Executive Committees of district and corresponding city Soviets of People's Deputies

Article 142. The Council of Ministers of a Union Republic shall coordinate and direct the work of the Union-Republic and Republic Ministries, and of state committees of the Union Republic, and of other bodies under its jurisdiction.

The Union-Republic Ministries and state committees of a Union Republic shall direct the branches of administration entrusted to them, or exercise inter-branch control, and shall be subordinate to both the Council of Ministers of the Union Republic and the corresponding Union-Republic Ministry, or the state committee of the USSR.

Republic ministries and state committees shall direct the branches of administration entrusted to them, or exercise inter-branch control, and shall be subordinate to the Council of Ministers of the Union Republic

Chapter 18
HIGHER BODIES OF STATE AUTHORITY AND ADMINISTRATION OF AN AUTONOMOUS REPUBLIC

Article 143. The highest body of state authority of an Autonomous Republic shall be the Supreme Soviet of that Republic.

Adoption and amendment of the Constitution of an Autonomous Republic; endorsement of state plans for economic and social development, and of the Budget of the Republic; and the formulation of bodies accountable to the Supreme Soviet of the Autonomous Republic are the exclusive prerogatives of that Supreme Soviet.

Laws of a Autonomous Republic shall be enacted by the Supreme Soviet of the Autonomous Republic.

Article 144. The Supreme Soviet of an Autonomous Republic shall elect a Presidium of the Supreme Soviet of the Autonomous Republic and shall form a Council of Ministers of the Autonomous Republic, that is, the Government of that Republic.

Chapter 19
LOCAL BODIES OF STATE AUTHORITY AND ADMINISTRATION

Article 145. The bodies of state authority in Territories, Regions, Autonomous Regions, Autonomous Areas, districts, cities, city districts, settlements and rural communities shall be the pertinent Soviets of People's Deputies.

Article 146. Local Soviets of People's Deputies shall deal with all matters of local significance in accordance with the interests of the entire state and of the citizens residing in the area under their jurisdiction, implement decisions of higher bodies of state authority, guide the work of lower Soviets of People's Deputies, participate in discussions of matters of Republic and national significance, and submit their proposals concerning them.

Local Soviets of People's Deputies shall direct state, economic, social and cultural development within their territory; endorse plans for economic and social development and the local budget; exercise general guidance over state bodies, enterprises, institutions and organizations subordinate to them; insure observance of the laws, maintenance of law and order, and protection of the rights of citizens; and help strengthen the defense capability of the nation.

Article 147. Within their powers, local Soviets of People's Deputies shall assure the comprehensive, total economic and social development of their area; exercise control over the observance of legislation by enterprises, institutions and organizations subordinate to higher authorities and located in their area; and coordinate and supervise their activities which are related to land use, conservation, construction, utilization of manpower, production of consumer goods, and social, cultural, communal and other services and benefits for the public

Article 148. Local Soviets of People's Deputies shall decide matters falling within the powers accorded to them by the legislation of the USSR and of the pertinent Union Republic and Autonomous Republic. Their decisions shall be binding on all enterprises, institutions and organizations located within their area, and on officials and citizens.

Article 149. The executive-administrative bodies of local Soviets shall be the Executive Committees elected by them from among their deputies.

Executive Committees shall report on their work at least once a year to the Soviets that elected them and to meetings of citizens at their places of work or residence

Article 150. Executive Committees of local Soviets of People's Deputies shall be directly accountable to both the Soviet that elected them, and to the higher executive and administrative body.

VII.
JUSTICE,
ARBITRATION,
AND PROCURATOR'S
SUPERVISION

Chapter 20
COURTS AND ARBITRATION

Article 151. In the USSR justice is administered only by the courts. In the USSR there are the following courts: the Supreme Court of the USSR, the Supreme Courts of the Union Republics, the Supreme Courts of the Autonomous Republics, Territorial, Regional and City Courts, Courts of Autonomous Regions, Courts of Autonomous Areas, district people's courts (including city courts), and military tribunals in the Armed Forces.

Article 152 All courts in the USSR shall be formed on the principle of the election of judges and people's assessors

People's judges of district (city) people's courts shall be elected for a term of five years by the citizens of the district (city) on the basis of universal, equal and direct vote by secret ballot. People's assessors of district (city) people's courts shall be elected for a term of two and a half years at meetings of citizens at their places of work or residence by a show of hands.

Higher courts shall be elected for a term of five years by the corresponding Soviet of People's Deputies.

The judges of military tribunals shall be elected for a term of five years by the Presidium of the Supreme Soviet of the USSR; and assessors, for a term of two and a half years by meetings of servicemen.

Judges and people's assessors are responsible and accountable to their electors or to the bodies that elected them, shall report to them, and may be discharged by them in the manner prescribed by law.

Article 153. The Supreme Court of the USSR is the highest judicial body in the USSR and supervises the administration of justice by the courts of the USSR and Union Republics within the limits established by law.

The Supreme Court of the USSR shall be elected by the Supreme Soviet of the USSR and shall consist of a Chairman, Vice-Chairmen, members, and people's assessors. The Chairmen of the Supreme Courts of Union Republics are ex officio members of the Supreme Court of the USSR.

The organization and procedures of the Supreme Court of the USSR are defined in the Law on the Supreme Court of the USSR.

Article 154. The hearing of civil and criminal cases in all courts is collegial; in courts of the first instance cases are heard with the participation of people's assessors. In the administration of justice, people's assessors have all the rights of judges

Article 155. Judges and people's assessors are independent and subject only to the law.

Article 156. Justice is administered in the USSR on the principle of the equality of citizens before the law and the court.

Article 157. Proceedings in all courts shall be open to the public Closed hearings are allowed only in cases provided for by law, with observance of all the rules of judicial procedure.

Article 158. A defendant in a criminal action is guaranteed the right to legal assistance

Article 159. Judicial proceedings shall be conducted in the language of the Union Republic, Autonomous Republic, Autonomous Region, Autonomous Area, or in the language spoken by the majority of the people in the locality. Persons who participate in court proceedings who do not know the language in which they are being conducted, shall be assured the right to become fully acquainted with the material in the case; the services of an interpreter during the proceedings; and the right to address the court in their own language.

Article 160. No one may be judged guilty of a crime and undergo punishment as a criminal except by the sentence of a court and in conformity to the law.

Article 161. Staffs of lawyers are made available to give legal assistance to citizens and organizations. In cases provided for by legislation, citizens shall be given legal assistance free of charge

The organization and procedures of the bar are determined by legislation of the USSR and of the Union Republics.

Article 162. Representatives of public organizations and of work collectives may participate in civil and criminal proceedings.

Article 163. Economic disputes between enterprises, institutions and organizations are settled by state arbitration bodies within the limits of their jurisdiction.

The organization and manner of functioning of state arbitration bodies are defined in the Law on State Arbitration in the USSR.

Chapter 21
THE OFFICE OF THE PROCURATOR

Article 164. Supreme power of supervision over the strict and uniform observance of laws by all ministries, state commissions and departments, enterprises, institutions and organizations, executive-administrative bodies of local Soviets of People's Deputies, collective farms, cooperatives and other public organizations, officials and citizens is vested in the Procurator-General of the USSR and in the procurators subordinate to him.

Article 165. The Procurator-General of the USSR is appointed by the Supreme Soviet of the USSR and is responsible and accountable to it and, between sessions of the Supreme Soviet, to the Presidium of the Supreme Soviet of the USSR.

Article 166. The procurators of Union Republics, Autonomous Republics, Territories, Regions and Autonomous Regions are appointed by the Procurator-General of the USSR. The procurators of Autonomous Areas and districts, and city procurators are appointed by the procurators of Union Republics, subject to confirmation by the Procurator-General of the USSR.

Article 167. The term of office of the Purcurator-General of the USSR and of all the lower-ranking procurators shall be five years.

Article 168. The agencies of the Procurator's Office exercise their powers independently of any local bodies whatsoever, and are subordinate exclusively to the Procurator-General of the USSR.

The organization and procedures of the agencies of the Procurator's Office are defined in the Law on the Procurator's Office in the USSR

VIII.
THE EMBLEM,
FLAG, ANTHEM AND THE
CAPITAL OF THE USSR

Article 169. The State Emblem of the Union of Soviet Socialist Republics is a hammer and sickle on a globe depicted in the rays of the sun and framed by stalks of wheat, with the inscription "Workers of All Countries, Unite!" in the languages of the Union Republics. At the top of the emblem is a five-pointed star.

Article 170. The State Flag of the Union of Soviet Socialist Republics is a rectangle of red cloth with a hammer and sickle depicted in gold in the upper corner next to the staff, and with a five-pointed red star edged in gold above them. The ratio of the width of the flag to its length is 1:2.

Article 171. The State Anthem of the Union of Soviet Socialist Republics is confirmed by the Presidium of the Supreme Soviet of the USSR.

Article 172. The capital of the Union of Soviet Socialist Republics is the City of Moscow.

IX.
THE LEGAL FORCE OF THE CONSTITUTION OF THE USSR AND THE PROCEDURE FOR AMENDING THE CONSTITUTION

Article 173. The Constitution of the USSR shall have supreme legal force. All laws and other acts of state bodies shall be promulgated on the basis of and in conformity with it

Article 174. The Constitution of the USSR may be amended by a decision of the Supreme Soviet of the USSR adopted by a majority of not less than two-thirds of the total number of Deputies of each of its chambers

APPENDIX 4

THE STATUTES (RULES) OF THE COMMUNIST PARTY OF THE SOVIET UNION (CPSU)

PREAMBLE

The Communist Party of the Soviet Union is the tried and tested militant vanguard of the Soviet people, which unites, on a voluntary basis, the more advanced, politically more conscious section of the working class, collective-farm peasantry and intelligentsia of the USSR.

Founded by V. I. Lenin as the advance detachment of the working class, the Communist Party has travelled a glorious road of struggle. It brought the working class and the working peasantry to the victory of the Great October Socialist Revolution and to the establishment of the dictatorship of the proletariat in our country Under the leadership of the Communist Party, the exploiting classes were abolished in the Soviet Union, and the socio-political and ideological unity of multinational Soviet society has taken shape and is steadily growing in strength. Socialism has triumphed completely and finally. The proletarian state has grown into a state of the entire people. The country has entered the stage of developed socialism.

Remaining in its class essence and ideology the Party of the working class, the CPSU has become the Party of the entire people.

The Party exists for and serves the people. It is the highest form of socio-political organization, the nucleus of the political system and the leading and guiding force of Soviet society The Party defines the general perspective of the country's development, ensures the scientific guidance of the people's creative activities, and imparts an organized, planned and purposeful character to their struggle to achieve the ultimate goal, the victory of communism

In all its activities, the CPSU is guided by Marxist-Leninist theory and its own Program, which defines the tasks of the steady and all-round advancement of socialism and of the further progress of Soviet society towards communism on the basis of the country's accelerated socio-economic develcpment.

The CPSU bases its work on unswerving adherence to the Leninist standards of Party life, the principles of democratic centralism, collective leadership, the comprehensive development of inner-Party democracy, the creative activity of Communists, criticism and self-criticism and broad publicity.

Ideological and organizational unity, monolithic cohesion of its ranks, and a high degree of conscious discipline on the part of all Communists are inviolable laws for the CPSU. Any manifestation of factionalism or group activity is incompatible with Marxist-Leninist Party principles, and with Party membership. The Party expels persons who violate the Program and the Statutes of the CPSU and compromise the worthy name of Communist by their behaviour.

In creatively developing Marxism-Leninism, the CPSU vigorously combats any manifestation of revisionism and dogmatism, which are utterly alien to revolutionary theory

The Communist Party of the Soviet Union is an integral part of the international communist movement. It firmly adheres to the tried and tested Marxist-Leninist principles of proletarian, socialist internationalism, actively promotes the cooperation and cohesion of the fraternal socialist countries, of the world system of socialism, and the international communist and working class movement, and shows solidarity with the nations fighting for national and social liberation, against imperialism and for peace.

I.

PARTY MEMBERS, THEIR DUTIES AND RIGHTS

1. Membership of the CPSU is open to any citizen of the Soviet Union who accepts the Program and the Rules of the Party, takes an active part in communist construction, works in one of the Party organizations, carries out Party decisions, and pays membership dues.

2. It is the duty of a Party member:

(a) to implement, firmly and undeviatingly, the Party's general line and directives, to explain to the masses the CPSU's domestic and foreign policy, to organize the working people for its implementation, and to work for the strengthening and expansion of the Party's ties with the people;

(b) to set a good example at work, to protect and augment socialist property, to work persistently for higher production efficiency, for a steady growth of labor productivity, for higher product quality, for the application of the achievements of modern science and technology and advanced experience in the national economy; to upgrade his professional skills, to actively champion all that is new and progressive, to make the maximum possible contribution to the acceleration of the country's socio-economic development;

(c) to be active in the country's political life, in running state and public affairs, to set an example in fulfilling one's civic duty, to contribute actively to the ever fuller implementation of the people's socialist self-government;

(d) to master Marxist-Leninist theory, to widen his political and cultural horizons, and promote in all possible ways the growth of the Soviet people's consciousness and their ideological and moral standards. To combat resolutely any manifestations of bourgeois ideology, private-property mentality, religious prejudices and other views and morals alien to the socialist way of life;

(e) to abide strictly by the standards of communist morality, to assert the principle of social justice which is innate in socialism, to put public interests above personal, to be modest and upright, responsive and considerate to people, to respond promptly to working people's requirements and needs, to be truthful and honest with the Party and the people;

(f) to disseminate steadily the ideas of proletarian, socialist internationalism and Soviet patriotism among the working masses, to combat manifestations of nationalism and chauvinism, to work actively for the consolidation of friendship between the peoples of the USSR and fraternal relations with the countries of socialism, with the proletarians and working people of the whole world;

(g) to help in every possible way strengthen the defense capability of the USSR; to struggle indefatigably for peace and friendship among nations;

(h) to strengthen the ideological and organizational unity of the Party, to safeguard the Party against infiltration by people who do not deserve the worthy name of Communist, to display vigilance, to keep Party and state secrets;

(i) to develop criticism and self-criticism, boldly expose shortcomings and work for their removal, to combat ostentation, conceit, complacency, and pettiness, to counter firmly all attempts at suppressing criticism, to combat bureaucracy, parochialism and departmentalism and all actions injurious to the Party and the state and to inform of them Party bodies, up to and including the CC CPSU;

(j) to pursue undeviatingly the Party's policy with regard to the proper selection of personnel according to their political, professional and moral qualities. To be uncompromising whenever the Leninist principles of the selection and education of personnel are violated;

(k) to observe Party and state discipline, which is equally binding on all Party members. The Party has one discipline, one law for all Communists, irrespective of their past services or the positions they occupy.

3. A Party member has the right:

(a) to elect and be elected to Party bodies;

(b) to discuss freely questions of the Party's policies and practical activities at Party meetings, conferences and congresses, at the meetings of Party committees and in the Party press, to put forward proposals; to express openly and uphold his opinion until the Party organization concerned adopts a decision;

(c) to criticize any Party body and any Communist, irrespective of the position he holds, at Party meetings, conferences and congresses, and at the plenary meetings of Party committees. Those who suppress criticism or victimize anyone for criticism shall be penalized strictly by the Party, to the point of expulsion from the CPSU;

(d) to attend in person all Party meetings and all bureau and committee sessions that discuss his activities or conduct;

(e) to address any question, statement or proposal to any Party body, up to and including the CC CPSU, and to demand an answer on the substance of his address.

4. Applicants are admitted to Party membership only individually. Membership of the Party is open to politically conscious and active citizens from among workers, peasants and the intelligentsia, all devoted to the communist cause. New members are admitted from among the candidate members who have undergone the established probationary period.

Persons may join the Party on reaching the age of eighteen. Young people up to the age of twenty-five may join the Party only through the All-Union Leninist Young Communist League (YCL) (KOMSOMOL)

The procedure for the admission of candidate members to full Party membership is as follows:

(a) Applicants for Party membership must submit recommendations from three members of the CPSU who have a Party standing of not less than five years and who know the applicants from having worked with them, professionally and socially, for not less than one year

Note 1. In the case of members of the YCL applying for membership of the Party, the recommendation of a district or city committee of the YCL is equivalent to the recommendation of one Party member

Note 2. Members and alternate members of the CC CPSU must refrain from giving recommendations.

(b) Applications for Party membership are discussed and a decision is taken by the general meeting of the primary Party organization; the decision of the latter is valid if not less than two-thirds of the Party members attending the meeting have voted for it, and comes into effect after endorsement by the district Party committee, or by the city Party committee in cities with no district division.

The question of admission to the Party may be discussed in the absence of those who have recommended the applicant for Party membership. Admission to the Party takes place, as a rule, at open meetings.

(c) Citizens of the USSR who formerly belonged to the Communist or Workers' Party of another country are admitted to membership of the Communist Party of the Soviet Union in conformity with the rules established by the CC CPSU.

5. Communists recommending applicants for Party membership are responsible to Party organizations for the impartiality of their description of the

political, professional and moral qualities of those they recommend and help the latter further develop their ideological and political awareness

6. The Party standing of those admitted to Party membership dates from the day the general meeting of the primary Party organization decides to accept them as full members.

7. The procedure of registering members and candidate members of the Party, and their transfer from one organization to another is determined by the appropriate instructions of the CC CPSU.

8. If a Party member or candidate member fails to pay membership dues for three months in succession without a good reason, the matter shall be discussed by the primary Party organization If it is revealed that the Party member or candidate member in question has virtually lost contact with the Party organization, he shall be regarded as having ceased to be a member of the Party; the primary Party organization shall pass a decision thereon and submit it to the district or city committee of the Party for endorsement.

9. A Party member or candidate member who fails to fulfil his duties as laid down in the Rules, or commits other offences, shall be called to account, and may incur a penalty: a warning, reprimand (severe reprimand), or a reprimand (severe reprimand) with note of this made in his registration card. The strictest Party penalty is expulsion from the Party.

In the case of minor offenses, Party education measures and influence should be applied--in the form of comradely criticism, Party censure, warning or reproof.

A Communist who has committed an offense shall answer for it, above all, to his primary Party organization. The primary Party organization will be informed should a Communist be called to account to the Party by a higher body.

Maximum attention must be given to discussion of the question of calling a Party member to Party account and the grounds for the charges preferred against him must be thoroughly investigated.

The Party organization gives the Party member a hearing, not later than a year after the penalty was imposed on him, to find out how he is rectifying his shortcomings.

10. The decision to expel a Communist from the Party is made at the general meeting of a primary Party organization. The decision of the primary Party organization to expel a member is adopted provided not less than two-thirds of the Party members attending the meeting vote for it, and takes effect after endorsement by the district or city Party committee.

Until the decision to expel the member is endorsed by the district or city Party committee, the Party member or candidate member retains his membership card and is entitled to attend closed Party meetings.

A person expelled from the Party retains the right to appeal, within two months, to the higher Party bodies, up to and including the CC CPSU

11. The question of calling to Party account a member or alternate member of the CC of the Communist Party of a Union Republic or of a territorial, regional, area, city or district Party committee, as well as a member of an auditing commission, is discussed by primary Party organizations and decisions to impose penalties are passed in conformity with the regular procedure

Party organization proposals for expelling a Communist from the CPSU are reported to the relevant Party committee of which he is a member. The decision to expel from the Party a member or alternate member of the CC of the Communist Party of a Union Republic or of a territorial, regional, area, city or district Party committee, or a member of an auditing commission, is adopted at the plenary meeting of the committee concerned by a majority of two-thirds of the membership.

The decision to expel from the Party a member or alternate member of the Central Committee of the CPSU, or a member of the Central Auditing Commission of the CPSU, is adopted by the Party congress, and in the interim between congresses, by a plenary meeting of the Central Committee by a majority of two-thirds of the CC CPSU members.

12. A Party member shall bear dual responsibility to the state and the Party for the violation of Soviet laws. Persons who have committed indictable offences are expelled from the CPSU.

13 Appeals by persons expelled or disciplined, as well as the decisions of Party organizations on expulsion from the Party, shall be examined by the appropriate Party bodies within not more than two months from the date of their receipt

II.

CANDIDATE MEMBERS

14. All persons joining the Party must go through a probationary period as candidate members in order to familiarize themselves more thoroughly with the Program and the Rules of the CPSU and prepare for admission to full membership. Party organizations must assist candidates to prepare for admission to full membership, and test their personal qualities in practical deeds, in the fulfilment of Party and public assignments.

The period of probationary membership shall be one year

15. The admission procedure for candidate members (individual admission, submission of recommendations, decision of the primary organization on admission, and its endorsement) is identical with the admission procedure for Party members.

16. On the expiration of the candidate's probationary period the primary Party organization discusses his admission to full membership and passes a decision on it. Should a candidate member fail to prove worthy during the probationary period, and should that candidate member's personal traits rule out admission to membership of the CPSU, the Party organization shall pass a decision denying his admission to membership of the Party; after endorsement of that decision by the district or city Party committee, he shall cease to be considered a candidate member of the CPSU

17. Candidate members of the Party participate in all the activities of their Party organizations; they shall have a consultative voice at Party meetings. Candidate members of the Party may not be elected to any leading Party body, nor may they be elected delegates to a Party conference or congress

18. Candidate members of the CPSU pay membership dues at the same rate as full members.

III.

ORGANIZATIONAL STRUCTURE OF THE PARTY INNER-PARTY DEMOCRACY

19. The guiding principle of the organizational structure, of the life and activities of the Party is democratic centralism, which signifies:

(a) election of all leading Party bodies, from the lowest to the highest.

(b) periodical reports of Party bodies to their Party organizations and to higher bodies;

(c) strict Party discipline and subordination of the minority to the majority;

(d) the obligatory nature of the decisions of higher bodies for lower bodies;

(e) collective spirit in the work of all organizations and leading Party bodies and the personal responsibility of every Communist for the fulfilment of his duties and Party assignments.

20. The Party is built on the territorial production principle: primary organizations are established wherever Communists are employed, and are associated territorially in district, city, etc., organizations. An organization uniting the Communists of a given area is higher than any component Party organization of that area

21. All Party organizations are autonomous in deciding local questions, unless their decisions contradict Party policy

22. The highest leading body of a Party organization is the general meeting or conference (for primary organizations), conference (for district, city, area, regional and territorial organizations), or congress (for the Communist Parties of the Union Republics and the Communist Party of the Soviet Union). A meeting, conference or congress is considered competent if it is attended by more than one half of the members of the Party organization or of the elected delegates

23. The general meeting, conference or congress elects a bureau or committee which acts as its executive body and directs all the current work of the Party organization

An Apparatus is set up at the CC CPSU, the CCs of the Communist Parties of the Union Republics, territorial, regional, area, city and district Party committees, for carrying out the current work of organizing and checking on the fulfilment of Party decisions and rendering assistance to the lower organizations in their activities.

The CPSU Central Committee defines the structure and the staff of the Party apparatus.

24. Party bodies are elected by secret ballot. Elections of the secretaries, deputy secretaries of Party organizations and Party group organizers at meetings of primary organizations with less than 15 Party members and of Party groups may be held, with the Communists' consent, by a show of hands. In these primary organizations, the procedure for the election of delegates to the district and city Party conferences is the same.

During elections all Party members have the unlimited right to challenge candidates and to criticize them. Each candidate shall be voted upon separately. A candidate is elected if more than one half of those attending the meeting, conference or congress vote for him.

The principle of the systematic renewal of the composition of Party bodies and of the continuity of leadership shall be observed in the election of all Party bodies—from primary organizations to the CPSU Central Committee.

25. The members and alternate members of the CC CPSU, the Central Committees of the Communist Parties of the Union Republics, the territorial, regional, area, city and district Party committees must, by their entire activity, justify the great trust placed in them. A member or alternate member of the Party committee who degrades his honour and dignity may not remain on the committee.

The question of removing a member or alternate member of a Party committee from that body is decided by a plenary meeting of the given committee. The decision is adopted if not less than two-thirds of the members of the Party committee have voted for it by secret ballot

The question of removing members of the CPSU Central Auditing Commission, or of the auditing commissions of local Party organizations from these commissions is decided by their meetings according to the procedure established for members and alternate members of Party committees

26. The free and effective discussion of questions of Party policy in the Party, in all its organizations, is an important principle of inner-Party democracy. Only on the basis of inner-Party democracy is it possible to ensure Communists' high creative activity, open criticism and self-criticism and strong Party discipline, which must be conscious and not mechanical.

Discussion of controversial or insufficiently clear issues may be held within the framework of individual organizations or the Party as a whole.

Party-wide discussion is held:

(a) on the initiative of the CC CPSU, if it considers it necessary to take counsel with the Party as a whole on a particular question of policy;

(b) at the proposal of several Party organizations at republican, territorial or regional level.

Broad discussion, especially discussion on a country-wide scale, of questions of Party policy must be so held as to ensure the free expression of Party members' views and preclude attempts to form factional groupings, to split the Party

The supreme principle of Party leadership is collective leadership, which is an absolute requisite for the normal functioning of Party organizations, the proper education of cadres, the promotion of the activity and initiative of Communists, and a reliable guarantee against the adoption of, subjectivist decisions, the manifestation of the cult of personality and violations of the Leninist principles of Party life.

Collective leadership implies personal responsibility for the matter in hand, constant control over the activities of every Party organization, every worker.

28. The CC CPSU, the Central Committees of the Communmist Parties of the Union Republics, and territorial, regional, area, city and district Party committees shall systematically inform Party organizations, in the interim between congresses and conferences, of their work and of the actions taken on the strength of critical remarks and proposals made by Communists.

It is an unbreakable rule for the Party committees, primary Party organizations to objectively and promptly inform the higher Party bodies of their activities and the state of affairs in their organizations.

29. Meetings of the activists of district, city, area, regional and territorial Party organizations and of the Communist Parties of the Union Republics shall be held to discuss major decisions of the Party and to work out measures for their implementation, as well as to examine questions of local significance

30. Standing or temporary commissions and working groups on various questions of Party work may be set up at the Party committees, and other forms can also be used to draw Communists into the activities of the Party bodies on a voluntary basis

IV.

HIGHER PARTY BODIES

31. The supreme body of the Communist Party of the Soviet Union is the Party Congress. Regular congresses shall be convened by the Central Committee not less than once in five years. The convocation of a Party Congress and its agenda shall be announced at least six weeks before the Congress.

Extraordinary (emergency) congresses shall be convened by the Central Committee of the Party on its own initiative or on the demand of not less than one-third of the total Party membership represented at the preceding Party Congress. Extraordinary (emergency) congresses shall be convened within two months and are considered competent provided not less than one half of the total Party membership is represented at them.

The rates of representation at a Party Congress are determined by the Central Committee.

32. Should the Central Committee of the Party fail to convene an extraordinary (emergency) congress within the period specified in Article 31, the organizations which demanded its convocation have the right to form an Organizing Committee, which shall enjoy the powers of the Central Committee of the Party, for the convocation of the extraordinary (emergency) congress.

33. The Congress:

(a) hears and approves the reports of the Central Committee, of the Central Auditing Commission, and of the other central organizations;

(b) reviews, amends and approves the Program and the Rules of the Party;

(c) determines the line of the Party in matters of domestic and foreign policy, and examines and decides the most important questions of Party and state life, of communist construction;

(d) elects the Central Committee and the Central Auditing Commission

34. The number of members to be elected to the Central Committee and to the Central Auditing Commission is determined by the Congress. Vacancies arising in the Central Committee are filled from among the alternate members of the CC CPSU.

35. In the interim between congresses, the Central Committee of the Communist Party of the Soviet Union guides the entire activity of the Party and the local Party bodies, selects and appoints leading functionaries, directs the work of central government bodies and public organizations of working people, sets up various Party bodies, institutions and enterprises and guides their activities, appoints the editors of the central newspapers and journals operating under its control, and distributes the funds of the Party budget and controls its execution

The Central Committee represents the CPSU in its relations with other parties.

36. The Central Auditing Commission of the CPSU verifies the observance of the established procedure for handling affairs, the work involved in examining letters, applications and complaints from the working people in the Party's central bodies, the correctness of the execution of the Party budget, including the payment, collection and accounting of Party dues, and also the financial and economic activities of the enterprises and institutions of the CPSU Central Committee.

37. The CC CPSU shall hold not less than one plenary meeting every six months. Alternate members of the Central Committee shall have a consultative voice at sessions of the CC plenary meetings

38. The Central Committee of the Communist Part of the Soviet Union elects a Politburo to direct the work of the Party between plenary meetings of the CC, and a Secretariat to direct current work, chiefly the selection of cadres and the verification of the fulfilment of Party decisions. The Central Committee elects the General Secretary of the CC CPSU.

39. The Central Committee of the Communist Party of the Soviet Union organizes the Party Control Committee of the CC

The Party Control Committee of the CC CPSU:

(a) verifies the observance of Party discipline by members and candidate members of the CPSU, and takes action against Communists who violate the Program and the Rules of the Party and Party or state discipline, and against violators of Party ethics;

(b) considers appeals against decisions of Central Committees of the Communist Parties of the Union Republics or of territorial and regional Party committees on expelling members from the Party or imposing penalties upon them.

40. In the interim between Party congresses the CPSU Central Committee may convene, should the need arise, an All-Union Party Conference to discuss pressing Party policy issues. The procedure of holding an All-Union Party Conference is determined by the CC CPSU.

V.

REPUBLICAN, TERRITORIAL, REGIONAL, AREA, CITY AND DISTRICT PARTY ORGANIZATIONS

41. The republican, territorial, regional, area, city and district Party organizations and their committees are guided in their activities by the Program and the Rules of the CPSU, carry out all work for the implementation of Party policy and organize the fulfilment of the directives of the CPSU Central Committee within the Republics, territories, regions, areas, cities and districts concerned.

42. The basic duties of republican, territorial, regional, area, city and district Party organizations, and of their leading bodies, are:

(a) political and organizational work among the masses, mobilization of Communists, of all working people for carrying out the tasks of communist construction, accelerating socio-economic development on the basis of scientific and technological progress, increasing the efficiency of social production, raising labor productivity and improving product quality, fulfilling state plans and socialist commitments, and ensuring the steady rise in the material and cultural standards of the working people;

(b) organization of ideological work, propaganda of Marxism-Leninism,, promotion of the communist awareness of the working people, guidance of the local press, radio and television, and control over the activities of scientific, cultural and educational institutions:

(c) guidance of Soviets of People's Deputies, trade unions, the YCL, the cooperative and other public organizations through the Communists working in them, and the increasingly broader involvement of working people in the activities of these organizations, development of the initiative and activity of the masses as an essential condition for the further in-depth development of socialist democracy;

(d) strict observance of the Leninist principles and methods of leadership, the affirmation of the Leninist style in Party work, in all spheres of state and economic management, securing the unity of ideological, organizational and economic activities, the strengthening of socialist law, of state and labour discipline, order and organization in all sectors;

(e) implementation of the personnel policy, education of personnel in the spirit of communist ideology, fostering moral integrity and a high sense of responsibility to the Party and the people for the work entrusted to them;

(f) organization of various Party institutions and enterprises within the bounds of their Republic, territory, region, area, city or district and guidance of their activities; distribution of Party funds within the given organization; regular reports to the higher Party body and accountability to it for their work.

Leading Bodies of Republican, Territorial and Regional Party Organizations

43. The highest body of republican, territorial and regional Party organizations is the congress of the communist Party of a Union Republic, the territorial or regional Party conference and, in the interim, the Central Committee of the Communist Party of a Union Republic, and the territorial or regional committee.

44 A regular congress of the Communist Party of a Union Republic shall be convened by the Central Committee of the Communist Party not less than once in five years. A regular territorial or regional Party conference shall be convened by the territorial or regional committee once every two-three years. Extraordinary (emergency) congresses and conferences are convened by the decision of the Central Committee of the Communist Party of a Union Republic, the territorial or regional committee, or on the demand of one-third of the total membership of the organizations belonging to the republican, territorial or regional Party organization.

The rates of representation at congresses of the Communist Parties of the Union Republics, at territorial and regional conferences are established by the respective Party committees.

A congress of the Communist Party of a Union Republic or a territorial or regional conference hears the report of the Central Committee of the Communist Party of the Union Republic or of the territorial or regional committee, and the report of the auditing commission, discusses at its own discretion other matters of Party, economic and cultural development, and elects the Central Committee of the Communist Party of the Union Republic or the territorial or regional committee, the auditing commission and delegates to the Congress of the CPSU.

In the interim between congresses of the Communist Parties of the Union Republics, the Central Committees of the Communist Parties may convene, whenever necessary, republican Party conferences to discuss topical questions concerning Party organizations' activities. The procedure for holding republican Party conferences is determined by the Central Committes of the Communist Parties of the Union Republics.

45. The Central Committees of the Communist Parties of the Union Republics, the territorial and regional committees elect buros, including secretaries of the committees. The secretaries must have a Party standing of not less than five years. The plenary meetings of the committees approve the heads of departments of these committees, chairmen of Party control commissions and editors of Party newspapers and journals

The Central Committees of the Communist Parties of the Union Republics, territorial and regional Party committees set up secretariats to attend to current affairs and verify the implementation of decisions.

46. Plenary meetings of the Central Committees of the Communist Parties of the Union Republics, of territorial and regional committees shall be convened at least once every four months

47. The Central Committees of the Communist Parties of the Union Republics, the territorial and regional committees direct the area, city and district Party organizations, inspect their work and regularly hear reports of the respective Party committees.

Party organizations of Autonomous Republics, and in autonomous and other regions forming part of a Union Republic or a territory, function under the guidance of the Central Committees of the Communist Parties of the Union Republics or respective territorial committees.

Leading Bodies of Area, City and District (Rural and Urban) Party Organizations

48. The highest body of an area, city or district Party organization is the area, city or district Party conference or the general meeting of Communists convened by the area, city or district committee once in 2-3 years, as well as an extraordinary conference or general meeting convened by the decision of the respective committee or on the demand of one-third of the total membership of the Party organization concerned.

The area, city or district conference (meeting) hears reports of the committee and the auditing commission, discusses at its own discretion other questions of Party, economic and cultural development, and elects the area, city or district committee, the auditing commission and delegates to the regional or territorial conference or the congress of the Communist Party of the Union Republic.

The rates of representation at the area, city and district conferences are established by the respective Party committee.

49. The area, city or district committee elects a buro, including the committee secretaries, and approves heads of committee departments, the chairman of the Party commission and newspaper editors. The secretaries of the area, city and district committees must have a Party standing of at least five years. The committee secretaries are approved by the respective regional or territorial committee, or the Central Committee of the Communist Party of the Union Republic.

50. The area, city or district committee sets up the primary Party organizations, directs their work, regularly hears reports on the work of Party organizations, and keeps a register of Communists

51. The plenary meeting of the area, city or district committee is convened at least once every three months

VI.

PRIMARY PARTY ORGANIZATIONS

52. The primary Party organizations are the basis of the Party.

Primary Party organizations are formed at the places of work of Party members—factories, state farms and other enterprises, collective farms, units of the Armed Forces, offices, educational establishments, etc., wherever there are not less than three Party members. If necessary, primary Party organizations may also be formed on the residential principle.

In individual cases, with the approval of the regional or territorial committee, or of the Central Committee of the Communist Party of the Union Republic, Party organizations may be formed within the framework of several enterprises that make up a production association and are located, as a rule, on the territory of one or several districts in the same city.

53. At enterprises, collective farms and institutions with over 50 members and candidate members of the CPSU, shop, sectional, farm, team, departmental, and other such Party organizations may be formed within one primary Party organization with the approval of the district, city or area committee.

Within shop, sectional, etc., organizations, and also within primary Party organizations with less than 50 members and candidate members, Party groups may be formed in the teams and other production units

54. The highest body of the primary Party organization is the Party meeting, which is convened at least once a month. In Party organizations with shop organizations, both general and shop meetings are held at least once every two months.

In large Party organizations with a membership of more than 300 Coimmunists, a general Party meeting is convened when necessary as scheduled by the Party committee or on the demand of several shop Party organizations.

55. To attend to current affairs, the primary or shop Party organization elects a buro for a term of two or three years. The number of its members is fixed by the Party meeting. Primary and shop Party organizations with less than 15 Party members do not elect a buro. Instead, they elect a secretary and a deputy secretary of the Party organization. Elections in these organizations are held every year.

Secretaries of primary and shop Party organizations must have a Party standing of at least one year.

Primary Party organizations with less than 150 Party members shall have, as a rule, no salaried functionaries relieved from their regular work.

56. At large enterprises and institutions with more than 300 Party members and candidate members, and if necessary at organizations with over 100 Communists, by virtue of specific production conditions and territorial dispersion, and subject to the approval of the regional committee, territorial committee or the Central Committee of the Communist Party of the Union Republic, Party committees may be formed, with shop Party organizations granted the rights of primary Party organizations.

The Party organizations of collective farms, state farms and other agricultural enterprises may form Party committees if there are no less than 50 Communists in them.

In individual cases, given the approval of the regional or territorial Party committee, or the Central Committee of the Communist Party of the Union Republic, Party organizations numbering more than 500 Communists may form Party committees in the larger shops, and the Party organizations in production sectors may be granted the rights of a primary Party organization.

The Party committees are elected for a term of 2-3 years. Their numerical composition is fixed by the general Party meeting or conference.

Party committees, Party buros and secretaries of primary and shop Party organizations regularly inform Communists of their work at Party meetings.

57. The Party committees of primary Party organizations with more than 1,000 Communists may be granted, with the approval of the Central Committee of the Communist Party of the Union Republic, the rights of a district Party committee in matters of admission to the CPSU, of keeping a register of members and candidate members of the Party and of considering the personal cases of Communists

These organizations may elect enlarged Party committees within which buros are formed to guide day-to-day work.

58. In its activities the primary Party organization is guided by the Program and the Rules of the CPSU. It is the political nucleus of a work collective, it conducts its activities in the midst of the working people, rallies them round the Party, organizes them to fulfil the tasks of communist construction, takes an active part in implementing the Party's personnel policy.

The primary Party organization:

(a) admits new members to the CPSU;

(b) educates Communists in the spirit of loyalty to the Party cause, ideological staunchness and communist ethics;

(c) organizes the study by Communists of Marxist-Leninist theory in close connection with the practice of communist construction and combats any manifestations of bourgeois ideology, revisionism and dogmatism, backward views and moods;

(d) ensures the growing vanguard role of Communists in work and in socio-political life, their exemplary behaviour in everyday life, hears reports of CPSU members and candidate members on the fulfilment of their statutory duties and Party assignments;

(e) acts as the organizer of the working people in carrying out the tasks of economic and social development, heads the socialist emulation movement for the fulfilment of state plans and commitments, the intensification of production, the raising of labor productivity and product quality, the extensive introduction of the achievements of science and technology and advanced experience into production, mobilizes the working people for tapping internal reserves, works for the rational, economical use of material, labour and financial resources, shows concern for the protection and growth of public wealth, for the improvement of people's working and living conditions;

(f) conducts political education and propaganda work, educates the working people in the spirit of devotion to the ideas of communism, Soviet patriotism and friendship among peoples, helps them achieve a high level of political culture, enhances their social activism and sense of responsibility;

(g) helps Communists, all working people get used to participation in socialist self-government, ensures the growing role of the work collective in managing the affairs of enterprises and organizations, guides the activities of the trade union, YCL and other public organizations;

(h) on the basis of extensive criticism and self-criticism, combats cases of bureaucracy, parochialism, departmentalism, violations of state, labor and production discipline, thwarts attempts to deceive the state, acts against negligence, waste and extravagance, works to affirm a temperate way of life.

The primary Party organizations at enterprises in industry, transport, communications, construction, material and technical supply, trade, public catering, communal and public welfare services, at collective and state farms and other agricultural enterprises, design organizations and drafting offices, research institutes, educational establishments, cultural and medical institutions, enjoy the right to control the work of the administration.

The Party organizations at ministries, state committees, and other central and local government and economic bodies and departments exercise control over the fulfilment of Party and government directives and the observance of Soviet laws by the apparatus. They must actively contribute to the improvement of the work of the appartus, the selection, placement and education of its staff, enhance their responsibility for the matter in hand, for the development of a particular sector and of public services, take measures to strengthen state discipline, resolutely combat bureaucracy and red tape, inform the appropriate Party bodies in good time of shortcomings in the work of the respective offices and individuals, regardless of the post the latter may hold.

Note. Primary Party organizations may set up commissions to exercise the right of control over the administration's activities, and the work of the apparatus in certain production spheres.

VII.

THE PARTY AND THE STATE AND PUBLIC ORGANIZATIONS

60. The CPSU, acting within the framework of the USSR Constitution, exercises political leadership of state and public organizations, directs and coordinates their activities.

The Party organizations, Communists working in state and public organizations see to it that these organizations fully exercise their constitutional powers and statutory rights and duties, and that they extensively involve working people in management and in deciding political, economic and social questions.

Party organizations do not supplant government, trade union, cooperative and other public organizations, and do not allow the functions of the Party and other bodies to be mixed.

61. Party groups are formed at congresses, conferences and meetings convened by state and public organizations, as well as in the elected bodies of these organizations with at least three Party members. The task of these groups is to carry out Party policy in the respective non-Party organizations, to enhance Communists' influence on the state of affairs in these organizations, to develop the democratic principles in their activities, to strengthen Party and state discipline, to combat bureaucracy, to verify the fulfilment of Party and government directives.

62. The work of Party groups within non-Party organizations is guided by the respective Party body: the CPSU Central Committee, the Central Committee of the Communist Party of the Union Republic, territorial, regional, area, city or district Party committee.

VIII

THE PARTY AND THE YCL

63. The All-Union Leninist Young Communist League is an independent public and political organization of young people, an active assistant and reserve of the Party. The YCL helps the Party educate the youth in the communist spirit, draw it into the practice of building the new society and running state and public affairs,

and raise a generation of harmoniously developed people prepared to work and to defend their Soviet Motherland.

64. The YCL organizations must actively promote Party directives in all spheres of production and social life. They enjoy the right of broad initiative in discussing and raising in the appropriate Party organizations questions related to the work of enterprises, collective farms, institutions or educational establishments, and directly take part in solving them, especially if they pertain to the work, everyday life, training and education of young people.

65. The YCL works under the guidance of the Communist Party of the Soviet Union. The work of the local YCL organizations is guided and monitored by the appropriate republican, territorial, regional, area, city and district Party organizations.

In carrying out the communist education of young people, in mobilizing them for the fulfilment of concrete production and social tasks, local Party bodies and primary Party organizations rely on the YCL organizations, support their useful initiatives, give them every assistance in their activities.

66. Members of the YCL who have been admitted to the CPSU cease to belong to the YCL the moment they join the Party, provided they are not members of elected YCL bodies and do not work as YCL functionaries.

IX.

PARTY ORGANIZATIONS IN THE ARMED FORCES

67. Party organizations in the Armed Forces are guided in their work by the Programme and the Rules of the CPSU and operate on the basis of instructions issued by the Central Committee. They ensure the implementation of the Party's policy in the Armed Forces, rally servicemen round the Communist Party, educate them in the spirit of Marxism-Leninism and boundless loyalty to the socialist Motherland, actively further the unity of the army and the people, concern themselves with enhancing troops' combat preparedness and with strengthening army discipline, mobilize servicemen for carrying out the tasks of combat and political training, for becoming skilled in the use of new hardware and weapons and for irreproachably fulfilling their military duty and the orders and instructions of the command.

68. Party work in the Armed Forces is guided by the CPSU Central Committee through political bodies. The Chief Political Administration of the Soviet Army and Navy functions as a department of the CC CPSU.

The chiefs of the political administrations of military districts and fleets, and the chiefs of the political departments of armies, flotillas and formations must have a Party standing of five years.

69. The Party organizations and political bodies of the Armed Forces maintain close contacts with local Party committees, and regularly brief them on the political work carried out in the military units. The secretaries of army Party organizations and chiefs of political bodies participate in the work of local Party committees.

X.

PARTY FUNDS

70. The funds of the Party and its organizations are derived from membership dues, incomes from Party enterprises and other revenue.

The CPSU Central Committee decides how Party funds are to be used.

71. The monthly membership dues for Party members and candidate members are as follows:

Monthly earnings	Dues	
up to 70 Roubles	10 kopeks	
71 to 100 roubles	20 kopeks	
101 to 150 roubles	1.0 percent	of the monthly earnings
151 to 200 roubles	1.5 percent	of the monthly earnings
201 to 250 roubles	2.0 percent	of the monthly earnings
251 to 300 roubles	2.5 percent	of the monthly earnings
over 300 roubles	3.0 percent	of the monthly earnings

72. Candidate members pay admission dues of two percent of their monthly earnings.

INDEX

ABOUT THE AUTHOR

LEO HECHT received his academic degrees (B.S., M.A., Ph.D.) from Columbia University with numerous honors including Phi Beta Kappa. He has also attended several other institutions including the University of Maryland, Georgetown University, New York City University, and the University of Hamburg, Germany. He was selected to participate in three Fulbright-funded faculty exchanges to Moscow State University. He also took part in several all-summer seminars sponsored by the National Endowment for the Humanities. He is the author of four books, many contributions to books, numerous articles in scholarly journals, and has presented countless papers at major academic conferences throughout the United States and in Moscow. In addition to his lengthy exchange programs he has taken numerous shorter trips throughout the USSR — from the Baltic Republics to the Transcaucasus and Soviet Central Asia. Because of his extreme interest in the performing arts in the Soviet Union he has, for the past seven years, been the editor of the journal Soviet and East European Drama, Theatre and Film. He has also been an active officer of the American Association of Teachers of Slavic and East European Languages.

Professor Hecht is Chairman of an interdisciplinary program in Russian Studies at George Mason University, the State University in Northern Virginia located in the suburbs of Washington, D.C. This allows him excellent access to persons and printed resources connected with his area of research interest.